MIDWIVES AND MOTHERS

BOOK FORTY-THREE
Louann Atkins Temple Women & Culture Series

Books about women and families, and their changing role in society

MIDWIVES AND MOTHERS

SHEILA COSMINSKY

The
Medicalization
of Childbirth on
a Guatemalan
Plantation

UNIVERSITY OF TEXAS PRESS
Austin

The Louann Atkins Temple Women & Culture Series is supported by Allison, Doug, Taylor, and Andy Bacon; Margaret, Lawrence, Will, John, and Annie Temple; Larry Temple; the Temple-Inland Foundation; and the National Endowment for the Humanities.

Requests for permission to reproduce material from this work should be sent to:
    Permissions
    University of Texas Press
    P.O. Box 7819
    Austin, TX 78713-7819
    http://utpress.utexas.edu/index.php/rp-form

♾ The paper used in this book meets the minimum requirements of ANSI/NISO Z39.48-1992 (R1997) (Permanence of Paper).

LIBRARY OF CONGRESS CATALOGING-IN-PUBLICATION DATA

Names: Cosminsky, Sheila, author.
Title: Midwives and mothers : the medicalization of childbirth on a Guatemalan plantation / Sheila Cosminsky.
Other titles: Louann Atkins Temple women & culture series ; bk. 43.
Description: First edition. | Austin : University of Texas Press, 2016. | Series: Louann Atkins Temple women & culture series ; book forty-three | Includes bibliographical references and index.
Identifiers: LCCN 2016018052| ISBN 978-1-4773-1138-7 (cloth : alk. paper) | ISBN 978-1-4773-1139-4 (pbk. : alk. paper) | ISBN 978-1-4773-1140-0 (library e-book) | ISBN 978-1-4773-1141-7 (nonlibrary e-book)
Subjects: LCSH: Midwives—Guatemala—Social conditions. | Traditional medicine—Guatemala. | Childbirth—Social aspects—Guatemala. | Maternal health services—Social aspects—Guatemala. | Plantation life—Health aspects—Guatemala. | Rural development—Health aspects—Guatemala.
Classification: LCC RG963.G9 C67 2016 | DDC 618.20097281—dc23
LC record available at https://lccn.loc.gov/2016018052

doi:10.7560/311387

In Memory of

Mary Goodrich Scrimshaw, Nevin Scrimshaw,
Brigitte Jordan, and Maria de la Cruz, comadrona

CONTENTS

ACKNOWLEDGMENTS

This work grew out of my concern for midwives, who are increasingly under attack by biomedical personnel and by international organizations such as the World Health Organization. In Guatemala, midwives and the mothers and infants they serve are experiencing a gradual loss of midwifery knowledge and attenuation of the midwives' role. My first contact with Guatemalan midwives was during my dissertation research in Santa Lucía Utatlán in 1968, which focused on decision making and health care.

I owe a great debt to the late Mary Scrimshaw and the late Nevin Scrimshaw, who introduced me to Guatemala in the summer of 1967 and gave me the opportunity to do that research. That year I went with Nevin Scrimshaw and the late John Gordon from the Department of Nutrition and Food Science at the Massachusetts Institute of Technology. They were working on studies through the Institute of Nutrition of Central America and Panama (INCAP). I had been working part-time in that department at MIT while studying for my comprehensive exams in anthropology at Brandeis University, where Mary Scrimshaw was also a graduate student. The Scrimshaws took me under their wing and were *en locus parentis* for me. Nevin encouraged me to conduct my research in Guatemala and helped me to obtain support through INCAP for my dissertation research. Under the guidance of Carlos Tejada, who was head of INCAP's education division, I carried out my research in the *aldeas* of Novillero and Chuchexic, in the town of Santa Lucía Utatlán. I am extremely grateful to INCAP for their material and intellectual support during my research.

In 1974, Nevin invited me to do research with Mary on the finca where he had been conducting a nutrition field school for clinicians and carrying out research. Mary and I were co-investigators carrying out various research projects in 1974, 1976, and 1978 and coauthors of several articles. During our initial research together, she introduced me to Doña María and the other people on the finca. I am extremely grateful to Mary for her friendship, intellectual stimulation and support.

I wish to thank the people of the finca, especially Doña María, Doña Siriaca, and my godson's family (the family of Estela Valdez Ruano), for their openness and willingness to share their lives with me, as well as Marina Galindo, who opened both her house and her heart to me and provided invaluable information about the finca. I owe a great debt to the *finquero*, Antonio Bischoff, and his family for their hospitality and openness, and for access to the finca. He has kindly given me permission to use the name of the finca, Finca San Luis. In previous publications, I used a peudonym, Finca San Felipe.

I also owe a debt of gratitude to the people of Santa Lucía Utatlán, especially Domingo Chavez and Paula Cochoy, who opened up their home and family to me; Lorenzo Tacán, who was my assistant, K'iche' tutor, transcriber, and K'iche'-to-Spanish translator; and Lorenzo's family. I am also indebted to the midwives and healers who let me observe their *costumbres* and explained them to me. In addition, I am grateful to the nuns who ran the clinic in Novillero and the health promoter program. They graciously provided shelter when I first arrived and allowed me to observe in the clinic and access health records. They also shared with me many meals and stimulating discussions.

I wish to extend a special acknowledgement to the late Rosalio Saquic Calel, of the Instituto Indigenista Nacional and originally from El Novillero, for his friendship, for his assistance in transcribing and translating recordings, and for sharing his knowledge of K'iche' culture.

In Guatemala City, Juan Foster and his wife, Mary Gene, provided me with companionship, food, and shelter when I came to the city from the field, and I am grateful for their kindness and hospitality. I owe their friendship to the late Toni and Lefty Robin of Philadelphia, who introduced me to them. Toni was a nutritionist from Philadelphia who had worked with Catholic Relief Services in Guatemala. They fell in love with the country and its people, bought a house in San Lucas Tolimán, and for many years had a business in Philadelphia selling textiles and crafts imported from Guatemala.

I also wish to express my gratitude to Juan Jose Hurtado, his late wife, and his daughter Elena and her husband Hernan Delgado. Juan is the epitome of a caring, humanistic physician, combining medicine and anthropology in his practice, his clinic, his research, and his teaching, especially in treating his Mayan patients with respect for and understanding of their culture. He is a rarity in the Guatemalan medical world and an inspiration to me and to many others. Elena, an applied anthropologist involved in many Guatemalan health and nutrition projects, including research on midwives, has provided both physical and intellectual sustenance when I have been in Guatemala City, and I am grateful for her kind hospitality, generosity, and sharing of information and ideas.

I also thank my research assistant, Blanca Estela Garcia, for her invaluable assistance, suggestions, support, and sensitivity in the field in Guatemala. Her companionship, friendship, and insights during our fieldwork are especially appreciated.

I give my appreciation to Robbie Davis-Floyd for her critical support and encouragement concerning my midwifery research over the years and for her constructive suggestions during the revision process. I would also like to thank the anonymous reviewers for their insights and helpful comments, and anthropologist and dear friend Karen Kerner for her significant input and contributions. I extend my gratitude to Anita Chary, Peter Rohloff, and their team from Wuqu' Kawoq for kindly reviewing the manuscript and making helpful recommendations. In addition, I wish to extend my thanks to copy editors Liana Silva and Meg Wallace for their thoughtful comments and critical editing. At the University of Texas Press, I am grateful to retired editor Theresa May for her original support of the project, and to her successor Casey Kittrell for his patience, sensitivity, and thoughtful suggestions, and to members of his staff, especially Lynne Chapman and Angelica Lopez.

The recent passing of Brigitte Jordan, on May 24, 2016, requires a special note of deep sorrow and sincere appreciation. Her influence on my work is evident throughout the book.

My interest in both midwives and ethnomedicine was stimulated and increased by my participation in various consultations and committees of the World Health Organization during the late 1970s and 1980s. These included the Interregional Consultation on Traditional Birth Attendants, the Action Programme on Essential Drugs (Social Science Network), and the Task Force on Indigenous Plants for Fertility Regulation. At that time the policy was to "make the best use of the great health manpower resource constituted by the traditional birth attendants" (Mangay-Maglacas and Simons 1986:5). I would like to express my gratitude to Amelia Mangay-Maglacas, who was chief scientist for nursing at WHO, for her support, idealism, and inspiration in believing that articulation between biomedicine and traditional midwives was possible, and that midwives could and should be trained in a respectful manner and utilized as part of the health system.

Rutgers University has been very supportive of my research both through sabbaticals and several grants from the Rutgers University Research Council over the years. The research in Guatemala on which the book is based had been approved by the Rutgers University Institutional Review Board.

I owe my deepest gratitude to my husband, Herbert Ershkowitz, for his understanding and support during my various trips to Guatemala and for critically reading my manuscript, and to my daughter, Anna, for her patience during my times away and for prodding me to finish the manuscript.

Parts of this book are based on my previously published articles, including "Childbirth and Change: A Guatemalan Study," in *Ethnography of Fertility and Birth*, 2nd edition, ed. Carol MacCormack (Prospect Heights, Ill.: Waveland, 1994); "Knowledge and Body Concepts of Guatemalan Midwives," in *Anthropology of Human Birth*, ed. Margarita Kay (Philadelphia: F. A. Davis, 1982); "Birth and Blame: Guatemalan Midwives and Reproductive Risk," in *Risk, Reproduction, and Narratives of Experience*, ed. Lauren Fordyce and Aminata Maraesa, 81–101 (Nashville, Tenn.: Vanderbilt University Press, 2012); "Childbirth and Midwifery on a Guatemalan Finca," *Medical Anthropology* 1, no. 3 (1977): 69–104; and "Midwifery across the Generations: A Modernizing Midwife in Guatemala," *Medical Anthropology* 20, no. 4 (2001): 345–78. Taylor and Francis has granted permission for use of material from *Medical Anthropology*. Material on *detención* and emmenagogues in chapter 4 and in the appendix on medicinal plants is drawn from my chapter "Midwives and Menstrual Regulation: A Guatemalan Case Study" in *Regulating Menstruation: Beliefs, Practices, Interpretations*, edited by Etienne van de Walle and Elisha P. Renne (University of Chicago Press, 2001). Part of the case study of Elena and some other material in chapter 2 appears in a chapter I coauthored with Mary Scrimshaw, "The Impact of Health on Women's Food-Procurement Strategies on a Guatemalan Plantation" in *Diet and Domestic Life in Society*, edited by Anne Sharman, Janet Theophano, Karen Curtis, and Ellen Messer (Temple University Press, 1991). University of Chicago Press and Temple University Press have granted permission for the use of these materials.

MIDWIVES AND MOTHERS

Midwives and Mothers examines the changes and continuities in the birthing system on a Guatemalan plantation (or finca) and its environs. Focusing on the midwives (*comadronas*) Doña María and her daughter Doña Siriaca, this analysis shows how a local population reacts to the increasing pressures of medicalization from national and international governmental and medical institutions and personnel.[1] According to a 1989 report, there were an estimated 20,000 *comadronas*, who attended over 80 percent of the births (Putney and Smith 1989). Today there are an estimated 23,000 midwives, of whom 16,000 have received some training (CARE 2015). These midwives still attend over two-thirds of the births in Guatemala and over 80 percent in many Maya areas. This local childbirth system has been and continues to be subject to a barrage of criticisms by biomedical experts, often well-intentioned, that may have unintended and even unfavorable results in terms of maternal and infant survival (Berry 2010).

This book is a study of birth, illness, death, and survival on a Guatemalan sugar and coffee plantation, Finca San Luis.[2] The story of María and Siriaca, who represent two generations of midwives, provides a lens for viewing plantation life and for understanding the impact of medicalization on Guatemalan people over the past forty years. Birth practices reflect the culture and reinforce the values of a society. They can also be an entry point for examining social life on the plantation and for exploring the relationships among cultural values, social organization, gender relations, and political economy (Davis-Floyd and Sargent 1997, 6).

To understand how birth is socially produced and culturally constructed, and the role midwives play, we must view birth and the midwife's role within the context of the plantation, including the constraints of poverty, poor living conditions, and problems of access to health care facilities.

Midwives and Mothers also addresses the relationship between knowledge, power, and the state. Specifically: How do midwives, doctors, and the government use the local ethno-obstetric model as well as the biomedical model of birth to establish authoritative knowledge, with women's bodies as the contested site? Authoritative knowledge refers to the knowledge on which decisions and actions are based (Jordan 1997:58). Key to establishing this authority is access to technology and the hierarchical distribution of knowledge, with the physician at the top and the local or traditional midwife and the mother at the bottom because their knowledge does not count (64).

Beyond the state, how are the linkages between international health policies and agendas manifested at the national and local levels? This study highlights how midwives are enmeshed in a political and economic context of medicalization and globalization in which different forms of knowledge, both indigenous and imported, and corresponding power relations are contested. In this chapter I discuss ethnographic fieldwork on the plantation, particularly as it relates to doing research on birth and reproduction. I also explore issues of reflexivity in terms of my relationship to Doña María, Doña Siriaca, and other women on the plantation, and I consider how those issues influenced the field research.

In the course of this study, we will see how the biomedical model differs from the local ethnomedical model of birth, which regards pregnancy and birth as resulting in an imbalance of hot and cold qualities and representing a normal but potentially dangerous state. During pregnancy, a woman is in a hot state, whereas postnatally she is in a cold state. This balance is also influenced by one's emotional state: anger, for example, is believed to cause miscarriage, premature labor, and other complications. Special attention will be paid to the role of anger as both an "idiom of distress" (Nichter 1981) and a manifestation of what Finkler (1994) refers to as "life's lesions," and to what this role tells us about social relations on the finca, especially gender relations and alcohol use and domestic abuse, which generate anger.

MEDICALIZATION

A major theme of this study is the impact of medicalization on childbirth and on the role of the midwife at this Guatemalan plantation. In its simplest and most basic sense, medicalization refers to the process by which various domains of life, such as reproduction and birth, are defined by the biomedical model in terms of disease: a physiological disturbance or an abnormal or pathological state. Thus described, a person with this condition or in this state should be treated medically, or the condition should be managed through biomedical intervention by the formal or professional health care sector or "skilled attendants."[3]

Eugenia Georges emphasizes the global and exclusive nature of this process: "Medicalization refers to a global process by which biomedicine has achieved the authority to redefine and treat an expanding array of individual life events and social problems as medical problems and ultimately to make exclusive claims over the body" (Georges 2008:1). This medicalization process is facilitated by international organizations such as the World Health Organization (WHO) and assumes that the same medical knowledge and procedures are applicable universally. The biomedical model that underlies medicalization is based on the assumption of the separation of the mind and body. When applied to childbirth, it holds that pregnancy is an abnormal state and a physical process and that other aspects of the person involved are irrelevant, including cultural, psychological, social, emotional, behavioral, and spiritual dimensions.

Medicalization assumes that someone who seeks help or health is a patient, which is regarded as a universal role within an individual physical body. This characterization ignores the possibility that multiple people may be involved in definition and treatment—that is, social as well as medical aspects of the "illness" may exist in the treatment (Harvey 2013), and birth may not be defined as a disease.

Medicalization is also based on the machine metaphor of the body. In regard to birth, it is based on what Robbie Davis-Floyd (1992) calls the technocratic model of birth, with the doctor repairing one part of the broken body as if it is isolated from any relationship to the rest of the body. It also implies the superiority of technology, the hospital as the locus for birth, the use of medications for pain or for speeding up labor, and the existence of hierarchical and authoritarian relationships among personnel and toward patients (Jordan 1993).

Other aspects of the medicalization of birth include withholding of information on the disadvantages of obstetrical medication, the expectation that women give birth in a hospital, elective induction of labor, separation of the mother from familial support during labor and birth, confinement of the laboring woman to bed, professional dependence on technology and pharmacological methods of pain relief, routine electronic fetal monitoring, chemical stimulation of labor, delay of birth until the physician's arrival, the requirement that the mother assume a prone position rather than an upright or kneeling one, routine use of regional or general anesthesia for delivery, routine episiotomy, and early clamping of the umbilical cord (Baer, Singer, and Susser 2003:14–15; Haire 1975).

The spread of medicalization contributes to physicians' and health institutions' increasing control over individual patient behavior. Social and economic problems, including poverty, become individualized. Michel Foucault has emphasized that medicalization expands the medical gaze, discourse, surveillance, and governmentality, in this case over the woman's body (Foucault 1975; Lupton 1997). Lynn Morgan and Elizabeth Roberts apply the concept of governmentality specifically to the area of reproduction. They define reproductive governance as "the mechanisms through which different historical configuration of actors . . . use legislative controls, economic inducements, moral injunctions, direct coercion, and ethical incitements to produce, monitor, and control reproductive behaviours and practices" (2012:243).

In the case of Guatemala, this reproductive governance works through state institutions, international organizations, and nongovernmental organizations (NGOs), and especially through midwifery training programs and increasing restrictions on the midwife's role. The sociologists Irving Zola (1972) and Peter Conrad (1979, 2007) have shown that medicalization has widened social control and that people internalize the "medical and therapeutic perspectives as a taken-for-granted subjectivity" (Conrad 2007:14). As we examine the process of the medicalization of birth among midwives and mothers on the finca in Guatemala, we will see how this process is gradually occurring within areas of compliance, resistance, and accommodation.

Medicalization entails a different relationship between the midwife and the mother and family than previously existed in the finca community. The biomedical system is based on a hierarchical model of social relationships, with doctors at the top and mothers at the bottom. In the local model of birthing, the midwife does not have such authority over the mother and her family. In the process of medicalization, however, the midwife is pressured to shift toward a more hierarchical and authoritarian relationship with the mother.

Conrad and Schneider (1980) propose that medicalization occurs at three levels: conceptual, institutional, and interactional. In their analysis of childbirth and midwifery, George Lowis and Peter McCaffery (2000) expand this general framework to five dimensions or levels: technological, conceptual, interactional, control, and gender/status. These five factors, which are closely interrelated but may change at different rates, constitute a dynamic framework for analyzing medicalization as it affects the role of midwives and women's reproductive health.[4] I apply this framework to examine the process and impact of medicalization at various stages of the birth process on María's and Siriaca's work as midwives.

The Technological Level

Obstetric technology and reliance on technical experts like doctors are perhaps the most important factors responsible for changing the status of the midwife, according to Lowis and McCaffery (2000). The success of technological innovation created doubts about existing techniques and procedures, thus challenging the legitimacy and authority of the midwife (26).

The Conceptual Level

At the conceptual level, medicalization redefines birth as a risky, hospital-based, medically managed process instead of a family- and community-centered event (Lowis and McCaffery 2000). This shift is accompanied by moves toward medical doctors rather than midwives being in charge. Sociocultural factors are considered either neutral or an impediment to the birthing process (McClain 1982). The power to define risk also shifts from the midwife and the mother to medical personnel. Biomedicine establishes cultural authority over the definition of health and disease and determines how, when, and where health care should be provided. Medical vocabulary is used only by medical personnel and excludes others from full participation in the birth process as maternity care becomes more standardized.

The Interactional Level

At the interactional level, physicians regard women in childbirth as medical problems. They treat women in childbirth with medication, medical technological intervention, and pharmacological resources, "managing birth without a close social and emotional relationship built up between the midwife, family, and community" (Lowis and McCaffery 2000: 27). Interaction is characterized by hierarchical relations with doctors at the top, then nurses, then midwives and patients in descending order. Characteristic of this hierarchy is the disdain and dismissal of treatments employed by midwives and mothers.

The Control Level

Who has control over pregnancy and birth? Is it the hospital, the doctor, the midwife, the in-laws, or the mother? A variety of decisions, such as where the mother gives birth, what position she uses, who receives the baby, and even how the mother may or may not behave during the delivery, are usually made by people other than the mother (Selin 2009:xvi). The process of medicalization transfers decision-making power from midwives to medical doctors. They gain control over the pregnancy and the birth by "redefining birth as dangerous and birth attendance as increasingly scientific . . . and by casting midwives as dangerously unskilled" (Lowis and McCaffery 2000:27). The midwife's loss of control over birth and her displacement by the obstetrician and hospital are a critical aspect of medicalization.

Medical personnel maintain sole control over access to technology, including the instruments and procedures that may be used in the birthing process, such as forceps, anesthesia, analgesics, surgery, ultrasounds, stethoscopes, and blood pressure cuffs. That control is reinforced by bureaucratization of medical institutions and is reflected in scheduling, the provision of official documents such as midwifery licenses and registration forms for births, and the reporting of births and deaths to the health center or vital registry.

The Gender/Status Level

The birthing experience may be viewed as largely a reflection of male domination and control. The transfer of control over childbirth from the midwife to the doctor represents also the transfer of control from females to males. The biomedical model derives from a male perspective, a perspective that translates into a power relationship of male dominance over the medical profession and the birthing process. Gender bias may also be reflected in decision making within the family, where the pregnant woman's preferences, such as the choice of a midwife or a hospital delivery, may be subordinated to the preferences of her husband or partner or of her in-laws. In addition to gender, other status dimensions that should be incorporated into the model are class and ethnicity. With respect to the role of the midwife, age is another aspect of status that needs to be considered.

By applying the above medicalization framework, I do not mean to deny the scientific benefits of biomedicine or romanticize midwives and ethnomedicine. Rather, I mean to show that biomedicine also includes nonscientific characteristics and nonbeneficial aspects, even though it is usually assumed to be scientific and beneficial. Furthermore, certain traditional birth practices have been shown to be beneficial and scientifically valid, although it is often assumed otherwise. These sorts of claims change over time as new discoveries are made. Ginsberg and Rapp explain that "while the benefits are undeniable, the spread of medical hegemony, through the introduction of hospital-based birth technologies, for instance, often displaces or competes with indigenous practices and may disorganize or extinguish local forms of knowledge" (1991:318).[5]

The biomedical model or paradigm is an abstract ideal type. Physicians and nurses practice and adhere to this model in various ways. One example of this variation is Guatemalan physicians' view of pregnancy and risk—that is, whether every pregnancy is at-risk, or whether pregnancy is a normal, healthy biological process (Dudgeon 2012:19-20). Proponents of both viewpoints agree with the physiological biomedical model of birth, but they differ in the degree to which they regard risk in childbirth as pathology or the result of an outside threat, or to which they understand such risk as danger inherent in the birth process itself. Similarly, midwives vary in the extent to which their practice reflects an ethnomedical model and incorporates or rejects aspects of biomedicine.

One of the major drivers of medicalization is the pharmaceutical industry (Conrad 2007:132). Medicines may be prescribed or recommended by a doctor, nurse, folk healer, or curer (such as a shaman, herbalist, spiritist, or midwife); or they may be self-prescribed or prescribed by a layperson and sold by a pharmacist, salesperson, or traveling vendor. In a study of finca residents' resource utilization, 59 percent of the study sample used pharmaceuticals in their initial treatment, as did 57 percent of those seeking help from a second resource (Cosminsky 1994). These included oxytocin injections, iron pills, antibiotics, vitamin injections, tonics, and common over-the-counter remedies such as Alka-Seltzer, aspirin, and acetaminophen. In Guatemala, as in some other Latin American countries, many pharmaceuticals can be acquired without a prescription. People can go directly to the pharmacy and either buy something they have used previously or ask advice from the pharmacist, who often acts as a lay doctor. They save money by bypassing the doctor or clinic, where they may receive a prescription but not the medication itself.

Sacralization is a countervailing process to medicalization and pharmaceuticalization. When healers or spiritists prescribe a remedy while they are possessed, this imbues the medicine with a sacredness that becomes a property of that medicine. It also gives authority to the healer—in some cases a midwife—who is prescribing the medicine. The belief that the midwife is a ritual specialist with a divine calling who has special dreams, who feels that God is guiding her hands during a massage, who hears voices of spirits, and who lights candles and says prayers are all aspects of the sacralization of birth that are a countervailing force to medicalization. For example, Siriaca prays and lights a candle to the statue of El Niño de Atocha before going to a birth, thus attributing protective and healing powers to Jesus. An opposite form of sacralization occurs with respect to the cult of Moreno Cañas, a Costa Rican physician who was murdered in 1937. People pray to him seeking cures and good fortune. Setha Low argues that by treating Moreno Cañas in a religious manner, adherents are sacralizing secular medicine and consequently demedicalizing control of their own health care (1982:527).

Thus, at the same time that medicalization of birth is happening, a process of demedicalization is also occurring. I argue that the medicalization of birth involves the demedicalization of the midwife's role and the birthing system that she practices. One of the aims of midwifery training programs is to upgrade midwives' practice by increasing their biomedical knowledge, which includes recognition of risk factors and obstetrical emergencies. However, the midwife's role is increasingly attenuated when it is stripped of its medical aspects, which are referred to skilled attendants. This leaves the midwife to function as a supportive figure and emphasizes her social, psychological, and religious roles, which medical personnel do not perform. As Low points out, Renée Fox has suggested that "medicalization and demedicalization are not opposing forces, but part of a reoccurring continuum in which each process responds to the other" (1982:531).

In the process of medicalization, biomedicine comes to be accepted—or in some cases is imposed—as the authoritative knowledge. Other forms of knowledge and ways of knowing become subordinated or lost. Women's voices and knowledge may become muted in this process. Although feminist theorists use the term *muting* to mean that women cannot realize or express their view of the world using the terms of the dominant male model (Moore 1988:3, citing Ardener 1975), the concept of muting may also be applicable to the biomedical model. Carol McClain (1989) raises the question of whether women healers' voices are muted. Some studies say that their voices are silenced, while others contend that they are not; which is true may depend on the existence of a separate male healing discourse. McClain does not discuss the muting of women's voices as represented in the local ethno-obstetric system in relation to the biomedical system.

From one point of view, medicalization may result in the acquisition of additional or new knowledge for Doña María and other women. This may increase the health and nutritional status of their clients and families, and consequently may lead to greater respect and empowerment. On the other hand, medicalization may result in the devaluation and loss of certain types of knowledge, decreased power and control within the family, and decreased respect within the community as community members become more dependent on the biomedical and commercialized health sector. In addition, this knowledge may not translate into behavioral change that results in better health and nutrition if women do not have access to and control of the economic resources needed to carry out biomedical practices; in some cases the knowledge may result in increased mortality and morbidity. Finally, discontinuation or loss of beneficial midwife practices may lead to an increase in birth complications and mortality (Berry 2010).

The issue of silencing or muting as part of medicalization is related to the issue of agency. Agency can be understood as the behavioral manifestation of voice. Although the term agency is often used in discussions of resistance, Wimal Dissanayake uses the term *agent* to "denote the locus from which an action can be initiated, whether it be one of reconfirmation or resistance mainly from the interstices between various subjective positions" (1996:x). Carole Browner and Carolyn Sargent define *agency* "as the socioculturally mediated capacity to act" (2011:13). From this perspective, not all individual actions are manifestations of agency. In this study, agency is involved in acceptance of as well as resistance to aspects of biomedicine. Nicole Berry argues that "agency is not defined by resistance. . . . It may also be defined by actively seeking to form alliance or cooperate or any other activity that does not involve conflict (2010:59). Furthermore, women's decision to give birth at home is "an explicit exercise of women's agency—women prefer to stay home. This preference speaks to the importance of kin ties in supporting women, as well as in subordinating them" (59).

Use of the term *agency* can thus be a two-edged sword. For example, is the midwife incorporating a new practice because she believes it is better, safer, and more advantageous, or because she feels she is forced to do so because of perceived or real threats from the doctor or the state? As Laura Ahearn writes, "agentive acts may also involve complicity with, accommodation to, or reinforcement of the status quo—sometimes all at the same time" (1999:13).

Agency is also closely related to autonomy. Zubia Mumtaz and Sarah Salway (2009) critique the view that the limited autonomy of women is a "key barrier to improvements in their reproductive health," contending that this approach is inadequate for several reasons, including an undue emphasis on women's independent, autonomous action and on women's access to and control over economic resources, and an erroneous assumption that uptake of reproductive health services is an indicator of autonomy (1349). Although their critique is based on a study in Pakistan, many of the issues they raise are also applicable to Guatemala, especially considering the way in which reproductive health programs, such as Safe Motherhood, and various midwifery training programs have been carried out (Berry 2010). "The autonomy paradigm has provided some insights into how gender inequities have impacted women's reproductive health," but it needs to be complemented by an approach that takes into account how the web of social relationships and various hierarchies and inequities operate "to shape women's experiences of reproductive health and illness" (Mumtaz and Salway 2009:1355). The social embeddedness of relations— friendships, loyalty, caring, and responsibility—is devalued when the focus is on individualism.

Does the concept of agency apply when a joint decision is made? Consider the case of Doña Juana. Juana was seriously ill and was having trouble breathing. One of her daughters, Julia, was taking care of her. Julia felt that she could not make the decision to take her mother to the hospital by herself. If she did so without consulting her siblings, they would be mad at her, especially if anything happened to Juana. So she had to wait until at least one of the other siblings arrived to consult with them about whether to take their mother to the hospital. Does Julia lack agency in this case? Or is she acting agentively by expressing the importance of the family, not just the individual, in decision making? This question reveals how the concept of agency often depends on the concept of individualism.

How do policies established at the state level, such as certification, licensing requirements, and restrictions on midwives' practices, affect the agency of midwives and mothers at the local level? The formal midwifery training courses run by Guatemala's Ministry of Health are not only a major source of biomedical knowledge and practices, but also a means by which government policies and regulations promoting the dominance and control of birth by the biomedical system are communicated and carried out. These policies also reflect medicalization as a global process, implementing agendas promoted by international agencies such as WHO, the Pan American Health Organization, the US Agency for International Development (USAID), and the World Bank.

These agendas have shifted over time. Whereas in the 1970s WHO promoted training programs for lay midwives ("traditional birth attendants," or TBAs, as they are referred to by biomedical professionals),[6] it has recently stated that such programs have failed to increase referrals to hospitals or to decrease maternal mortality. WHO is therefore now supporting the training of skilled attendants instead (Replogle 2007). Medical and development personnel use the term *traditional birth attendant* to refer to lay and "traditional" midwives and to those who assist women at birth but do not have biomedical training. Now they are referred to as "unskilled attendants" in contrast to skilled attendants; this reflects the hierarchical and control dimensions of medicalization.

Stacey Leigh Pigg (1997) and Sheila Cosminsky (1977b) discuss the inherent bias of the term *traditional birth attendant*. The term assumes that the midwife only attends the birth and does not provide prenatal or postnatal care. But in Guatemala, among both Mayans and Ladinos, the midwife plays a wide obstetrical, social, and ritual role. The term *midwife* (Spanish *comadrona*; K'iche' *iyom*) is a more accurate and more encompassing term. As Pigg points out, *TBA* refers to societal features that development aims to change. Rapp (2012:232) refers to this shift in terminology as a ping-pong game in which biomedical experts label birth attendants as competent or incompetent without attending to the specifics of their gender and of the training itself. Too often the shift produces costly abstractions rather than teamwork in the interest of medical service. Berry (2010) shows how the transition from considering local midwives as competent and worthy of training to considering them incompetent and thus not worthy has created havoc and confusion in the Safe Motherhood project in Sololá, Guatemala. Both María and her daughter Siriaca fall into the TBA category, according to medical personnel, although the "traditional" parts of their practice differ and have changed over the generations, with Siriaca having much more exposure to biomedicine than her mother.

In the course of this study, we will see how the biomedical model of birth differs from the local ethnomedical model, which regards pregnancy and birth as resulting in an imbalance of hot and cold qualities and representing a normal but potentially dangerous state. During pregnancy, a woman is in a hot state, whereas postnatally she is in a cold state. This imbalance is also influenced by one's state of emotions, especially anger, which is believed to cause miscarriage, premature labor, and other complications. I pay special attention to the role of anger as both an "idiom of distress" (Nichter 1981) and a manifestation of what Kaja Finkler refers to as "life's lesions" (1994), and I consider what this tells us about the social relations, especially gender relations, within the finca, including alcohol use and domestic abuse, which generate anger.

METHODS

It has been my privilege to follow Doña María and Doña Siriaca since 1974, when I met them during my first trip to the plantation. At that time I was carrying out a study of illness behavior and health care utilization with Mary Scrimshaw, my co-investigator. That research was part of a larger, interdisciplinary, "ecological assessment of nutritional status" on the plantation, conducted under the supervision of nutritionist Nevin Scrimshaw, which began in 1970 and continued through 1976. Baseline data had been gathered in 1970, including anthropometrical results, dietary studies, information about food beliefs and practices, reproductive histories, morbidity rates, demographic and sociocultural characteristics of the finca population, and interviews with residents, including the midwife María. On subsequent trips we updated some of this information, including reproductive histories, and added additional information regarding economics, work, gender, and health care.

During that time, I became particularly interested in Doña María and her midwifery role. I had been conducting research with Mayan midwives in the western highland *aldeas* (villages) of El Novillero and

Chuchexic, which are part of the town of Santa Lucía Utatlán, where I had carried out my dissertation research in 1968 and 1969. My earlier work focused on ethnomedicine, decision making and health care, and I was affiliated with the Institute of Nutrition of Central America and Panama (INCAP). That research included studies of the Mayan midwives in the village, as well as of other healers (Cosminsky 1972).

In 1974 and 1976 I returned and conducted extensive interviews and observations with three K'iche' Maya *comadronas* and one Ladina *comadrona*; I also collected medicinal plants that they used. In 1978, we returned to the finca. The focus of that study (Scrimshaw and Cosminsky 1991) was women's productive and reproductive strategies and the allocation of resources between food and medicine. Whereas most studies had focused on families that were doing poorly and asked why they struggled, we were interested in why some families had good health and nutrition records in comparison to others— or in what has since been called "positive deviance" (Zeitlin, Ghassemi, and Mansour 1990). Given that most male workers on the finca earned approximately the same amount as one another and that males had less leeway than females to engage in other economic activities, we hypothesized that it was the women's strategies and control of resources that made the difference in the health and nutritional status of the households, especially because women were the ones that made most of the decisions in those areas.[7]

We were also interested in the impact of seasonality: we compared the lean or hungry season, when corn and cash are scarce, to the peak season, when both are more plentiful, because the availability of resources and women's use of options and strategies differ in each of these seasons.[8] We also observed and interviewed several healers and religious specialists whom people used both on and off the finca.

During our fieldwork, we noticed what seemed to be an increase in infant bottle-feeding. Thus, in 1979 I returned to conduct a study on infant feeding practices and the impact of bottle-feeding. I found that doctors played an important role in encouraging bottle-feeding. If a woman delivered in the hospital, the baby was often given sugar water in a baby bottle. In other cases, if a mother had problems breast-feeding, the doctors blamed her health condition or the quality of her milk, and encouraged her to bottle-feed with commercial formula. The medical profession thus reinforced the idea that infant formula was better than the mother's milk and bottle-feeding was a positive practice. As Penny van Esterik states, "Medicalization of infant feeding refers to the expropriation by health professionals of the power of mothers and other caretakers to determine the best feeding pattern of infants for maintaining health" (1989:112).

While I was doing research on the finca, Doña María was very open and willing for me to accompany her on her rounds. On several successive trips in the 1970s and 1990s, I interviewed and observed Doña María extensively. Because of the respect people accorded her, the forcefulness of her character, and the authority of her position, my association with her helped me to gain women's confidence and to gather information that might have been more difficult to obtain otherwise.

During the 1980s, when the violence in Guatemala prevented me from returning, one of María's daughters, Doña Siriaca, began practicing as a midwife and took over that role from her mother. Siriaca now attends most of the births on the plantation and in neighboring areas. The last time I saw María was in July 1996. At that time she rarely practiced midwifery because her sight was deteriorating and she was having trouble walking, but she still practiced divining and healing. Doña María died in October 1997. People on the finca say that many attended the funeral and that it was announced on the radio because she was widely known and respected.

Data on the plantation population from 1970 to 2013 provide an unusual longitudinal perspective. Both María and Siriaca were included in a sample of thirty-five households that participated in the 1978 study that provided us with detailed information on their families. Additional interviews with and observations of Siriaca and her clients were carried out in 1993, 1996, 2000, 2010, and 2013. During these visits I focused on changes on the finca, followed up with the families still living there, and engaged in intensive interviews with and observations of Siriaca. Like her mother, Siriaca was very hospitable and generous with her time and information. She let my assistant and me accompany her on her visits to various clients.

PLACE IN THE LITERATURE

Most anthropological studies of Guatemala have been carried out among highland Mayan populations, as was my own earlier work. With the exception of Bossen (1984), which includes a chapter on plantation women, hardly any studies of plantation systems in Guatemala have been published, although a significant proportion of local populations live and work in these settings. The research that has occurred on plantations has mainly been on Mayan seasonal migration to cotton, sugar, and coffee plantations, not on settled plantation populations, and has been concerned with the terrible conditions faced by migrant workers (Hoyt 1955). Very little research has focused on migrants' health conditions, although they have been reported to be among the worst in the country (USAID-Guatemala 1977). Jude Pansini (1980:222) reports, "According to INCAP data, the highest malnutrition and mortality rates in the country are registered on these farms." Pansini carried out an ethnographic study of a finca on the south coast, focusing on ethnicity and its relation to religion and social and economic class. This finca is corporately owned by an international company and thus is different from Finca San Luis, where the owner (*finquero*) and his family play a crucial role in the running of the plantation. A different and previously lacking perspective is provided by Elizabeth Oglesby, who has interviewed sugar refinery owners, *finqueros*, and sugar cane workers and has analyzed the changes in labor policies and their implications (2004, 2010, 2013).

Although few studies of fincas have been carried out, several recent studies have been made of Mayan midwives in the highlands of Guatemala, usually as part of a larger project. For example, David Carey Jr. (2006), in his historical study of highland Kaqchikel Mayan women, includes a chapter on a Mayan midwife named Germana, covering the years 1931–1966. Many of Germana's beliefs and practices and her respected status in the community are similar to those of María and Siriaca, as well as the criticisms made of them by biomedical personnel and the pressures to change. Barbara Rogoff (2011) has written a longitudinal study of a Mayan midwife and her family in the town of San Pedro la Laguna on Lake Atitlán. Having access to Lois and Benjamin Paul's notes and photographs from their fieldwork in San Pedro going back to the 1940s, she is able to place the continuity and changes in birth practices in the context of the development and modernization of that town.

The impact of the global Safe Motherhood Initiative in Sololá and Santa Cruz, another town on Lake Atitlán is the focus of work by Berry (2006, 2008, 2009, 2010). She examines the different meanings of motherhood, birth, and birth-related death among midwives, villagers, and biomedical personnel. Berry argues that Safe Motherhood policies not only have failed to decrease maternal mortality locally but may actually increase the number of maternal deaths, in part due to the lack of cultural understandings of both self and family. Several articles have appeared concerning indigenous midwives in Guatemala and Mexico, including their interaction with the formal medical system (Putney and Smith 1989; Berry 2006; Foster, Anderson, Houston, and Doe-Simkins 2004; Callister and Vega 1998; Cosminsky 2001b; Glei and Goldman 2000; Goldman and Glei 2003; Hinojosa 2004; Hopkinson 1988; Hurtado 1984; Hurtado and Saenz de Tejada 2001; Maupin 2008; Paul 1975; Paul and Paul 1975; Pebley, Goldman, and Rodriguez 1996; Roost, Johnsdotter, Liljestrant, and Essen 2004; Wilson 2007). Sarah Proechel (2005) has written a study on Mayan midwives in the highland town of Concepción Chiquirichapa. Since the time of her research, the midwives in that town, who have an effective organization (ACAM—Asociación de Comadronas de Area Mam), were able to raise money with the assistance of an American midwife to build a maternity center, which they run and in which they attend deliveries. This is a different model of integrating biomedicine and Mayan midwifery (Christiana 2011).

The present study is the only one based not in the highlands but on a coastal plantation and in a mixed Maya-Ladino population. Covering the years 1970–2013, it is the only longitudinal study of a finca.

In the following chapters, I describe the plantation setting that provides the context, constraints, and structure within which people are born, live, and die, and in which the midwife or *comadrona* practices. A comparison of Doña María and her daughter Doña Siriaca highlights the continuities and changes in the role of midwives over this forty-year period. I use the medicalization and midwifery model of Lowis and McCaffery (2000) to analyze the impact of medicalization on the birthing process from prenatal care to management of labor and postpartum stages, and on the midwife's role, including her role as healer for illnesses related to women's reproductive health and for various children's illnesses. Family planning programs and contraception are also part of medicalization.

Medicalization is promoted through policies and midwifery training programs from international organizations, government agencies, and nongovernmental projects. A variety of these programs have been and are currently being carried out in Guatemala. I examine the possibilities for accommodation or articulation between biomedicine and the ethno-obstetric system, and I make several recommendations for facilitating more effective relations among biomedical personnel, midwives, and mothers.

MARÍA'S WORLD: THE PLANTATION | *Chapter 2*

*I do not know if coffee and sugar are essential to the hap-
piness of Europe, but I well know that these two products
have accounted for the unhappiness of two great regions
of the world: America has been depopulated so as to have
land on which to plant them: Africa has been depopulated so as to have the people to cultivate them.*

J. H. BERNARDIN DE SAINT PIERRE (1773), QUOTED IN
SIDNEY MINTZ, *SWEETNESS AND POWER: THE PLACE OF
SUGAR IN MODERN HISTORY* (1985)

Towering royal palms line the entrance to Finca San Luis (figure 2.1),
leading to the administration building and the *finquero*'s house, with
its tennis court and swimming pool. The latter has largely been unused
in recent years, but it is a reminder of a past way of life. The entrance
to the plantation used to be open, but now it has an iron gate and an
armed guard, reflecting the violence and crime that has increased in
the area since the Guatemalan civil war broke out in the 1980s.

Along the way are some of the workers' houses; the rest are located
in a compact area on a grid of pathways north and east of the administrative offices. Fields of sugarcane border the main road to the finca,
with views of the volcanoes Santa María and the smoking Santiaguito
in the distance.

Periodically the latter deposits wind-blown ash on the finca, which
is located in the southwestern part of the town of San Luis, Retalhuleu. It is connected to the Pacific Highway by a road that is 6.5 kilometers in length and is passable year-round. Against this backdrop live
Doña María and Doña Siriaca.

In this chapter I describe the environment and the conditions of poverty under which the finca women live, work, and give birth; the decisions midwives and their clients make; and the actions they take. After
a brief historical overview of sugar and coffee production in Guate-

FIGURE 2.1. *Entrance to the finca and the administration building, or* oficina. *Royal palms line the path, and the* finquero's *house is on the right (1996).*

mala, I trace the continuities and changes over the last forty years as people have adjusted to the forces of medicalization and globalization.

THE PLANTATION ECONOMY AND LAND DISTRIBUTION

The term *finca* is used in Guatemala to describe a wide variety of farms that are used for commercial agriculture, for cattle raising, or for both, and that employ one or more permanent or temporary workers who usually live on the finca with their families. A finca may be owned by an individual, a family, a company, or the state.[1]

According to Werner Ascoli (1970), this use of the term *finca* dates back to around 1850, when large-scale cultivation of coffee began in Guatemala. Rapid increase in the production of coffee brought about an influx of foreigners who bought land for growing coffee, as well as Guatemalan Ladinos (non-Indians) who also bought Indian communal lands. David McCreery mentions that for towns of the *boca costa*, the area in which Finca San Luis is located, "coffee hit the local economy and society as a tidal wave, engrossing land and converting local inhabitants into *colonos* (resident workers) or day laborers on the *fincas*" (1990:107).[2]

In the past, from the time of the Spanish conquest to 1944, labor for these farms was provided through various types of forced labor (*encomiendas*, *mandamientos*, *repartimientos*, vagrancy laws, debt servitude, and so on) that were supported through government policies and regulations. Forced labor was abolished in the 1940s, so plantations had to compete for free wage labor. Laurel Bossen explains: "In times of labor scarcity, they attempt to increase the security of their hold on the labor force by maintaining resident workers (for whom they must ensure year round maintenance) with migrant workers who are contracted on short term in accordance with the fluctuating labor needs of the plantation" (1979:33). Whereas in the past the finca used migrant workers from the highlands during the height of the cane harvest, today there seems to be sufficient labor locally for them not to employ migrant workers.

Guatemala faces extreme inequality in land distribution between small landholdings (*minifundias*) and large haciendas and plantations (*latifundias*). According to the World Bank, Guatemala is one of the countries with the most skewed land distribution in the world (2004:60). An estimated 2 percent of the population owns over 65 percent of the arable land.[3] Only 0.2 percent of the fincas are over ten *caballerías* in size (about 1,100 acres), but these larger fincas constitute 36 percent of the cultivated area.[4] Finca San Luis, which is 12.5 *caballerías* in size, falls into this top 0.2 percent (Ascoli 1970). However, it is relatively small compared to the large sugar finca of over 5,200 on which Bossen carried out her research (Bossen 1984:133).

Guatemala is also characterized by a very high proportion of people in poverty and by very high rates of child malnutrition. The distribution of income and wealth is highly skewed. The wealthiest 10 percent of the population receives almost half of all income; the top 20 percent receives two-thirds of all income. According to the most recent World Bank poverty assessment in Guatemala, the poverty rate has declined but is still very high at 53.7 percent in 2011. However, in rural municipalities, which represent 44 percent of the country's population, "almost eight out of ten people are poor" (World Bank 2014). While there has been some improvement in poverty in general, there has not been with respect to extreme poverty, largely due to the increase in food prices (World Bank 2009:viii). Furthermore, Guatemala's num-

TABLE 2.1. CHARACTERISTICS OF FINCA SAN LUIS

	1976	1996–2000	2010
Population	690	400	313
Households	130	52	45
Production	coffee	coffee	no coffee
	cattle	no cattle	cattle—mechanized milking
	sugar cane	sugar cane	sugar cane-hauling, mechanized
	panela, bagasse	no *panela*	raising pigs
Workers	full time: 53; temporary: 210	temporary: 130	temporary from finca: 130; others from outside and from refinery

bers on social and nonmonetary indices such as infant mortality, maternal mortality, maternal illiteracy, and water and sanitation facilities are among the worst in the Western hemisphere, and chronic child malnutrition is among the worst in the world. These indicators of poverty characterize much of the rural population, including that of Finca San Luis.

Finca San Luis was established around 1842 and has been owned by the same family since 1890 (table 2.1). The current owner is of Swiss, Scottish, and Guatemalan ancestry, and is married to an American. His grandfather was originally from Scotland but moved to Mexico, then came to Guatemala. He bought the farm during the expansion of coffee production as it became Guatemala's major export crop. The chimney from the defunct sugar processing plant that used to make unrefined brown sugar, or *panela*, bears the date 1861. Around that time, coffee accounted for 90 percent of Guatemalan exports (COVERCO 2000:4). Today, coffee accounts for a lower proportion of exports. Nevertheless, In 2015, it was still the leading export (Observatory of Economic Complexity 2015).

The amount of coffee produced fluctuates according to the price of coffee on the international market. Thus Guatemala has become vulnerable to changes in the supply and price of coffee on the world market. When the price decreased due to an increase in production in Brazil, Ethiopia, and the Ivory Coast, and more recently in Vietnam, Guatemalan *finqueros* diversified agricultural production. Sugarcane, cotton, bananas, cattle, cardamom, lemongrass oil and most recently palm, have become important commodities. Palm is currently the country's third-largest export, primarily for cooking oil, but the high prices reflect the global demand for its use in biofuels (Rosenthal 2013).

After the market in coffee crashed in 2002 with the expansion of coffee production in Vietnam, the owner of Finca San Luis stopped growing coffee. He said that today the demand is for high-quality, especially organic or fair trade coffee that grows better at higher altitudes than the finca, so it is not worth it for him to go back to growing coffee because he cannot successfully compete. This change has had a significant impact on women's role on the finca and their access to cash, since picking coffee during the harvest season was their primary source of income. Much of the way of life described in this volume revolved around the importance of coffee, especially to women and their families; it has dramatically changed in a number of ways since 2003.

Some of the land previously used for coffee is now used as pasture for dairy cattle or for more cane fields. When coffee was the primary crop in Guatemala, sugar was produced primarily for the local market. With the decline in coffee, sugar cultivation has expanded.[5] Within the past few years, finca owners have been following a policy of diversification. On Finca San Luis, the owner has started planting rubber trees, and his son has started raising and selling pigs. Neither of these requires the same amount of labor as do sugar and coffee. The owner has also rented out land to others to use as a nursery for coffee and other plants.

Finca San Luis is 12.5 *caballerías* plus 37 *manzanas*, or 1,384 acres (560 hectares) (Ascoli 1970). In the 1970s the finca also grew lemongrass and raised cattle, but by 1979 the owner had sold off most of the cattle and had turned over some of the pastureland to coffee. In 1996 approximately 7 *caballerías* were planted in sugar, 3.2 in coffee and 2 in African palm. When the coffee price dropped so low in 2002, he turned again to raising dairy cattle. In 2010, 6.25 *caballerías* were planted in sugar, 2.25 were pasture for thirty cows, and 15 *manzanas* had lemon trees.

By 1980, the owner had sold off about 200 acres, which were divided into small plots. "To help my people, I sold pieces of land to my workers," he said. "I sold it so cheap, stupidly at Q100/*cuerda*, and they could buy on credit. They sold it for five or ten times the price to outsiders." (Antonio Bischoff, 1996, personal communication). Several former Finca San Luis residents, including at least two of María's daughters and two of her sons and their families, had bought land and until recently were living in the area. Nevertheless, some of the former finca families living in the area worked as temporary workers for the finca.

In 2000, many people expressed the fear that they would be flooded by the Samalá River, which runs through the area. Boulders from the eruptions of the Santiaguito volcano caused a change in the course of the river and increased the danger of flooding from the river. By 2010, most of the residents had relocated to a new location, Nuevo Pomerrosal, under the *municipio* of San Felipe. Only a few families remained in the previous area of Pomerrosal, although the river had not yet flooded the area.

HOUSING AND LIVING CONDITIONS

Conditions on the plantation reflect the poverty of the finca population. These poor conditions contrast with those described by Bossen (1984:134) for the Finca El Cañaveral, which had houses for the permanent workers with cement floors, electricity, access to running water, and outhouses. Even though the *finquero* of San Luis provides housing, it is poor and overcrowded. Most is constructed with wooden boards for the walls, a corrugated metal roof, and a dirt floor on a raised foundation. During one interview it started to rain, and we had to shift chairs several times to avoid the drips from the leaking roof. Juan, the head of the household, said that the *finquero* would not fix the roof, and he did not want to spend the money himself because his family did not own the house and did not know how long they would be living in it.

The majority of these houses were constructed in rows. About a third of the housing units are single, freestanding houses built in the same style. The average house is twenty-five by fourteen feet. Many have been subdivided into two or more rooms with boards or bamboo. Some houses have lean-tos or room additions for cooking, sleeping, or storage made out of wood or local cane and thatch. A few houses, such as those of the administrator, the teacher, and the carpenter are constructed of cement block with raised cement floors.

FIGURE 2.2. *Typical finca housing and main street (1978).*

The average household on the finca consists of five to six people but some have as many as fourteen. Most are nuclear families but several are three-generation extended families. Beds are commonly shared by several people. According to Merrill Read's 1970 study of Finca San Luis, the average number of people per bed was 2.1, increasing to 2.8 in households having young children. Such crowding facilitates the exchange of infectious disease. Latrines were virtually nonexistent, and only a few houses, such as the administrator's and the teacher's, had indoor facilities. Defecation occurred in the fields, woods, or nearby streams (Read 1970). This situation has hardly changed up to the present, except now there are fewer houses.

Cooking is done over a wood fire, with the wood either on the floor or on a raised wooden platform made filled with dirt. Three rocks or bricks are placed in the fire to support the cooking utensil, in the traditional Mayan fashion. Some families have a raised hearth on a concrete base. Several families have built a shed or extension for the cooking area, which decreases the amount of smoke inside the house.

Between 1970 and 2000, water on Finca San Luis was supplied primarily from two public taps, or *pilas*, and was not potable. Women and children carried the water to the houses, where it was stored in large, often open or exposed, jugs. The streams that traverse the finca were used for washing clothes, dishes, and bathing.

When I returned to the finca in 2000, I saw that important changes had been made. In 1999 several taps with potable water were installed on the plantation. The population was less than half of what it had been due to people leaving voluntarily or being forced to leave. The houses of the departing families were then knocked down. According to the finca owner's son, these would eventually be replaced by better housing for the smaller workforce that would be left after reorganization of the finca.

By 2010 the finca owner had provided outdoor sinks and taps for several families. However, the houses were still basically the same, only there were fewer of them. Being able to wash clothes and dishes in the sinks that were provided instead of in the streams is an important labor saver for the women in the household, and it is healthier than washing clothes and dishes in the stream.

Another change in the 1990s was that many people had televisions, although they still did not have electricity. People used car generators to power the TVs, even if they had no cars. By 2010, most families had

FIGURE 2.3.   *Children fetching water at the main fountain* (pila) *(1978).*

FIGURE 2.4.   *Washing clothes, dishes, and bodies in a local stream on the finca (1978).*

FIGURE 2.5. *Household outdoor tap and sink* (pila) *provided by the finca (2013).*

electricity—usually enough power for one light bulb and for their TV if they had one. The electricity was also used to charge cell phones, which several people now owned.

FINCA ORGANIZATION AND TYPES OF WORKERS

The finca owner (*finquero* or *patrón*) lives in Guatemala City and visits the finca once or twice a week. Previously, he and his family used to stay more often and for longer periods, but since the *violencia* (civil war) in the 1980s, and with the increase in crime in Guatemala and various incidents in and around the finca, they have considered it too dangerous to stay overnight. However, when I returned in 2000, the owner's son and his family had moved in and were staying on the finca. By 2010, the son had school-age children and had moved back to Guatemala City. He was spending a couple of days each week on the finca, as was his father.

The *finquero* is also responsible for providing a number of basic services, including a school, teachers, a water supply, rations, and maintenance of social security benefits for permanent workers (Read

1970:11). Rations consist of *panela*, firewood, coffee, and corn. These rations do not need to be provided for temporary workers.

The finca is organized hierarchically, with the highest position being held by the administrator, who is responsible for day-to-day management. The administrator influences many of the decisions and policies concerning the workers, decisions on work assignments, housing, land allocation, and living conditions. Next in the hierarchy is the office assistant, who manages payroll and other fiscal matters. Workers are organized into the following categories: salaried workers (*meseros* or *empleados*), permanent workers (*colonos*), and temporary workers (variously referred to as *temporales, eventuales, ganadores,* or *voluntarios*).

Among the workers, the salaried workers hold the highest status and are paid a set salary rather than wages that are determined by the amount or the area worked. Salaried workers include the office manager, accountant, chauffeur, tractor driver, carpenter, cook, and gardener. They are assigned to housing that is usually freestanding and somewhat larger than that of the other workers.

Finca San Luis had a permanent population of resident laborers and their families. These *colonos* were tenant farmers who received housing and small plots of land (*milpas*) for cultivation of their food crops, as well as wages for their labor. Married *colonos* were provided with eight *cuerdas* of land (one *cuerda* = 625 square meters) for cultivating crops for personal consumption or sale. Unmarried *colonos* received six *cuerdas*. *Colonos* who had been designated as *caporales* (field supervisors) had higher status and more privileges; they received more land and rations.

Although the finca used to also contract with seasonal migrants from the highlands, it no longer needs to do so and instead hires temporary labor from within the finca and the surrounding area. Because they do not work for more than three months at a time, the *finquero* doesn't have to pay government benefits, such as social security and indemnification (Read 1970). However, the *finquero*, has allowed some of them to live on the finca, primarily those who are sons or daughters of former *colonos*. These *ganadores* receive four *cuerdas*, but usually of poorer land or land that is in a less desirable location. Guatemalan law supposedly protects them from being unjustifiably fired.

The use of these temporary workers means less dependence on migrant workers. In 1996, 25 percent of the workers lived on the finca and 75 percent were from outside, mostly from the adjacent village, or *aldea*. Today cheaper temporary day labor sourced mainly from outside the finca is used instead, and there is no requirement that plots of land for crops be provided for them. Fewer migrant workers were being used each year. In 1970, about fifty were used during the peak of the coffee season (September to November). To my knowledge none have been used since 1993. The changes in labor policy on the finca are part of a larger policy incorporating private-public relationships governing labor. Elizabeth Oglesby (2013) examines these changes involving the elimination or eviction of resident workers from fincas and increases in refineries' and plantations' hiring of temporary workers from outside. The changes were instituted by the National Sugar Foundation (FUNDAZUCAR) and the landowners as a way of increasing their control of the labor force.

AGRICULTURAL PRODUCTION ON THE FINCA

Two interdependent production systems coexist on the plantation: the commercial production of cash crops, such as sugarcane and coffee, and peasant production of subsistence crops like corn and beans. Most of the latter are used for the workers' subsistence, but occasionally workers sell some corn to pay for necessities like medical care.

Subsistence Crops

There are two harvests of corn and beans. The first harvest, referred to as the *temporada*, is in June and July. The second, which is less productive, is the *segunda*, in December and January. The yields from these harvests are usually not sufficient for the household's food supply for the year and must be supplemented by purchased food. All families buy these staples at some point before the *temporada*, sometimes as early as April. During this lean season there was also no coffee to pick when coffee was grown on the finca. Therefore cash employment is essential for food supply, and dependence on the husband to buy corn is highest at this time, because the wife does not have any cash.[6] According to S. Ryan Isakson, "The returns from subsistence-oriented agricultural activities provide a necessary complement to the low wages that they receive in the labor market. The resiliency of the Guatemalan peasantry . . . is underpinned by its participation in multiple forms of economic provisioning" (2009:753). Several families have bought land off the finca if they were able to, because they were no longer being given land on the finca or because of the insecurity arising from the possibility that they could be forced to leave the finca.

In 2000, instead of receiving plots of land, workers were allotted strips or rows (*surcos*) in the cane fields to plant their corn and beans. This disposition included land given to widows and retired workers.[7] When I returned in 2010, those workers were no longer being given rows in the cane fields; the *finquero* was again allocating small plots of land to some of these workers. This change might be related to the practice of burning the cane fields before the harvest.

Everyone still plants some *milpa*. The social value and meaning of planting *milpa* is still very important with respect to gender roles. Men are responsible for planting the corn, and women plant the beans between the corn. Ideally men are supposed to provide corn for the household—whether it is from the *milpa* or purchased with cash. Women are also responsible for weeding, or *limpiando la milpa*. When they go out to the fields to weed, they often pick wild greens that they cook and eat in soups or with tortillas.[8] Although people regard these greens as a food of last resort, they are very important nutritionally. Isakson points out that several unquantifiable, nonmarket values are associated with the cultivation of *milpa*: "It is a multidimensional asset: to reduce its value to the single rubric of a monetary price would sacrifice meaning for measurement" (2009:753). *Milpa* is an expression of cultural identity that fortifies social bonds, offsets the uncertainty of the market, and rejects the complete commodification of food, even though its cultivators participate in the market economy (Isakson 2009:755). Although Isakson is writing about Mayan agriculture, much of this meaning of making *milpa* seems to hold for the mixed finca population as well.

Some families have fruit trees in their patios and will sell the fruit in the market in Retalhuleu to get a little cash. They also may plant various herbs to use in cooking and healing. Other economic activities that people, especially women, engage in to extend their cash are establishing small stores or corn mills (for which they have to get permission from the *finquero*), selling sodas on payday and during fiestas, making and selling tamales on payday, making and selling flavored ices, raising small animals (chickens, turkeys, and ducks), selling eggs, and sewing clothes. In the 1970s, some women would buy milk produced from the finca cattle and make cheese, which they would sell for the equivalent of $.25 a packet. However, when the owner sold off all the cattle, that opportunity to make some cash was lost. Today the

FIGURE 2.6. *Mother making a hole with a machete in which her daughter plants beans in between the rows of corn planted by her father (1978).*

finca has dairy cattle, but all of the milk is collected mechanically and sold to a dairy.

Sugar

Another source of income is from cutting sugarcane. The season for cane on the finca runs from November through July. The finca used to have a processing plant for unrefined brown sugar (*panela*). Mill workers received payment on the basis of unit of *panela* produced, with proportional pay for sugarcane cutters and haulers. Income for this activity frequently totaled the equivalent of $1.25/day, a higher income than they usually earned from cutting the cane at that time. Women and children also carried *bagasse* (the waste pulp left after sugarcane is pressed) in large baskets, then spread it out to dry. Although one woman said the work was hard ("este trabajo es duro") and they did not get paid much, it was an extra source of income.

However, by 1979 the mill was no longer being used and all the cane was sent to a refinery to be processed into white sugar, in part because the price of sugar had gone up and sending the cane to the refinery was more profitable than making brown sugar for local consumption or sale. According to the finca's administrator, they needed to run the *panela* processing plant at night to make it profitable, and people did not want to work those hours. According to some of the workers the *finquero* would have had to pay overtime, which would cost him more; others said he closed the plant because it was more profitable to sell to the sugar refinery.

Some large sugar plantations with refineries have mechanized planting, cultivation, and other aspects of sugar production, but this has not happened yet on Finca San Luis. Workers still plant, cultivate, and cut cane by hand. However, by the time I returned in 2010, the finca had mechanized the process of hauling the cane into trucks through contracts with a sugar refinery, which also was providing a large percentage of the temporary workers. By then the finca was hiring only a few local workers, maybe twenty to thirty.

The administrator explained that they now use the CAT system—corte, alce, y transporte—which refers to cutting the cane, gathering it, and transporting it. This system was introduced in Guatemala in 1980 (Wagner 2007:211). The cane is burned a few hours before the cutting to facilitate the work of the cutters. The burning reduces the trash (*basura*) and keeps away vermin such as rodents, spiders, and

FIGURE 2.7. *Man cutting sugarcane (1978).*

snakes. According to Wagner (2007), on some fincas that do not apply this system, cutters light fires "by accident." If the fires are not set in a controlled manner, taking into account the direction and intensity of the wind, major damage can occur. Mechanized cane cutting, which does not involve burning, began in the decade of the 2000s and has been constantly increasing throughout Guatemala, but as of 2010 such mechanization was not employed on Finca San Luis.[9]

Coffee

During August through November, many extra laborers were needed for harvesting coffee. Women and children picked coffee to earn additional income that was critical to the maintenance of the family. Women and children earned less than men for picking coffee. For example, while men were paid Q1 (US$1) for a *quintal* (one hundred pounds) of coffee, while women and children got the equivalent of $.60–.70 per *quintal*. The finca also had a *beneficio*, a processing plant where coffee was spread out to dry, graded for different qualities, processed, and made ready for shipping.

The finca's tenants, especially the women, looked forward to the coffee harvest. They went out with their children, who helped them pick coffee and kept the income they made. Coffee harvest was the time when women could pay off debts and buy medicines, clothes, and other household items.

Coffee was not only critical economically but also important socially. Women often worked in groups of related families, which promoted female bonding. The coffee harvest was a time when women would get together with other female relatives or neighbors at lunch break and socialize and share food. In the words of one mother:

> We get together with our children, with companions. I go with my sister and my cousins. At lunch we eat together. We exchange tortillas. Some bring beans and rice, some a little meat or herbs, and we divide. After lunch, we say many thanks and go back to work. This is a good time of the year. It is hard; we must get up at 3:00 or 4:00 a.m. to complete our household tasks, but we are content, tranquil because we earn our own money. It is ours. We can eat a little better or buy clothes for the children and ourselves. (Cosminsky and Scrimshaw 1981:53)

THE COMMUNITY OF THE FINCA

According to the baseline 1970 study, the permanent population of Finca San Luis was 652 persons. Over half of the workers then employed at the finca were born on Finca San Luis. Among the 134 workers who were born on the finca, 58 percent had two parents who were

FIGURE 2.8.   *Woman picking coffee while carrying her infant (1978).*

also born on the finca, and another 14 percent had one parent who was born there (Read 1970). Some of the parents not born on Finca San Luis were from nearby fincas, such as Finca Buena Vista. Others were from highland towns such as San Cristobal, Totonicapán, and Quetzaltenango. Of those workers not born on the finca, most had been living there between twenty and forty years; some for over fifty years. The finca was thus a stable community, with many families living there for several generations. This residential stability also promoted family stability, with husbands and partners staying and playing a role in maintaining their families. This stability was mentioned by the *finquero*, who said, "I've been pretty lucky. I haven't had too many problems. Most of the people have been here for years. I know them" (1996, personal communication).

The population of the finca in 1976 was 690, half of whom were female. The finca had 53 permanent workers and 210 temporary workers, 96 of them male and 114 female. In 1996, according to the office manager, there were 130 workers. All of these workers were temporary, (*eventuales* or *voluntarios*), and there were no longer any *colonos*. However, for one of the *quincenas* (fifteen-day work periods) in January 1996, there were only seventy-nine workers. This was not during the coffee season, when the number of workers would increase. In contrast, in September 2010 only thirty men from the finca were working there, ten of whom were actually retired.

The elimination or displacement of the *colonos* follows a pattern that is being carried out increasingly on Guatemalan fincas (Oglesby 2013). Some former *colonos* have relocated to adjacent communities or moved to Guatemala City. When a house becomes empty because someone has died or moved, it is knocked down so no one else can use it. Several people expressed their anxiety about not knowing whether or when they will be forced to move. The *finquero* has said he would not force widows of *colonos* to move.

However, Finca San Luis is a complex community that is undergoing change. Finca policies are changing in response to new labor laws, economic conditions, the political situation, and crime rates. The most drastic of these changes is the elimination of the *colonos* and the hiring of only temporary workers, in addition to the end of coffee cultivation. Yet the *finquero* has allowed the *colonos* and their families to stay and keep their houses so far. Several of the surrounding fincas have followed a pattern of eliminating all *colonos* and resident workers except for a skeleton crew who work full time, and using only part-time or temporary workers beyond that. The trend now is to hire part-time workers for no more than three months at a time, so the employer will not have to pay the required government benefits. This strategy is financially beneficial for the *finquero*. In 1996 several people expressed fear that this was what would happen on Finca San Luis as well, and said they didn't know what they would do if that happened.

When I returned in 2000 the owner's son was managing the finca. Beginning in 1999 he reduced its resident population and knocked down houses. Whereas in 1970 there were 124 houses, and in 1976 there were 130 houses, in 2000 there were 52, and in 2010 only 45. The population size went from 690 in 1976, to 400 in 2000, and to 313 in 2010. The sons of *colonos* had to leave if they were not working on the finca, even if they and their parents had worked there for many years, and especially if their parents had died or retired. More and more people who lived outside the finca, either in the adjacent *aldeas* or in nearby areas, were being hired, rather than those individuals living on the finca. According to the administrator of the finca, these young men did not want to work on the plantation but sought jobs in town or at the nearby Coca-Cola plant; according to some of these men, they wanted to work on the finca, but the administrator had refused to hire them.

Compared to the 1970s, families today on the finca are more unstable. There are more young single mothers living with their natal families and more absentee fathers and fathers not recognizing paternity. In addition, more young males have migrated to the city or are working on road construction or on other fincas, leaving fewer male partners for the young women on the finca. There are also a number of cases of young women and girls who have gone to work as maids for families in Retalhuleu or Guatemala City, have become pregnant, and have asked the grandmother to raise the child on the finca so they can continue working. They send money whenever they can to help with the raising of their child.

HOUSEHOLDS

In 1970, the majority of households on the finca were nuclear (47.5 percent) but many were extended or multigenerational (36 percent). The remaining were single parent and children (7.7 percent) and single without children (8.8 percent). The average household size was 5.6 persons, although households ranged from large three- or four-generation families with eighteen inhabitants at one extreme, to single-person house-holds, usually of a widow or widower, at the other. The majority of households were headed by a couple. Often another couple lived in the same household, such as the householder's son and his wife and their children. Even though most of the unions were common law rather than the result of a formal church or legal ceremony, they tended to be stable. Eighty-six heads of households were asked the duration of their present union; the average was eighteen years, with many having been together for thirty years or more (Read 1970:14).

Household composition changes and shifts with the stage in the do-mestic cycle. This affects how much money the family has, its food needs, and the sufficiency of the food supply. These factors are in turn influenced by illness and health status, including reproductive health, which affect the ability to work, earn money, and pay medi-cal expenses. For a young family, the high dependency ratio affects the mother's food provisioning behavior, the family income, and expenses. By comparing the households of the midwives María and Siriaca, and a typical finca mother, Elena, in 1978, 1996, and 2000, we can see the impact of these changes and the survival strategies used to maintain a household on the finca.

María's Household

María's house, like the others, was made of wood, with a metal roof and a dirt floor, but it was freestanding and larger with three rooms. The size of her home reflected the large size of her household. The largest room was a combined living and sleeping area; a smaller room was a partitioned-off section in the back for a bedroom; and the third was the kitchen. There were five beds. María's household was made up of a large extended family. Between 1970 and 1996, the number of people and the composition of the household varied, reflecting differ-ent phases of the domestic cycle as María's children and their spouses, in-laws, and grandchildren moved in and out. In 1970, fourteen peo-ple lived in the house. In 1976, that number increased to eighteen peo-ple. By 1978, some had moved out, and ten people were living there. In contrast, in 1996 only María, her husband, and a granddaugh-ter lived in the house. At times María's mother-in-law also lived with them, until she passed away. Sometimes a married son, his wife, and their children were part of the household. María was also raising two grandchildren.[10]

A heavy workload fell on the three women in this household, who procured and prepared food (weeding and cleaning the milpa, grinding corn, making tortillas, cooking, going to the market) and performed other household duties (fetching water, washing, ironing, caring for children, and so on). In addition, they picked coffee on the finca during the coffee season, and they worked on their own small plots of land, which were provided by the finca owner for their corn and beans. One of María's daughters or granddaughters would sometimes accompany her on her house calls at other fincas. She also went to the bush or *monte* to gather herbs and went to the market in San Felipe or Retalhuleu every other Sunday.

María used a variety of strategies to extend her resources. For example, she had a large brick oven at the back of her yard in which she baked bread, especially for the Day of Ascension. She also let other people use the oven, for which she charged a fee. She raised pigs in conjunction with other finca residents. These people would raise the piglets, and when they were sold, the person who raised them would receive half of the money from the sale, and María would receive the remaining half. After her own children, her *comadres* would have priority to raise the pigs.

Raising pigs was an important survival strategy; it was like having savings in a bank. Residents of the finca raised pigs to be sold to others when a monetary need arose rather than to be eaten by themselves. A piglet costing the equivalent of ten dollars would sell for forty to sixty dollars, depending on the size and health of the animal. Money from the sale of animals was frequently used to defray medical expenses or to buy food in times of scarcity.

According to a 1978 order by the plantation owner, people could raise pigs only if the pigs were restrained by being tied up or kept in a pig sty to prevent them from getting into the fields and destroying the crops. Unrestrained pigs would be shot. A shooting incident happened that year while I was interviewing one of María's daughters-in-law. There was a sudden uproar outside, and everyone ran out of the house excitedly. The finca administrator had shot two of her pigs, and María's son was bringing them back dead in a wheelbarrow. The family ate two pounds of the meat, gave some to María, and sold the rest. People did not have refrigeration or any way of preserving the meat, so it had to be disposed of rapidly. By the time I returned in 1993, the plantation owner prohibited people from keeping pigs at all. Because women are responsible for the care of small animals, including pigs, an important survival strategy for women had been drastically curtailed with this prohibition.

María's husband and sons contributed a portion of their pay for the support of the household. It is general practice on the finca not only for husbands to give a portion of their salary to their wives for food and household expenses but also for their children who are working and living in the house to contribute. For example, for a two-week period in May 1978, María received a total of $34 (Q34) from her husband, three sons, and one grandson.[11]

Siriaca's Household

Siriaca's house has two main rooms, which are made of wood with a tin roof and dirt floors. One side adjoins another house. She has two couches and four beds. She had added a separate room that she uses as a kitchen. In 1978, her six children, her husband and herself—eight people in all—were living in the household. In 2010 there were seven people, including one of her daughters, her daughter's husband, and their four children. They were staying with her because her son-in-law, who works as a mason, was temporarily out of work due to the rainy season.

Her husband, Vidal, had fallen off the sugarcane truck in 1977 while working and had hurt his chest. He had pain in his chest "como aire" (like air) and had problems after that, including not being able to work regularly. He went to the Social Security Institute (IGSS) where they took X-rays and gave him some pills. During the time we were on the finca in 1978, he fell again and hurt his ribs. He went to the IGSS again, where they gave him an injection and pills, but they didn't help. He felt very weak. In addition, he had recurrent sore throats and chest and stomach pains. Because his body was in a hot state from working in the sun, he drank herbal teas that were considered *fresco* (cool).

As the symptoms continued, Vidal went to the San Cayetano clinic in San Felipe. He became worse, with diarrhea and wheezing in addition to the stomach and chest pains. Over the next few months, he took more herbal remedies and some Terramycin pills. He consulted a spiritist, who prescribed herbs, patent remedies, compresses, and plasters. The spiritist referred Vidal to another spiritist in the city of Quetzaltenango who performed invisible operations. Vidal saw him at least four times, during one of which he had an invisible operation. In addition to the costs of the treatment, Vidal had to pay bus fare, and he lost wages. The expenses that we were able to track during our stay, from March to August 1978, were over fifty-five dollars, not counting loss of wages. This was a big drain on the household. It happened before Siriaca started practicing as a midwife.

Siriaca's husband died in 1989 from cancer of the esophagus. He had gone to the cancer hospital in Guatemala City, but was told the cancer was too advanced to operate. Siriaca attributed it to working with pesticides unprotected for so long. When he died, the *finquero* initially gave her Q18 per month (Q6 for each of three children, the equivalent of $2.57). In 1996 she was receiving Q110 per month ($14.38) from the Social Security Institute because of his death. In 2010, she was receiving Q220 per month ($27.50).

Elena's Household

Elena was one of the mothers in the 1978 study and is still living on the finca with her family. In 1978, Elena was twenty-seven years old and had four small children, three girls and one boy, ranging from one to ten years old. Her husband, Orlando, was a *ganador* (temporary worker) and the only full-time wage earner. On average, he was making the equivalent of seventeen dollars per *quincena* (fourteen-day pay period) during the lean season, from April through July. That year everyone in the family was sick. At various times Elena had fever, chills, sore throat, cough, swollen glands, diarrhea, stomach cramps, and urinary bleeding. At one point she was diagnosed with malaria. All the children suffered on and off from colds, cough, fevers, and diarrhea. In addition to having diarrhea, the baby was vomiting and had fever sores and conjunctivitis. The family spent the equivalent of over sixty-seven dollars, seeking help from the public health clinic, private physicians, injectionists, shamans, diviners, and spiritists, and using a variety of herbs, patent remedies, pharmaceuticals, injections, prayers, and rituals. They sold corn several times in order to buy medicine and food. Sometimes this meant selling corn for below the market rate. Elena had increased her gathering of a variety of greens to substitute for meat, beans, and rice. Elena also borrowed money from the *finquero* to pay off food and medical debts. This amount would be deducted from her pay when she picked coffee during the harvest starting in October.

Because she was often sick and the children were always sick, Elena hadn't been able to work like some of the other women or go out and clean the fields. She said she was ashamed, (*me da vergüenza*) because they had nothing: "If there was no sickness, we would have some money, but since we are sick, there is none."

By October, the situation had greatly improved. The baby was well. Elena was picking coffee and with the girls' help earned the equivalent of twenty dollars. Her husband earned thirty-seven dollars for the *quincena* October 14–27, more than double what he had been earning in July and August. He gave Elena ten dollars and paid off several of their debts. They also had corn from their harvest, compared to July 1978, when she bought a hundred pounds of corn (one quintal) for two weeks, which cost eleven dollars. Now Elena bought eight pounds of meat and three pounds of fish, costing $5.85, and twelve pounds of beans. This was much more than the one pound of meat and two pounds of beans she had bought in the *quincena* May 28-June 10.

Elena gave birth to another boy in 1979 and a girl, Francisca, in 1984. The boy died when he was three years old. Thus Elena had six children, of whom four daughters and one son survived.

Elena's husband, Orlando, had an accident in 1993 when he fell from the cane truck while loading and was pierced by a piece of cane that tore his intestines. He went to the hospital, and they told him not to lift heavy things. He retired after that. He gets the equivalent of about twenty-five dollars per month from Social Security. At that time, he couldn't make *milpa* because he was sick, and they had to buy corn. When he felt better, he worked, taking care of his family's and others' *milpas*.

Elena's two oldest daughters work in Guatemala City, one as a maid for the owner of a finca, and the other as a cook for a family. They give Elena some money each month. They have also bought some land in the *aldea* outside the finca. The former daughter's male partner, with whom she had a son, abandoned her, and Elena is raising the child on the finca. They have been concerned about keeping him in school so he can get as much education as possible. His mother gives some money to Elena to help with expenses. Elena's two youngest daughters ironed and washed for a couple in Retalhuleu for a time, but as of 2010 they were back living with Elena on the finca. The youngest daughter, Francisca, had a son in 2011 as a single mother and is raising the child in Elena's house. She had prenatal care from both Doña Siriaca and the prenatal clinic but had to deliver in the hospital. This was her first child, and Siriaca is not allowed to deliver firstborns. Although Francisca had a normal birth, she had difficulty breastfeeding.

She said she tried various herbal remedies but they did not help. She said that the insufficiency of her milk may have been caused by antibiotics she took for a urinary infection while she was pregnant. She had to buy infant formula for the baby, which was an additional expense for the family. The baby also developed asthma, which entailed more medical expenses.

Elena is frequently ill with flu (*gripe*), anxiety, high blood pressure, and nervios, and she has trouble walking because of pains in her feet and legs. When she went to the doctor because of headaches, he told her she had *alta presion* (high blood pressure) and *nervios*. He prescribed some pills and injections, which she is supposed to keep taking. However, she cannot afford to take them continuously as prescribed. Orlando is no longer working and has had continuing problems and pains because of his earlier injury. Although they sell sodas, primarily during holidays, they are constantly experiencing financial and health problems. No longer having the opportunity to earn money from picking coffee has put additional strains on Elena's largely female household. In order to help with the family expenses, in 2015 Francisca went to work in Guatemala City for the family who employed her oldest sister, who had broken her arm and was having trouble working. Francisca left her little boy, who was four years old in 2015, on the finca with her mother, father, and one of her older sisters.

Both Orlando and Vidal were injured in work accidents involving falls from a cane truck. The accidents affected their ability to work regularly and thus put additional financial burdens on their households. It is impossible to know whether pesticides played a role in Vidal's cancer of the esophagus. Little information is available concerning occupational hazards such as accidents related to cutting cane and chemical exposure to pesticides.[12] This is an area of needed research.

ETHNICITY

The ethnic composition of the plantation reflects the enduring complexities of ethnicity in Guatemala. In the academic literature on Guatemala, people are referred to either as Indians (*indígenas* or *naturales*) or as Ladinos. The Indians are of Mayan ancestry, and there are over twenty different Mayan groups with distinct languages and cultural identities. The Ladinos are loosely defined as all nonindigenous groups; they are of European or mixed European and indigenous origin, speak Spanish, wear Western clothing, are oriented to European or Western culture, and do not self-identify as Mayan. The distinction is largely a cultural one, and as David Carey Jr. explains, a Maya can stop speaking his or her native language, wear Western clothing, associate with Ladinos, and identify himself or herself as Ladino (Carey 2001:285). However, non-Indians of upper socioeconomic status, such as the plantation owner, usually refer to themselves as *guatemaltecos* and do not use the term *Ladino*.

The population of Finca San Luis is of mixed heritage, consisting mainly of second and third generation Mayan migrants from various parts of the highlands. In a 1970 survey in which heads of household were asked to classify themselves and their spouse, 67 percent identified themselves or their spouse as *indígena* or *natural*, and 39 percent identified themselves or their spouse as Ladino. In 10 percent of the families, one parent was Ladino and the other was *natural* (Read 1970). However, most of those who self-identify as *natural* are ladinoized—that is, they speak Spanish as their mother tongue and wear Western dress. Another term of identification that is increasingly being used by people on the finca is *campesino* (peasant or farmer).

In 1970, approximately one-third of residents said they spoke a Mayan language. However, I never heard any Mayan languages spoken in public, and only a few older people still remember some of the Mayan language they once spoke. Nowadays everyone speaks Spanish. Some inhabitants wore an Indian skirt and retained certain Indian cultural traits, including birth and curing beliefs and practices—for example, a belief that being exposed to an eclipse is dangerous because it can cause cleft palate, birth deformities, and miscarriages. Those who migrated from elsewhere were from various Indian towns or areas and in some cases spoke different languages—such as K'iche' or Mam—so they had to speak Spanish to communicate with each other.

Status differences exist between Indian and Ladinos and among Ladinos. For example, most of the salaried workers, such as the cook for the finca owner and his family, the chauffeur, tractor drivers, the administrator, the office manager, and the teachers, were Ladinos and had better housing than other finca residents. People in these positions had higher status than Ladinos who worked in the fields (Pansini 1977). Some of the Ladino males had sexual liaisons with Indian women. For example, Veronica, a Maya woman, mentioned that her first two children were fathered by a Ladino when she was living on a different finca, before she moved to Finca San Luis with her present husband, who is also Maya. There were also a number of interethnic couples who were married, especially among the children of the earlier migrants. I knew of at least two other married couples on the finca in which the husband was Indian and the wife was Ladina. More common in Guatemala were interethnic relations between a Ladino male and Indian female.[13]

María is an Indianized Ladina, which is unusual. She was born a Ladina, but at age fourteen married an Indian whose family was living on the same finca as hers (Finca Buena Vista) and originally came from the highland town of Totonicapán. They lived under her mother-in-law's roof for several years. During that time she had to learn K'iche', and according to her daughter, she was mistreated and abused by her husband's family. Eventually, in the 1970s, María became a shaman, or daykeeper (Sp., *zahorín* or *chiman*; K'iche', *ajq'ij*) in the Mayan tradition, apprenticing with a shaman from whom she learned the ancient Mayan ritual calendar, prayers in K'iche', and how to divine with the *tsité* seeds and heal. She was already a practicing midwife and spiritist.[14] All of these roles are considered divine gifts for which practitioners are supernaturally selected. Siriaca does not identify herself as Maya or Ladino, but as *mezclado*.

EDUCATION

In 1970, the *finquero* provided a two-room schoolhouse for the first three years of school, paying for the salary of two teachers. Back then, the first grade had forty-three students and the combined second and third grade class consisted of thirty-one students (Read 1970). Although Guatemalan law requires six years of school, most students did not attend more than three years, except for those who repeated grades. During the peak work periods, especially coffee-picking time, attendance dropped because children helped their parents. Children who wanted to continue school for the second three years of primary school had to go to San Sebastián, about five miles away, which meant taking the bus to school, buying lunch, and paying for incidental expenses, which was impossible for many families. Secondary school was in Retalhuleu, with estimated costs of sixteen to eighteen quetzals a month, which was not affordable for most finca families. Some students did attend primary or secondary school off the finca. They came from the elite families, such as those of the teachers, the administrator, and the chauffeur, who had the highest incomes on the finca. Most of the finca women were illiterate, though a few of the younger women were semiliterate.

In 1996, students were going to the school in adjacent Pomerrosal, which went up to the sixth grade and had 115 students and four teachers. The *finquero* said he had closed the finca school and combined it with the one in Pomerrosal. They had a food program in which *atole* and lunch were provided for the students. However, because of the poverty of many of the families, many students did not stay in school but left to help their parents work, especially during the coffee season.

By 2010, the school in Pomerrosal had been closed because most of the families had moved away and a new school had been built on Finca San Luis that was also open to the children from one of the adjacent fincas. There were about 125 students from kindergarten through 6th grade at the school. If students wanted to continue their education, they had to go to school in the adjacent *aldea* or in Retalhuleu, which involved additional transportation costs. In 2013, there were eighty-nine students at the finca school, seventy-one in primary grades and eighteen in preprimary (kindergarten). One of the neighboring fincas now had its own school, which may account for the decline in numbers at the Finca San Luis school. The NGO Centro Ecuménica de Integración Pastoral (CEIPA) had helped paint murals on the school's outside walls and provided supplies to the students. In general, more students are attending school today and at higher grade levels than when I first came to the finca. As finca life becomes more precarious, families are putting more emphasis on education as necessary for the future of their children.

RELIGION

In 1978, all the families on the finca were Catholic. By 2000, the administrator, who had cancer, and his wife had converted to evangelical Christianity. By 2010, several other families had converted to evangelicalism. At least five older women who had converted said it was because they had been sick, or in one case, a child had been very sick with seizures, spirit possession, and *susto* (fright). In each case the sick person had gone to a doctor or local healers, and nothing had helped. Then one of the children or another relative who had converted took the sick person to an evangelical service. There everyone prayed for the person, who got better (sometimes temporarily) and eventually converted. In one of these cases, the sick person was diagnosed by the pastor and treated for spirit possession; in another one the sick individual had been diagnosed as being bewitched. Healing is thus still sacralized, and traditional causes, such as witchcraft, are still assigned to illnesses, in contrast to the disease paradigm of the biomedical system.

Conversion to evangelicalism provides a new community and support system to substitute for the old one that is being torn apart. In a situation in which anxieties abound concerning the increased crime in the area and the possibility of being displaced or evicted from the plantation, conversion to the new faith provides reassurance. Walter Adams and John Hawkins suggest that faith healing such as that offered by Pentecostal Protestantism provides an inexpensive replacement for the deteriorating traditional healing practices: "The faith healings and the psychosocial support offered by these new religions constitute important health resources for those without adequate social or financial assets." The expansion of such religions is "a response not only to social and economic stress but also to deteriorating access to health care" (2007:229). Although Adams and Hawkins are referring to the Mayan populations of Santa Catarina Ixtahuacan and Nahualá, their argument also applies to the situation on the finca, where the new religions have become an emergency release valve and social support system in place of Guatemala's inadequate physical and mental health care system in rural areas.

NUTRITION AND HEALTH

When I first arrived, general health and nutritional status of the Finca San Luis population was poor, as shown in surveys carried out in 1970, 1972, and 1976. According to Richard Sobel (1977) 47 percent had first-degree malnutrition, 40 percent had second-degree, and 4 percent had third-degree (Scrimshaw and Cosminsky 1991).[15] Currently malnutrition rates in Guatemala are very high, among the worst in the world, and the highest in the Americas. Recent national surveys cited by the World Bank (2014) report that 49.8 percent of children under five are considered stunted, a measure of chronic nutrition. These rates are often 50 percent higher for the indigenous Maya, who represent at least 40 percent of the total population (Chary, Diaz, Henderson, and Rohloff 2013). Gastrointestinal and respiratory infections are the most frequent diseases among children. Measles and whooping cough occur epidemically. They may exacerbate malnutrition and result in serious complications or death.

Although no quantitative data exists for malnutrition on Finca San Luis for recent years, the situation does not appear to have changed much. When I returned in 1993 for the first time since 1979, some people asked me if I could look at their children and asked if the doctors who had been there previously were returning because they perceived that there was more child malnutrition.

During my stay in 2000, a baby suffering with one of the worst malnutrition cases I had ever seen died. The mother, Carmela, was holding the fifteen-month-old baby on her lap. He was trying to hold a bowl and tilt it toward himself, but was too weak to do so. He looked very emaciated, with his rib cage showing. According to Carmela, the baby had not nursed or drunk water for five days. She was now giving it *suero* (oral rehydration solution) to drink. The baby had a fever and pyelitis.[16]

Carmela had gone to the health center in Nueva El Palmar, but they didn't give her any medicine for the baby. Meanwhile, she had given the baby amoxicillin and Alusor (kaolin) for the diarrhea, and Nistatina, an antibiotic and antifungal medication also used for candidiasis, or *fuego de la boca* (thrush), which she had bought in the pharmacy. She had also taken the baby to see a well-known healer off the plantation who told her to take the baby to the hospital. Siriaca gave her some money to buy a bag of powdered chicken soup with noodles. She also told her to take the baby to the hospital. Carmela refused, saying she was afraid to because the baby might die in the hospital, and it was better that he die at home. Her mother had done the exact same thing years before with one of her own children. She waited too late before taking him to the hospital because she was afraid of the hospital, and he died. One of the reasons people give for their reluctance to bring someone seriously ill to the hospital is that if the person dies there, they have to pay to have the body brought back for burial. Carmela's baby died two days after we first saw him, and he was buried in the finca cemetery.

Women also have poor nutritional and health status. At least 70 percent of the women between twenty and thirty years of age were either pregnant, lactating, or both (Cosminsky and Scrimshaw 1981). Only 8 percent of the pregnant women and none of the lactating women met the recommended dietary level for caloric intake (Gilbert 1976). At the same time, a heavy physiological demand is placed on the pregnant or lactating woman, including an increased need for calories and essential nutrients, which in most cases was not met. This failure was reflected in the lack of weight gain in several pregnant women whom we were able to track.

Chronic malnutrition among the rural poor in Guatemala worsened with the onset of the crisis in coffee prices (US Department of State 2003). Because coffee picking was finca women's primary source of cash, which they used for food, medicines, and the paying of debts they may have incurred in the course of treatment for illness, and because women make most of the decisions concerning food and health care in the household, they were particularly hard hit by the decline in coffee production. Both child and maternal nutrition on the finca are areas in which more research is needed. Although there have been such studies, especially of child nutrition, in the highland Maya areas, little research has been conducted on fincas and in other rural wage labor contexts (Chary, Dasgupta, et al. 2011; Chary, Messmer, et al. 2013).

In some other parts of the country, including Quetzaltenango and Guatemala City, obesity, diabetes, and dietary changes have been a major recent concern (Yates-Doerr 2012, 2015). In 2010 and 2013, people on the finca had a greater awareness of diabetes than before, and several people said they had been diagnosed with diabetes; a team of doctors had visited the finca around 2009 and tested people for diabetes. It is impossible to know whether there has been a discernible increase in incidence of the condition or whether only awareness has increased because there are no baseline data and people were rarely diagnosed previously. However, diabetes has been of increasing concern in Guatemala and has been attributed to increased consumption of fast foods, processed or packaged snack foods, carbohydrates, and soda.

HEALTH CARE

Health conditions and environmental sanitation on Finca San Luis are deplorable and result in high rates of respiratory and diarrheal diseases. People often use multiple resources in the course of treating an illness. Treatment options have varied over the years and exist in a pluralistic medical system that includes the professional, folk, and popular sectors (Kleinman 1978). On the biomedical side, or professional sector, there are the National Hospital in Retalhuleu; the private hospital Hilario Galindo (formerly San Cayetano), in San Felipe; the health centers in the towns of Retalhuleu, San Sebastián, and Mulua; the public health clinic in San Felipe; and private doctors in all these places. In addition, in the 1970s a private doctor who was a friend of the *finquero* visited the finca monthly, did health exams, and started a family planning program to distribute contraceptives. Specialists and healers in the popular and folk sectors include spiritists, *quemadores* (burners and diviners), *ajq'ij* (shamans, or daykeepers), *curanderos*, herbalists, *hueseros* (bonesetters) midwives, injectionists, and traveling vendors. Many of these prescribe both herbal and pharmaceutical medicines, as well as carrying out healing rituals (Cosminsky 1987; Cosminsky and Scrimshaw 1980; Scrimshaw and Cosminsky 1991).

In addition, people know about a large number of herbal remedies and patent remedies, and they self-medicate. Last but not least, several pharmacists operate in the various neighboring towns. For most medicines, including antibiotic injections, people do not need prescriptions, so they can obtain them directly from the pharmacy without going to a doctor. Pharmacists thus may act as lay doctors (Cosminsky 1994). With regard to reproductive health, including pregnancy and birth, most women today use both midwives and the prenatal clinic.

SUMMARY

During the 1970s, Finca San Luis was a stable community. This stable community no longer exists. Among the most important changes were the cessation of coffee production and the elimination of *colonos*, or permanent workers, and reliance on temporary workers, with a consequent reduction in the finca population. As one woman said, crying, "No hay cafe, no hay trabajo, no hay pisto. Ahora la vida es mas dura y mas triste. Antes era mas alegre" (There is no coffee, no work, no money. Life is harder and sadder now. Before it was happier). These or similar words were repeated by several women, especially older women when I returned to the plantation in 2010, after an absence of ten years.

Although I had first been to the finca in 1974 and had made intermittent trips over the next four decades (with an absence during the 1980s due to civil war violence), 2010 was the first time I heard these words said so frequently. Life has always been difficult on the finca, but during my last trip things seemed different. These women's words referred not only to the loss of money but also the loss of community and agency, for the women became more dependent on the males in the family. The result of not growing coffee has been the economic marginalization of the finca women. With less access to and control of resources by women, increasing government regulations, and a reduction in the size of the finca population and consequently fewer births, the role of the midwife has been greatly affected. Her role and the implications of these changes are the subject of the next chapter.

THE ROLE OF THE MIDWIFE: MARÍA AND SIRIACA

Chapter 3

*The locus of the sacred is the body, for the body is the
existential ground of culture.*

THOMAS CSORDAS 1990:39

"Buenos días," I called out from the open doorway of Doña María's
house after dodging the two turkeys in her front yard that seemed to
be guarding the house. The *patio* (yard) contained various plants, including medicinal ones, several chickens, the two turkeys, and a pig in
a sty. María invited me in and pulled up a wooden chair for me to sit
on. In the background one could hear chickens crowing, children playing, the radio blasting, and the slap-slap sound of one of her daughters
preparing tortillas in the kitchen.

Despite her modest surroundings, María was one of the most influ-
ential people on the plantation and in neighboring villages because of
her role as a midwife. In fact, she was the most frequently mentioned
by women we surveyed when we asked them who was the most respected woman on the finca. She is also one of the most interesting
and forceful people I have met during my many years of fieldwork.

In this chapter, I analyze the role of the midwife as epitomized by
María and her daughter Siriaca. I emphasize the social and ritual aspects of the midwife's role, and explain how they became midwives
through both divine calling and situated learning. The traditional
midwife's role is broader than that presented in the formal midwifery
training courses and in the clinics and hospitals that focus only on
birth as a physiological phenomenon. Biomedical training narrowly
defines the midwife solely as a birth attendant (Berry 2006; Maupin
2008). However, the Guatemalan traditional or lay midwife's role also
includes prenatal and postnatal care. This continuing care involves not
only the physical aspects of birthing, but also the social and ritual aspects. The midwife is a spiritual guide as well as a healer. She is an

agent of both change and cultural preservation. She is a cultural broker between the biomedical and the ethno-obstetric systems.

In the pages that follow I first discuss the role of the midwife as represented by María. I then talk about the similarities and differences in the way her daughter Siriaca carries out that role. I contrast paths of recruitment and training through embodiment and situated learning with the formal and didactic teaching methods in the biomedically oriented training programs.

MARÍA

María agreed to let me accompany her when she visited her clients. On this particular day we left her house and walked down a dirt path to visit Candelaria for a prenatal examination and massage. Children we met on the way greeted María, bowed their heads for her to touch them, and kissed her hand. María explained that a relationship of respect always exists between a midwife and the children she has delivered. Many of the children she delivered also became her godchildren.[1] Several adults we met greeted María with "buenos días, Comadre"— literally "comother," a term used reciprocally between a child's mother and godmother. These were all signs of respect were indicative of María's high status in the community. She and her husband were godparents to over eighty-five children, far more than anyone else on the plantation and over three times more than any other couple.[2]

María was born in 1919 on Finca Buena Vista. Her mother died when she was six years old. After a brief period her father left her with her godparents at another plantation. When her father was asked to be a foreman at Buena Vista, she moved back there with him, so that is where she grew up and met her husband.

He was a K'iche' Maya originally from the highland town of San Cristobal, Totonicapán, but his family had migrated to Buena Vista for work. María and her husband moved to Finca San Luis around 1942. She married when she was fourteen years old, and they were together for sixty-four years. She died July 5, 1997, and he died September 14, 1997. Siriaca said that after her mother died, her father didn't want to eat and was constantly crying. She said that he died from *tristeza* (sadness).

A marriage between an Indian male and a Ladina is very unusual, even today. Cases of intermarriage or intermixture usually involve an Indian female and a Ladino male. In the social and ethnic hierarchy of Guatemala, Ladinos consider Ladinas to be of higher status than Mayas and under stricter social restraints—especially unmarried girls, who are considered as off-limits for marriage to Maya men. María's father was against the marriage, so the young couple eloped, and thereafter her father would not let her enter his house. Initially she lived with her husband's family, although they also opposed the marriage.

According to her daughter Siriaca, María had a terrible time during her early married life because her husband's family mistreated, scolded, and beat her. Siriaca learned about her mother's past because sometimes at dinner, in front of her husband, María would talk about how terribly they had treated her. One problem she had when they got married was that she did not understand the language they spoke, K'iche' Maya. After four years she learned to understand and speak it out of necessity, but they would laugh at her when she was trying to learn it.

María did not get pregnant for the first four or so years of her marriage, which contributed to her being teased, mocked and abused by her in-laws. They considered her barren and said that she looked like a man because she had no hips. She said her first birth was difficult, with eight days of pain, pushing, and exhaustion, with no midwife present to assist. Finally, her grandparents and father asked the finca owner for his car to take her to the hospital; otherwise she would have died. She stayed three days in the hospital, where the doctor gave her intravenous liquids and she gave birth to a baby boy. Her mother-in-law did not believe that María's husband was the father because she claimed the baby's skin was darker than expected. She suspected María's *compadre*. After María's initial difficulty having children, she had twelve children, five boys and seven girls, one stillbirth, and two miscarriages, and she proved herself to be a dutiful wife and mother. Such large families are by no means unusual among the plantation population.

María started practicing midwifery in 1946, when she was about twenty-seven years old. The first child María delivered was her own. After her first delivery in the hospital, a midwife delivered her next three children. However, she delivered her fifth child by herself out of necessity because the midwife had died and no one was available. Shortly after that, she delivered a neighbor's baby successfully, and gradually more people began asking her to assist in childbirth. She also personally delivered the rest of her next seven children. She said she was ashamed or embarrassed (*tenía vergüenza*) to look for another midwife. After that she attended most of the mothers on the finca in the and surrounding areas, as well as her daughters and daughters-in-laws. María said she learned midwifery by herself, through experience:

> I don't know how I learned because the work, the experience itself showed me. When I went to receive classes with the doctors, I knew all this but as one should never be disobedient, I went and I paid attention to what the doctor said. . . . I did what I had learned because I saw that with this, it went well. . . . Still until today when there is a case, I do what is necessary. (1978)

After María moved to Finca San Luis and had been practicing for three years, the owner told her she should get her license because there was no licensed midwife on the finca.[3] A license would protect María against any legal problems resulting from her assistance at births. She had to go to the town of San Felipe, where the nurse from the public health center tested her and gave her a license. Some years later, in 1953, the government required midwives to take an official training course in order to be licensed (Carey 2006:46; Hurtado and Saenz de Tajada 2001). Around 1960, María went to classes in Retalhuleu for a year and received a certificate and *cédula* (identification card). To get the *cédula* renewed each year, she had to take a blood exam in Retalhuleu. She also had to go to the city of Quetzaltenango to have her lungs examined for tuberculosis. These trips, which María took at her own expense, were costly in both time and money.

Instructors strongly emphasized these documents during a midwifery review class held in Retalhuleu. The papers included not only the midwifery certificate, but also documents verifying immunizations and the results of a blood test and lung X-ray. The nurse asked the assembled midwives what papers they should have and what their importance was. It seemed that an inordinate amount of class time was spent going over these papers.

Gwynne Jenkins (2000) stresses that the documents are a mechanism by which the birth process is being medicalized and midwives integrated into the government bureaucracy. They also represent a way in which the state increases its control over midwives. With the use of these papers, the midwife herself—her body and her person—is also being medicalized. She has to prove that she is normal and not an unhealthy threat or danger to her client. That is, she is taught not only that the process of birth is risky and dangerous, but that she herself might be dangerous to others and therefore must have her lungs and blood checked to prove she is normal and not diseased. Although this certification may be viewed as a positive step in protecting the birthing mother, increasing control over the midwife and the medically negative view that the midwife herself might be dangerous is also being communicated.

Although María initially talked about becoming a midwife in empirical terms and explained how she started practicing by chance or necessity, she later mentioned that her being a midwife was a divine mandate; it was her destiny, calling, or gift (Sp. *don*).

> I was very sick; my hands and feet had stiffened, contracted, and shriveled up. I was sitting and then fell, as if having an attack. I thought I was going to die. . . . My husband brought a shaman to the house, who said that if I did not receive the work of a midwife, my fingers and toes would not get better. This was a punishment because I did not want to receive (*recibir*) the midwife's calling. Finally when I received, I recovered little by little. (1996)

María was also a spiritist and a shaman, diviner, or daykeeper (K'iche' *ajq'ij*), both of which involved her being very sick, then diagnosed and treated by a spiritist and by the same shaman who revealed her divine calling as a midwife.[4] She apprenticed with the shaman to learn the Mayan 260-day ritual calendar, prayers, and divination procedures that use the red *tz'ite* seed (*Erythrina corallodendron*). The symptoms of the illnesses that she suffered appear similar to the "snake illness" described by Tedlock (1992:54); that is one of the illnesses shamans can get.

Because María is a Ladina, for her to become a shaman in the Mayan Indian tradition was most unusual. A midwife experiences the same types of signs, such as dreams and a severe illness, as do shamans and other religious specialists. To become a midwife is not something you just do or are; it is a mandate or calling you receive from God or the spirit world. María said that she prayed to God to help her and to give her knowledge to be able to work at the time of a birth. The spirits of *las comadronas invisibles* (invisible midwives) helped her. She explained that two of them in particular, Cecilia and Isabel Castellanos, acted as her guardians or protector spirits and assisted her.

Similar spiritual assistance is reported in various highland villages. William Douglas reports that in Santiago Atitlán "there were thirteen Marías, two of which were considered as *Mero Jefes* (main bosses) and that each midwife had two specific Marías from the remaining eleven that were her personal guardians" (1969:145). This belief is similar to that of the Yucatecan midwives who recount dreams during which they say they learned from *diosas* (goddesses). Robbie Davis-Floyd and Elizabeth Davis write about Canadian and US midwives who talked about an inner voice or "inner knowing" telling them what to do, which they attribute to "intuition" (1997:326). This inner knowledge is based on connectedness—physical, emotional, intellectual, and spiritual—with the mother, the child, the father, and the midwife herself (324). Such an intuitive way of knowing parallels the spiritual and embodied way of knowing of both María and Siriaca.

An older midwife on the plantation, Doña Juana, occasionally attended births. She said no one had taught her to cure or deliver. It was her *destino* (destiny). She said she would dream when she was going to see a pregnant woman. She was unlicensed and had not taken any training courses. She said somewhat defensively that she helped only if María was not available. The two women were sisters-in-law, their husbands being brothers, and their relationship was strained. Juana said that María had taken over her practice when she was sick. However, women expressed more confidence in María, possibly because she was licensed, and Juana was not. Juana has since passed away.

María described her role as difficult and demanding:

> At times they call me at midnight; sometimes they come to look for me when the night enters; at times I go early. . . . If the patient is serious—that is, pains at each half hour, at each ten minutes, at each five minutes, at each three minutes—then I go immediately. When they are *primíparas* [first-time mothers], it is difficult—they don't know. Then I am going to be delayed. At times that I go at night, I spend the whole day there, until the following day. I go over there to Canton Barrio, and the fincas of Monte Cristo, Buena Vista, Tambor, Filadelfia, San Juan, Los Fuentes. It takes two and a half hours by foot to get to Tambor, or Monte Cristo. (1993)

SIRIACA

Siriaca, one of María's daughters, has now taken over most of her mother's practice and is the only practicing midwife on the plantation (figure 3.1). Siriaca began practicing at around thirty-four, a later age than her mother. At that time she still had very young children, which limited her activity. She had six children, five girls and one boy. In addition, her mother was still an active midwife.

FIGURE 3.1. *The midwife Doña Siriaca, María's daughter (2010).*

Siriaca learned midwifery skills at least partly by accompanying her mother: "She gave me all the instructions." However, one day she found herself obligated to assist in two births.

Two pregnant women had no one to attend them. They came to get my mother, but she wasn't there. I went to help one of the women and ended up delivering the baby. From there they called me for the other woman because my mother was still not home. The baby was already born, and they were waiting for the placenta. I went and waited for it to come. I hadn't had any experience so I didn't do any massage, just waited. However, this family was gossipy and my brother overheard them talking—saying why was I attending the birth, I didn't know anything, and the woman was going to die. They were going to look for a car to take her to the hospital. But they didn't really want to go to the hospital because they were afraid of the hospital. They went to get my mother, and when my mother arrived, the placenta had already come out. My brother scolded me, "Don't be doing favors for this kind of people because they were gossiping that Elvira was going to die. If she died, they were going to put you in jail. When someone comes, tell them you don't know anything and don't go because if one dies, you die with them," he told me. Thus I was not going to do these favors, and I went there with my mother to see if she had come back. She came to cut the cord, then left for another pregnant women in the *aldea* (village). Then they came and said my sister was in labor. My brother had just scolded me that I shouldn't do these favors, and now my sister is telling me she has a lot of pain. I can't let her die. I lay her down in the bed, and in a short time the baby was born. I treated the baby and everything. Then when my brothers heard the baby cry, and only I was there. Someone went on bicycle to get my mother again. She came in a car, and when she arrived, I had already done everything. She said, "let me see what you did." Then I took a piece of twine, and I measured four fingers width because I had heard her say four fingers, and tied it. She said that it was good. I was burning the cord when she arrived.[5] It is good, she told me. (1996)

Her mother's approval when she arrived after the birth and observed Siriaca treating the cord validated Siriaca's practice. María told Siriaca that she would have to take a course. María would present her to the health center because she herself was old and there would be no one to help the people. She would speak to Siriaca's husband, and if he gave permission, then she would take Siriaca the following week. Siriaca's husband agreed that it was good and that Siriaca should go if she had time. Siriaca remembers, "I went to the center. I went twenty days, daily, daily. I received my title and diploma. But I attended my sister before I took the course, seventeen years ago." Now that baby has just had her first baby, whom Siriaca also recently delivered.

Like her mother, Siriaca voices concerns about the demands and difficulties of being a midwife. However, she adds the possibility of being assaulted and robbed, especially at night. She says the roads and paths are very dangerous now, and she mentions specific examples of recent attacks on and robberies of neighbors. This is a reflection of a generalized feeling of uneasiness and fear due to increased crime since the end of the Guatemalan civil war. Siriaca prays to God before she leaves to go out, and she believes that God accompanies and protects her. This protection is linked to the belief that the midwife has a divine mandate.

DIVINE INTERCESSION

The paths of recruitment and the training undertaken by María and her daughter are typical of those reported elsewhere in Guatemala, primarily among Mayan midwives. These include a belief in a divine mandate, as revealed by signs such as dreams, visions, being born with a caul, bodily movements or twitches, finding symbolic objects like shells; fighting a serious illness; having a mother or grandmother who is a midwife; and necessity or mutual aid (Cosminsky 2001a, 2001b; Paul 1975; Berry 2010; Rogoff 2011).

One midwife from Chuchexic, a hamlet of the highland town of Santa Lucía Utatlán, told me that when she was young, she had found a red and white mirror in which she saw the face of a white-haired woman. This was interpreted by a diviner as being the face of Santa Ana, the patroness of childbirth, and the red symbolized the fire of the sweat bath that Mayan midwives use in her practice. Another midwife said she had dreams that she was hurrying on a road, out of breath, which portended an imminent birth. Yet another midwife said that she experienced internal body tingling or twitches as air or wind inside her body. Such bodily movements and many of these other signs are important experiences of shamans in Guatemala and are used in divining, where they are referred to as "the blood speaking" (Tedlock 1992:134). For any specific midwife, recruitment may involve any of these. They are not mutually exclusive and are often combined (Cosminsky 2001a, 2001b, 2001c; Paul 1975; Paul and Paul 1975).

María wanted to take Siriaca to the shaman, who would do a ritual to protect her, because María believed that being a midwife brings envy and that someone could take negative actions against Siriaca. But Siriaca refused, saying:

> My confidence is in God and to God only I pray. I don't need to visit anyone else. I don't have faith in those people. I learned to go to Mass, to pray, to speak directly to God. I go through him and get help from him. I get up early; sometimes people would come for me at midnight or 2:00 in the morning. The Lord goes with me. He helps me and everything turns out well. (2000)

Siriaca's statement indicates a change in her beliefs that had occurred in an earlier period. In 1978, I accompanied her on a visit to a spiritist who had a hospital of invisible operations in Quetzaltenango. This was for a consultation for Siriaca's husband, who had fallen off a cane truck and was having pains in his stomach and chest. At that time she believed that the spiritist's treatment might help. Before going to the spiritist, her husband had gone to the Social Security hospital, where he had received some pain pills, but he was still having problems. Her husband died in 1989 of cancer of the esophagus. Siriaca and many other people on the finca attributed his death to the effects of insecticides that the men must spray on the crops, usually without protection. I do not know whether the death of her husband or other factors influenced Siriaca's change in attitude to being negative toward spiritism and to practicing a more orthodox Catholicism. She came to believe that as a Catholic she should not believe in spiritism. On the other hand, spiritists, including her mother, still considered themselves to be Catholics.

Both María and Siriaca acknowledged sacred or spiritual sources of knowledge and divine assistance. Although Siriaca did not mention any signs such as dreams or illness, like her mother she experiences bodily sensations such as twitches in her fingers, especially between her thumb and forefinger, that portend or indicate that someone is going to give birth. If the twitches are on her left hand the birth will be delayed, but if they are on the right, the birth will be quick. Siriaca believes these feelings are signs from God. She also said that sometimes a particular type of bird, the *pixcoy*, comes and crows, which is a signal that someone is going to come for her.

María communicated with spirits of *comadronas invisibles*, who were her guides and gave her advice on massaging, on how to correct something if there was a problem, and on which medicines to use. She prayed to God and asked him for help. She had a large altar in the main room of her house (figure 3.2). It was decorated with colored tinsel and foil; sacred objects; pictures of Mary, Jesus, and various saints; and a cross covered with silver and blue foil. María prayed for her clients at this altar and lit candles for them before the birth. After the birth, she burned a candle on her altar and prayed for the protection of the mother and newborn. She also conducted spiritist consultations at this altar.

For shamanic or daykeeper (*ajq'ij*) consultations and treatments María had a separate, smaller altar, which she kept in a cane-and-thatch structure in the yard. On that altar were two wooden crosses, pictures of San Simón Tadeo and San Pascual, and a statue of Maximón. These are popular folk saints that have particular significance in Guatemala. They syncretize Mayan and Catholic elements and are often used in healing ceremonies (Pieper 2002). When someone came for a consultation or to ask a question, María laid out the divining seeds (*tz'ite*) and counted them out according to the Mayan ritual calendar (*tzolkin*) to divine the answer or the cause of the problem (figure 3.3).

FIGURE 3.2. *María and her house altar (1978).*

FIGURE 3.3. *María laying out the divining seeds at her second altar (1978).*

Sometimes María used her shamanistic role to divine the cause of birth or gynecological complications and treated the complications accordingly. One woman, Veronica, was having vaginal bleeding and pains, which María diagnosed as resulting from fallen womb or prolapsed uterus (*descompostura*). She massaged Veronica and gave her herbs to drink. However, through the use of *tz'ite* and the Mayan ritual calendar, she divined that the cause of Veronica's problems was an "evil burial" in her yard by a spurned former boyfriend. María returned that night and found the material that had been buried, disposed of it, and ritually cleansed the area. Thus the treatment involved both material and spiritual aspects.

Another case in which María demonstrated her role as ritual specialist was that of Rosa, a fifteen-year-old who was pregnant with her first baby and having recurring nightmares that she would have a difficult birth, would have to go to the hospital, and would die. Her dreams reflect the general fear of the hospital and the attitude that the hospital is a place to die. Rosa went to a spiritist, who, while in trance, said that the baby would die, but that the spirit would save her. However, María said that Rosa was having these dreams because her mother had cursed her for becoming pregnant without getting formally engaged first. Customarily the boy's family makes a formal request, or *pedido*, during which they bring gifts to the future bride's family. Rosa's family never received such gifts because of the pregnancy and thus were deprived materially of what they thought they were owed, as well as feeling ashamed of Rosa's out-of-wedlock pregnancy. By divining the cause of Rosa's bad dreams and ritually removing the curse, María helped allay Rosa's anxieties, and Rosa eventually had a normal delivery.

Siriaca, on the other hand, does not believe in the spirits of the dead midwives from whom her mother says she receives advice. She attributes her own success to God. She believes that the births are in Jesus' hands and that God guides her:

> When a mother is very sick, I pray, but to God. I ask God that when I go to see a pregnant woman, that it is not in my hands, that it is in the hands of Jesus. I pray to Jesus that the doctors will come promptly to help us so the woman recovers and the child comes without any problem, and God listens to me. But like my mother, no, I do not believe in that [the spirits of dead midwives], only in God. Above all, I ask that God goes with me to attend a birth,

knowing that it is a life that comes, a human life. Thanks to God I have not had problems. (1996)

Although Siriaca did not experience all the signs that her mother had, like her mother she believes that her work as a midwife is a gift from God. She says, "I understand that God has blessed me with this work because if I did not have this work I would be picking stones on the river's beach, but thanks to God that he gave me this work."

Siriaca has a small altar with a statue of the *El Niño de Atocha* (the Child of Atocha). She explains:

> The child is Jesus, and they say that he was like a light for the community. He talked with the children, he gathered together the bones of animals, the feet, the hands, and blew on them, and then it was a dog, a duck, or whatever class of animals it was. He would make dolls from paper, put them in a little thing of water and blow on them, and it became a duck or something else. For that reason, they say he was the light of the world; for that they say the child of Atocha is *La Antorcha* (the Torch). (2000)

Before she leaves for a delivery, Siriaca kneels in front of the altar and asks God to give her his blessing and accompany her on the road and at the hour of birth. "I say that it is not my hands, but Jesus' hands. I know it is the hands of Jesus. It is very beautiful that he walks with me" (1996).

In 2013 Siriaca had another statue that she also prayed to, *El Niño Divino* (the Divine Child Jesus). She had been given the statue by her cousin, who had become evangelical and thus couldn't keep the statue. The image is supposed to have miraculous powers of fertility and healing.

Siriaca acknowledges divine assistance, as does her mother, but uses an idiom that is more acceptable to herself while still recognized by her clients. This process of sacralization (Low 1982), which attributes a divine basis to some of their sources of knowledge and to their practice, is one way that María and Siriaca maintain their authoritative knowledge and keep their voices from being muted by the secular biomedical system and the pressures of medicalization. The view of birth as a sacred process reinforces the midwife's role in this contested area of control and contrasts with the medicalized view of birth as a potential disease or abnormal physiological process. In the sacralized view the body, both that of the mother and that of the midwife, is sacred, not just a physical entity, and it embodies messages from God or a spirit, manifested as dreams, twitches, and sickness. From María's and Siriaca's perspective, the sacredness of birth and midwife's role and knowledge are part and parcel of their everyday lives. In contrast to the biomedical view, birth is not separate from the moral, social, and spiritual domains of finca life.

LEARNING: EMBODIED AND SITUATED

While María was still alive, Siriaca accompanied her on her visits, during which she learned by doing as well as by observing. Her mother showed her what to do by guiding her hands over the woman's abdominal area. She learned from her mother how to estimate the due date, detect the position of the fetus, massage the mother, give the postpartum bath, and prescribe herbs and treatments for various illnesses and birth problems. She learned other practices from the midwifery training course and classes. Some of these practices have conflicted with what she learned from her mother, including cutting the umbilical cord before the placenta has been delivered and cauterizing the cord. Others have provided additional knowledge, such as the importance of examining the mother's eyes for signs of anemia.

The knowledge or skills learned in this manner are embodied; they involve "the ability to do rather than talk about something" (Jordan 1993:192). Brigitte Jordan describes the midwife Juana guiding her hands: "The midwife is less likely to talk than to guide the hands. . . . The knowledge is in the hands and is transferred by the hands. It is truly embodied knowledge" (Jordan 1993:192). During some of my prenatal visits with María, she would take my hand with hers on top of it and guide it to feel where the baby's head was, to feel the position of the baby and massage the mother. At first I was embarrassed because I could not feel or distinguish anything. María persisted, with her hand on mine, until I could feel the head. Similarly, she showed me how to tell when the baby was due by determining how much of her hand fit in the space between the top of the abdomen and the pubic bone; she took my hand and guided it so I could also measure the space. One time when a woman was in labor and bent over a table to ease the pains, and María was pushing downward on the woman's abdomen with her hand, she took my hand and asked me to continue pushing downward while she looked to see how the baby was coming.

Similar situations occurred eleven years later, and again in 2010 and 2013 when I accompanied Siriaca on prenatal visits. For example, two of the women who had gone to the prenatal clinic were told that their babies were in a sitting position and that they would need cesareans. In each case, during her visit Siriaca took my hands to show me that the head was in the correct position. In this way, she was both exerting her authority by teaching me in front of her clients and also using me to validate her conclusion and authoritative knowledge over that of the doctor. She then said that maybe the baby had turned since the doctor's examination. She did not say the doctor was wrong, but maintained that the knowledge obtained through her methods was authoritative. In both these cases she prevented cesarean operations; the babies were delivered vaginally without any problems.

Learning through apprenticeship, family relations, pragmatism and bodily experiences are not only drastically different ways of knowing than those used in the training courses, but are discredited and denigrated by the biomedical system. Jean Lave and Etienne Wegner (1991) refer to this type of experiential learning as situated learning. Situated learning is characterized by participation in social practice. That is, it occurs in a social context. In midwifery, becoming a midwife depends on participation in births and others' social recognition of one's experience, which then leads to more experience and validation of one's identity as a midwife. In María's case, the social world included supernatural agents such as the spirits of dead midwives, as well as family members and the community. In Siriaca's case, it includes God or Jesus, whom she believes accompanies her and guides her.

According to Lave and Wegner (1991), situated learning involves a gradual move from legitimate peripheral participation toward full participation in a particular occupation or specialization. They refer to the Yucatecan midwife's apprentice, who first does activities like running errands, then gives massages, then assists with delivery, and finally deals with the placenta as the last stage of full participation. However, María did not do a midwifery apprenticeship, and the first birth she attended was that of her own child. Siriaca, on the other hand, participated peripherally in the birth process while accompanying and learning from her mother, although during the first birth she attended she participated fully by necessity. During the next delivery she attended, her mother arrived to check on the birth before the final treatment of the cord. In this birth, Siriaca was not yet fully participating in the social community; the mother's parents were critical of her and had not yet accepted her status as a legitimate midwife.

These examples show how the move from legitimate peripheral to full participation in situated learning concerns not only participation in the whole process but also recognition by the social community. It takes time to establish one's reputation and status as a respected midwife. According to the San Felipe vital registry, María delivered only four babies in San Felipe in 1950, then she increased that number to fourteen by 1959. In 1954 one of her own was born dead while she was attended by another midwife. María attended only two births on the finca that year. At that time, at least three other midwives living on the finca were also active. By the 1970s one of these midwives had moved off the plantation, one had died, and the other hardly practiced; she only attended a few cases when María was not available. This last midwife was María's sister-in-law. She said she had the calling or the gift (*don*), but she had never gone for a training course and thus did not have a license.

In the 1970s an average of twenty-seven births per year occurred on the finca, and most of them were attended by María. In 1972 she had attended twenty-eight out of thirty-six births on the finca and eighteen off the finca in the surrounding areas, for a total of forty-six births. In 1975 twenty-five out of thirty births on the plantation were attended by María, as well as several births in nearby areas. Those that María did not attend were attended by another midwife who was not from the finca or took place in the hospital. These are minimal figures because both births and deaths are underreported in the vital registry (Kielmann 1970). Also, María was illiterate and did not keep any records. People are supposed to register the births of their own children, indicating who attended the birth, at the vital registry in San Felipe, at which time they receive a birth certificate. However, not everyone on the finca registered family births and deaths.

In contrast, Siriaca is required by the health center to keep a record book in which she records the date, sex, name, weight, and place of each birth. Siriaca had only two years of primary school, but she can read and write to a certain degree and is able to keep these records. In 1991 she attended thirty-one births, thirteen of which were on the finca proper and seven of which were in the adjacent area of Pomarrosal. The rest of the reported births were on neighboring fincas and in the aldea adjacent to the Finca San Luis.

For both María and Siriaca the increasing figures over the years indicate increasing acceptance by the community of their midwife status. In 1995, from January to September, Siriaca attended thirty-one births, eleven of which were on the finca proper. In 1999 she attended forty-four births. In 2000 she had already attended thirty-two births by July. The decreasing number of finca births reflects the decline in the size of that population; Siriaca is attending more and more off-finca births. In July 2000 I accompanied Siriaca when she visited twenty of her clients, only seven of whom lived on the plantation. Each birth entails several prenatal and postnatal visits. A visit may include examinations, massages, and herbal baths, which are very time consuming but are not recorded. In addition, a midwife may treat various related gynecological conditions, such as *descompostura*, and children's illnesses such as the evil eye.

The situation in which Siriaca found herself when she attended her first three births in one day reflects another aspect of Guatemalan life: high birth rates. The average birth rate for the years 1971–1975 on Finca San Luis was 39.5 per 1,000 population. This figure is based on the civil registry records, which do not include all births.[6] By 1995 the country birth rate was lower, at 38, and by 2014 it was estimated to have dropped to 25.5 (Index Mundi 2015), reflecting a trend of lower birth rates, but Guatemala's birth rate was still the highest in Latin America. By way of comparison, the current US birth rate is 13.42 births per 1,000 population (Index Mundi 2015). Recent interviews with families on the finca indicate they desire smaller families and are having fewer children than their parents.

In the 1970s a variety of programs were training midwives and health promoters in family planning and were distributing contraceptives. Knowledge of modern contraception expanded the midwife's role. In the 1980s many of these programs were curtailed, reflecting both a change in US aid policy under Ronald Reagan, of reducing or stopping funding to international family planning programs, and the violence in Guatemala toward community health workers.

The role of the midwife is broader than that defined by biomedicine, which refers to the midwife as a traditional birth attendant. In reality, the midwife's role includes prenatal and postnatal care, as well as delivery. In Guatemala it also includes ritual and social aspects. For example, in the midwifery training class, the nurses told midwives that they should not wash the clothes of the women they attended. If they did so, they should charge extra. But this was an important part of the midwife's role in various parts of the country. Women deliver while fully clothed, and thus their clothes are soiled with the blood from the delivery. María said that she washed the clothes if the woman had no one to help her. Siriaca, on the other hand, does not wash the women's clothes. She says that it is not part of her role. In some places, like San Marcos, midwives still wash clothes, but she does not. She follows the biomedical guidelines in this instance. Thus, some of the social aspects of the midwife's role have been curtailed, as well as the ritual aspects, because the biomedical model promoted in the training programs focuses only on the medical aspects of birth.

KINSHIP RELATIONS

Both María's and Siriaca's lives illustrate the importance of kinship relations as part of the social community involved in learning the role and being accepted as a successful midwife. On Finca San Luis, as in most of Guatemala and Latin America, gender ideology is based on a patriarchal model in which the father or husband is considered the authority figure within the household. The fact that María asked Siriaca's husband for permission for Siriaca to go take the training course reflects the husband's authority in decision making within the family. María also showed respect for her son-in-law by asking permission, and he showed respect for María by granting it. This may have been the reason that María rather than Siriaca asked for his permission. Siriaca mentioned that the husbands of some of her sisters would not let them be midwives.

Lois Paul (1975) has suggested that supernatural recruitment to the midwife role is a divine mandate that one must follow or suffer severe consequences, and it functions as a way of counteracting a husband's possible opposition to his wife practicing. The husband's opposition often stems from the freedom of movement enjoyed by a midwife and the midwife's increased exposure to risks, such as going out at all hours of the night. Usually if a woman goes out at night she may be suspected of adultery or she may be attacked. A husband may also object because of the disruption in the household duties of the wife, such as preparing meals for the husband and children, since she may have to spend many hours away, sometimes overnight, waiting for a woman to give birth. Usually a woman gets up at 4:00 AM to prepare the tortillas for her husband to eat for breakfast and take out to the fields. If the midwife is called in the middle of the night or has to stay overnight for a delivery and no one is at home to perform her household duties, tensions might arise within the family. Siriaca says:

Thank God my husband did not get angry. Sometimes when I went with my mother, the time would go by, as my mother doesn't walk very fast, and when I arrived late I was worried that my husband would be angry, but no. . . . He would say it is okay if you are accompanying your mother. Meanwhile, since all is in order, the food, the clothing, you can go to accompany your mother. (2000)

If the midwife still has small children, childcare support from other family members is critical. Similarly, if she cannot go to the market, she will have to depend on other family members to go for her. For example, María's daughters would sometimes pick up food or necessities for her at the market when she was unable to go because of her work. Midwives often do not attain their full practice until past menopause when they have fewer childcare responsibilities.

On the other hand, kinship entails certain obligations on the part of the midwife. María attended the births of her daughters and daughters-in-law (figure 3.4). One of Siriaca's first deliveries was her sister's baby. She felt obligated by family ties and could not refuse to assist. This sense of obligation continues today, and Siriaca treats relatives free of charge. At one point her pregnant sister-in-law Norma

FIGURE 3.4. *María with two of her daughters and their daughters, whose births she attended (1978).*

was having chills, pain in her back, and cramps in front. Siriaca examined her, then massaged her legs and thighs with rubbing motions downward toward the torso, as well as in the abdominal area to calm her pain and to help the baby get in the right position. She also had her drink black coffee with *esencia maravillosa*.[7] She did not charge Norma for the massage or treatment. She delivered her niece's baby in 1996 and did not charge her for attending the birth or for prenatal and postnatal visits, including massages and herbal baths.

Underlying this closeness of kin ties is the value of reciprocity. When I visited Siriaca in July 1996, she said that the week before she had had no money and no corn. July is often a difficult month. It is during the lean or hungry season, after people have run out of corn from the previous harvest and before the new corn is harvested in August. In addition, the coffee picking season had not yet begun, so income was low. Every fifteen days Siriaca was using two *arrobas*, or fifty pounds, of corn, which cost Q60 (then about US$10). She prayed to God for help. She said she did not know what she was going to do. Then suddenly her cousin, whom she had treated for *descompostura* without charge because she was a relative, gave her a gift of one arroba of corn, which enabled her to get through the next week. This action reinforced Siriaca's faith that if she performs her role as a midwife willingly, "God will provide."

Siriaca's first deliveries also illustrate the strength of sibling ties. Her brother wanted to protect her so he told her not to attend births because she did not yet have a license. She was torn between listening to her brother and her sense of obligation to her sister, who was in labor and whom she felt she must help despite the risks to herself. This conflict also shows the intrusion of the state into the family: a licensed midwife must attend every birth; otherwise, the attending woman is considered to have committed a crime and can be subject to legal action.

This need for legality is the major reason María said she would present Siriaca to the health center to register her so she could take a midwifery course and receive her license. Meanwhile, Siriaca continued learning from her mother.

Siriaca, however, is not training anybody. Two of her daughters are interested in working in the health field, but as health promoters, not midwives. One of her daughters took two health promoter courses and was allowed to run a small dispensary on the finca. She had also learned to give injections, but only used disposable syringes and needles brought by the patient; she did not sell them. The finca owner paid her a salary of Q200 (about $33) per month, but he sometimes owed her money. Her husband took blood samples for malaria testing and put the blood on a slide that was eventually collected by someone from the Ministry of Health. The finca owner had let her use a space in the store room, which had very minimal facilities, not even a chair for the patient to sit on. When I returned in 2013, she was no longer running this dispensary, and it had been closed.

Although María and Siriaca treat their relatives for free, they are expected to, and do, charge their clients for treatments. In 1978 María charged five dollars to attend a birth. This fee included all the prenatal visits and massages, the delivery, postnatal baths, and treatment of both mother and baby. This was the same fee charged for a consultation with a physician in town. (The basic wage on the plantation at the time was $1 to $2.80 per day.) In one of the review classes María took, the nurse told the midwives that they should be charging ten dollars because they had a license. She seemed to be unaware of the realities of the situation. María said that if they charged more than the unlicensed midwives, people would not use them. The accepted rate in 1996, which Siriaca charged patients, was Q50 (US$8.33). In 2010, the rate had risen to Q250 ($30). In 2013, it was Q300 ($39).

The midwife is usually called when a woman is three months pregnant. She goes monthly to examine and massage the woman, more frequently in the last month. She then attends the birth and follows it with two postnatal baths and massages of the mother and examinations of the baby. She is usually paid after the birth. However, if the woman goes to the hospital for whatever reason, the midwife receives nothing. However, because of the current restrictions on the midwife's practice, such as not attending first-time mothers, Siriaca is now charging separately Q15 per massage if a woman wants a prenatal or postnatal massage and bath.

Siriaca points out that a major problem experienced by midwives is that often people do not pay. If someone has to go to the hospital, they have to pay Q50 each way for a car, plus the expenses in the hospital, which may amount to another Q50, for a total of Q150. These costs are one reason people do not go to the hospital. Even when the midwife recommends hospital treatment because of complications, as she has been told to do by the training program and the health center, people often cannot afford it. The Ministry of Health and its hospitals can handle only about 20 percent of births in Guatemala (Hurtado and

Saenz de Tejada 2001). Since that estimate was made, there has hardly been any expansion of the national hospital system, so hospitals are often overcrowded. The midwife is thus indispensable, especially in rural areas.

SUMMARY

In this chapter I discuss various aspects of the midwife's role, as personified by María and her daughter Siriaca. These include recruitment and training of midwives and some of the physical, social, and ritual characteristics of their role. These, as well as some of the traditional obstetric practices, are being targeted by the medical profession through its training programs and government regulations. In the process of medicalization, the midwife's role is being attenuated (Berry 2006; Maupin 2008).

The following chapters examine the birthing system and the changes occurring in that system through the eyes and voices of María, Siriaca, and the women they serve.

Prenatal care is an important aspect of the role of the Guatemalan midwife. This care involves determining the age and position of the fetus, the expected due date, the health of the baby, and the health of the mother. The midwife provides treatment if there are any problems, provides advice concerning dietary and activity prescriptions and proscriptions, and refers the pregnant woman to the prenatal clinic for routine exams, for problems such as pre-eclampsia, and for tetanus injections and vitamins. The midwife's exam and care is usually provided in the client's home, often with other members of her family present, such as her mother or mother-in-law.

The point in a pregnancy when a women arranges for a midwife to examine her varies according to how many children she already has and whether her earlier pregnancies were easy or difficult. A pregnant woman or her husband will usually call the midwife early for a first pregnancy—around the third month. In these cases, the selection of the midwife is usually made by the parturient's mother or mother-in-law. If the client is young, her mother may talk to the midwife first and either bring the midwife to the house or bring the girl to the midwife to be examined to determine whether indeed she is pregnant.

MASSAGES

The massage, *masaje* or *sobada*, is considered by both the midwife and the mother to be one of the most important aspects of prenatal care. This is a service that the clinic does not provide. The massage serves a number of functions for both the mother and the fetus. It is believed to help promote an easier birth and to ease any discomfort or pain that the woman might have. The physical contact also provides emotional support for the woman. Massage is said to *acomodar* the baby—that is, align or adjust the baby and make it comfortable.

Doña María and I arrived at Elena's house for a prenatal visit.

"Buenos días, Doña Elena," María called, while knocking on the open door. Elena invited us in, and we all exchanged greetings. María asked how Elena was feeling. Elena said that she had been feeling badly and that she hurt all over from her back to the front of her abdominal area. Elena laid down on the bed, a hard wooden platform on which was placed a thin straw mattress and a blanket. María asked for some coals from the fire in a bowl and some cooking oil.

María rubbed the oil into her hands while warming them over the hot coals. The warmed oil prevented her cold hands from causing too sharp a contrast to Elena's bodily heat from her pregnant condition. She loosened the sash of the Elena's skirt, lowering it to just above the pubic area, and raised the blouse to just above the abdomen, thus preserving Elena's modesty. With her warmed, oiled hands María felt the position of the baby, located the baby's head, and measured the height of the abdomen with her fingers in order to estimate the due date of the baby. She gently but firmly massaged the abdominal area, moving her hands in opposite directions across the abdomen and along the sides and palpating the top (figure 4.1). María told her she was due in about one month and fifteen days. Elena thanked María, and they arranged the time for the next massage.

Siriaca massages her clients in the same manner as her mother. She says the oil helps the hands move more easily. It also helps her to *arreglar* (adjust) the position of the baby, who looks for *el camino* (the path). Sometimes she also massages the mother's calves and thighs, holding her legs up and rubbing downward. Siriaca says this "prevents cramps or problems with the legs. The nerves or tendons in the legs become distended and this helps them. The leg massage also helps the blood flow."

Knowing how to massage is the epitome of embodied knowledge for the midwife. From María's and Siriaca's perspective, it is divine knowledge. María learned how to massage not only experientially by experiencing massage herself and observing the midwife doing it, but also from the spirits of the *comadronas invisibles*, who told her what to do and guided her if necessary, thus sacralizing the procedure and the knowledge on which it is based. María explained:

There are persons who come with the baby *atravesado* (transverse). Then I ask protection. There are invisible midwives, true spirits. They tell me if the pregnancy is good, that I should massage her this way, like on the right or on the left, in order to fix it. When the day arrives, now she comes well. It is not across, by means of the spirits.

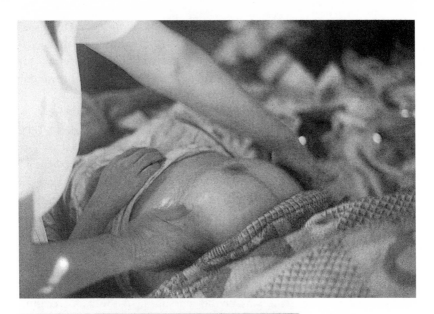

FIGURE 4.1.
*María doing a
prenatal massage
with warm oiled
hands (1976).*

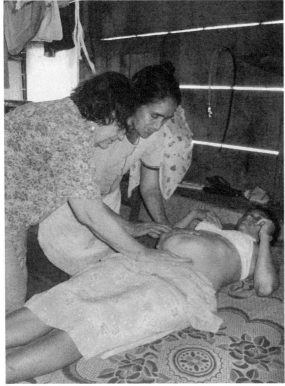

FIGURE 4.2.
*Siriaca shows
the author how
to feel the fetus
and estimate the
due date during a
massage (2010).*

Although Siriaca learned by observing her mother, she says she knows how to massage because "God is in my hands" and guides them. Although the source of the knowledge of massaging is different for mother and daughter, for both massage is sacralized: the knowledge comes from a sacred or divine source.

Almost every time I observed a prenatal massage with María or Siriaca, they took my hand and had me feel where the head of the baby was and showed me how to estimate when the baby was due (figure 4.2). Siriaca also asked if the woman had felt any movement. When we were visiting Luciana, whose estimated date was in a week, the baby kicked during the massage, while Siriaca was guiding my hands, and we all laughed, saying the baby was getting impatient.

In 1996 Siriaca would not charge separately for the massages and prenatal care, even though if a woman delivered in the hospital she would not get paid for anything. However, by 2010 the situation had changed. Siriaca had several clients who were going to deliver in the hospital but to whom she was giving massages, so she was charging separately for each massage. This was primarily due to restrictions on the midwives, who were not permitted to deliver first-born babies. According to Siriaca, "The doctor prohibits it. A midwife can lose her license and thus the right to practice if she attends a mother who is having her first child." Siriaca also gives prenatal massages to women who plan to have a hospital delivery in order to have a tubal ligation because they didn't want any more children, but they still want the massages. These cases speak to the importance that mothers still place on the massage and to their confidence in the midwife.

By 2010 Siriaca no longer heated her hands before massaging. She explained, "The doctor said that it is not necessary. It makes the hands hot, and then after the massage washing them in cold water is bad, because it can cause arthritis. The doctor said it is not necessary because the baby has its own heat inside the mother." Although I did not interact with this doctor and thus do not know what the doctor believed, the effect was ironically to reinforce the importance of the hot-cold balance—that idea that too strong a contrast can cause illness. Whereas the midwife was concerned about the contrast of her cold hands on the hotter body of the pregnant woman, the doctor expressed concern about the effect of the contrast on the midwife's hands.

Traditionally the midwife warms her hands before the massage to make the oil rub on more easily, but it also soothes the woman. However, by the time she finishes the massage and washes her hands, they are no longer warm. Due to the impact of medicalization, Siriaca now asks if the woman has some oil, lotion, or Vaseline that she can rub on her hands before massaging the woman, but she doesn't heat them. In even this minor way, the hierarchical relationship of the doctor's authority over the midwife is reinforced.

Biomedical personnel and the midwifery training programs have tried to discourage the midwives from doing massages and especially from doing external versions—the process by which a breech or sideways baby is turned to a head-down position. They are concerned that the midwife may apply too much pressure and cause the placenta to become detached. Whether this has actually happened or how many times it has happened is unknown. However, the midwives are told to refer any case that might involve malpresentation to the hospital.

About sending a mother to the hospital, Siriaca says:

> If it is high risk, they go to the hospital. They are births that I am not going to commit myself to. If I see that the baby is sitting. . . . I am going to ask if they feel movement here. If she says no, I touch the head, touch the soft behind. . . . Go to the health center. If it's three or four months, no. . . . At six months, she should go to prenatal care at the health center. There the doctor will put the apparatus to see where the heart is.

After the massage, Siriaca typically examines the eyes of the pregnant woman to see if she has anemia. If Siriaca suspects that she does, she tells her to go to the clinic to get iron pills. She also examines the nipples to see if they have everted sufficiently for breast-feeding. If not, she shows the woman how to massage them so the baby will be able to breast-feed after the birth. She also gives the pregnant woman nutritional advice, mentioning what foods she should and shouldn't eat.

PRENATAL EXAMINATIONS

The midwife usually examines and massages and the expectant mother once a month until the last month, when ideally she visits the woman once a week.

Examination of the abdominal area is the midwife's primary method of determining the state and progress of the pregnancy (table 4.1). However, both María and Siriaca mentioned various other bodily changes that indicate pregnancy. These include the size and shape of the breasts, the swelling and height of the abdomen, the color

TABLE 4.1. PRENATAL CARE

	María 1970–1979	Siriaca 1996	Siriaca 2010
Exam	Massage—sacred; warmed, oiled hands	Same	Massage—uses oil or balsam but does not warm hands
	Checks position of baby; does external version if she thinks it is necessary	Same	Does not do external version
	Estimates due date—measures height of fundus manually	Same	Same
	Checks for signs of preeclampsia—swelling of face and hands, headache; if positive, refers to clinic	Same	Same
		Checks eyes for anemia, refers woman to clinic for iron pills if anemia may be present.	Same
Dietary advice	Food prescriptions and proscriptions follow the hot-cold principle	Same	Same
	Should drink milk and eat eggs for vitamins	Same	Same
	Food cravings should be fulfilled; if not, can cause miscarriage	Same	Same
	Recommends prenatal vitamins	Same	Same
Injections	Does not give injections	Gives vitamin injections	Gives vitamin injections
Causation of problems	Hot-cold imbalance	Same	Same
	Strong emotions, especially anger	Same	Same

TABLE 4.I. (*CONTINUED*)

	María 1970–1979	*Siriaca 1996*	*Siriaca 2010*
Diagnosis and treatment of problems	For delayed menstruation: herbal remedies	Same	Same
	To prevent miscarriage: massage, apply a plaster, baths with avocado pits	Same	Same
Emergency plans			Helps family make plan

of the nipples and dark pigmentation markings on the mother's face or across the nose. Sexual differentiation of the fetus is believed to be indicated by such markings too. If the baby is a boy, the woman gets dark markings on her face, whereas with a girl, she does not. Also, the nipple area gets very dark if it is going to be a boy, and is lighter if it is going to be a girl. The markings are believed to be caused by the strength of the baby's blood, and a boy's blood is considered stronger or hotter than a girl's. The position of the baby can also encode sexual differentiation. If its position is more to the right side, it is believed to be a boy, and if more to the left side it is expected to be a girl. A male fetus will cause the woman to have trouble sleeping, but with a female the woman will have pain but it passes and she can sleep. María also said that the pregnant woman gets a vacant or empty look in her eyes (Cosminsky 1982a:200).

María provided the following example, which I conveyed in third person in a previous publication:

One woman showed María a dress she had bought for her daughter. María said it would be better if it were pleated because her daughter was very pale and maybe she was pregnant. The mother said she was pale because she doesn't cover herself in the night. María asked her, "Aren't the girl's eyes very strange?" The mother said it was because she got fever in the night from bathing. María said, "Look don't get angry at what I am going to say, but Martha is pregnant." The mother said, "No! How could that be, she's still studying." María said to me jokingly, "Maybe this is what she studied." "No." the mother said, "the child doesn't know anything yet because she hasn't gotten her period yet. She is 15 years old." "Take care because she is pregnant," María said. The mother insisted that her daughter couldn't be pregnant. Then in 1 month and 15 days, she gave birth to a little girl. The mother asked her who the father was. She mentioned 3 different boys, 2 of whom denied doing anything. The third was a boy who was staying with them in the same house who did "this bad thing." (María, cited in Cosminsky 2001c:264)

In this case, the mother was trying to enforce the value placed on premarital chastity, with attempts to keep up appearances and maintain a good reputation for the girl and the family. The mother's ignorance of the daughter's condition also reflects the common lack of communication between daughters and mothers about sexual matters, which are culturally unacceptable to discuss. The negative attitudes toward premarital sex are reflected in the woman's statement that the boy had done "this bad thing."

During the examination, if the midwife feels the baby is not in a correct position, she is supposed to refer the woman to the clinic and to the hospital for delivery. However, she may attempt to manipulate the fetus by external version, turning the baby *poco a poco* (little by little). If she feels that the baby is transverse or feet first, "the woman can do exercises, placing her head toward the ground and stretching, ten minutes daily; then the child will turn, because the head weighs more than the body. The head falls in order to be able to give birth. If it doesn't turn, she has to have a cesarean" (Siriaca 2000).

Some of Siriaca's clients were told during a prenatal exam at the clinic or health center that the baby was transverse or sitting and that she would have to have a cesarean, only to have Siriaca examine her and disagree. For example, Alicia was in her ninth month and was told by the doctor at the prenatal clinic that the baby was breech and that she should schedule a cesarean delivery at the hospital. Siriaca examined her and insisted that the baby's head was in the correct position, and Alicia did not need a cesarean. She took my hands and had me feel where the head was, and I discovered that her evaluation was correct.

In another case the woman said that the doctor showed her the sonogram and said she would have to have a cesarean section. Siriaca examined her and insisted that the baby was in a good position with the head downward; again she had me feel where the head was, thus using me to validate her conclusion. She said that maybe the baby had turned since the doctor's examination. She was thus able to exert her own authoritative knowledge without directly confronting the doctor.

During various field visits over the years, at least four other similar cases occurred while I accompanied Siriaca for prenatal examinations. However, if Siriaca does detect a malpresentation during her exam, she will tell the woman she should deliver at the hospital.

Today the clinic may give the woman a prescription for an ultrasound if they think there may be a malpresentation or other complication. Even if the baby seems to be normal, at least one of the health centers will urge women to have an ultrasound. This conveys an underlying message about the superiority of technology. However, a woman who goes to a health center or private facility that gives ultrasounds must pay for the expense of another trip and the cost of the ultrasound. The public health clinics and centers in the towns near Retalhuleu do not have ultrasounds available. If a woman cannot afford an ultrasound, her anxiety concerning her pregnancy may increase.

On the basis of a prenatal exam at the clinic, a nurse told Lucia that she should have an ultrasound because there might be a danger of placenta previa, in which case she would need to deliver in the hospital. She told Siriaca, who got a prescription for the ultrasound for her when she went to the health center for a monthly review session. I accompanied Siriaca when she gave Lucia a prenatal exam and massage, and she said everything was normal. However, Siriaca did give her the prescription for the ultrasound that she had gotten for her. Lucia had the ultrasound, which showed that everything was normal, and Siriaca delivered the baby in the home when it was time without any complication.

Siriaca cooperated with the clinic by getting the prescription for the ultrasound and giving it to Lucia. Thus even though Siriaca's exam contradicted medical advice, she still supported biomedical authority by getting the prescription for the ultrasound, which ironically supported her authoritative knowledge as a midwife. She also contributed to the medicalization process by agreeing to the use of ultrasound technology.

PREVENTION

Midwives issue prescriptions and proscriptions that are a form of preventive medicine because they attempt to keep the body in balance and thereby prevent miscarriages and various birth complications.

María and Siriaca, like other midwives, offer advice to women about their diet and activities. Several of their prescriptions and proscriptions are based on the assumptions of the hot-cold principle or humoral medicine. A pregnant woman is considered to be in a hot state: blood is usually classified as hot, and she accumulates blood in her body during the nine months of pregnancy, which puts her in a hotter state than normal. She must take care to avoid certain medicines and foods, such as chili, that might cause an excess of heat in the body. María advised specifically against beef soup, which is too strong and too hot for a pregnant woman, especially if she gets angry, which is also a hot state.

A pregnant woman must also avoid very cold foods because her excess heat makes her vulnerable to attacks of cold, and too great a contrast is considered dangerous. Cold foods include beans, pork, cabbage, certain greens, and eggs. Cold foods also give the woman colic. She should eat foods that are considered neutral (*templado* or *fresco*), such as tortillas and chicken soup.

Aside from the hot-cold principle, food restrictions depend on the health of the mother. During the pregnancy she can eat everything unless she is sick. Some women said that during the first trimester they ate very little and had little appetite because they felt nauseous. Some said that fried foods made them sick. María said she advised them to eat milk and eggs even if it made them sick, and even though they are cold foods, because they are nourishing and the stomach can become accustomed to them. However, mothers did not seem to follow that advice. They mentioned the difficulty of obtaining milk on the finca, for example. Also, Guatemalan adults have a high rate of lactose intolerance, contributing to the preference not to drink milk. Some people also believe that eating too much or drinking milk might cause the baby to become too big and result in a difficult delivery.

María advised pregnant women to eat vegetables and greens because they have vitamins. They should also eat root crops, plantains, bananas, milk, fish, chicken soup, and meat, especially liver and wild animals like rabbit. María said, "when the mother doesn't nourish herself, the baby comes out very little, wrinkled and sick; sometimes the baby can't stand it and it dies." If they don't have milk, mothers should buy Incaparina, a high-protein food supplement in the form of a powder that one mixes with water. Siriaca also advises pregnant women to drink orange juice. She said that not drinking orange juice may cause the baby to be in a sitting or transverse position.

Because they don't drink orange juice. They don't eat fruit. They don't nourish themselves with prenatal vitamins. For that reason the baby is transverse or sitting. If they drank orange juice or lemonade, ate fruits or greens, or drank vegetable drinks, Incaparina, . . . then they would have strength. . . . For that reason, the baby is transverse. The doctor says that orange juice provides a lot for pregnant women. They have to drink at least once daily, but at times they don't have it.[1]

Other food proscriptions have a sympathetic or metaphorical basis, such as restrictions against eating twinned fruits like the chayote (*Sechium edule*) to avoid having twins (Rogoff 2011:167), or rabbit meat to avoid having multiples. On the basis of the same principle, a pregnant woman should not point at or make fun of someone who is injured or has a disability because that can mark the baby or cause the baby to be born with that condition. Meanwhile, biomedical personnel attack dietary restrictions and tell the midwives and pregnant women that they should eat everything (Cosminsky 1977a, 1982b).

Both María and Siriaca incorporated nutritional information that they learned in the midwifery courses and from other biomedical personnel, such as the importance of taking vitamins and eating foods that are high in certain vitamins and advised their clients accordingly, although they did not usually differentiate among the vitamins. They largely maintained the traditional folk classification of foods according to their hot and cold qualities, but the impact of medicalization on midwifery is shown by María's and Siriaca's emphasis on the importance of milk and eggs. Even though they are considered cold and were traditionally avoided by pregnant and, especially, lactating women, now they are considered nutritious and good for the mother. Rather than trying to change the traditional beliefs, midwives could ease the discrepancy between the two models by suggesting the addition of a hot substance like cinnamon to neutralize the coldness of the milk or eggs (Harwood 1971) or by recommending foods such as chicken soup, which is neutral, to accompany greens that are classified as hot.

However, these restrictions do not really change pregnant women's diet. Expectant mothers follow the rules on a pragmatic basis, and most restrictions remain ideals. The extent to which they are actually followed and why is an empirical matter for investigation. The situation appears to be similar to that reported by Carol Laderman (1983) for Malay women: their usual diet does not contain most of the proscribed foods anyway, so following proscriptions does not represent a change in their diet.

Doctors express concern because of the poor nutritional status of pregnant and lactating women in Guatemala (McGuire 1976). I argue that poor nutrition is due primarily to poverty and lack of access to certain foods rather than to the imposition of cultural dietary restrictions during pregnancy. In a study by D. Gilbert (1976), only 8 percent of pregnant women and no lactating women were meeting the recommended dietary level for calories, protein, riboflavin, or niacin.

In a different sample of eleven pregnant women, there was an overall reduction in dietary intake during pregnancy, a time when more calories are needed. There was also very little if any weight gain among most pregnant women on the finca. The mean dietary intake of pregnant women was 1,632 calories while the mean caloric requirement for them was 4,199 calories, and the intake for nonpregnant women was 2,022 calories while their requirement was 3,769 calories (Frazao 1976:58). Although I do not have recent statistical data on dietary intake for the women on Finca San Luis, some women on the finca whom Siriaca sees have mentioned that buying beans and meat is difficult because of the increase in prices, so they are consuming less protein than before. The growth of the baby comes from the depletion of woman's own stores, potentially worsening her nutritional status and increasing her and her fetus's vulnerability to complications and low birth weight.[2]

María and Siriaca warn that a pregnant woman should also not expose herself to contrasts of physical temperature. The time of the day should influence her activities. She should not bathe in cold water late in the day when the air is cool or too often in one day, or the baby will be born with a cold or the mother might have pains. One pregnant woman in her seventh month whom María came to examine said she felt some pain and thought it was because she had bathed in cold water. Another mother, Sara, said:

> You feel much heat when you are pregnant, so you drink water. One feels much heat especially in the last month or so. You should bathe almost daily, but in warm water. They say that if you bathe a lot, the baby comes with a cold. Going in the river may cause knots in the legs or leg cramps, and cold water might cause the mother to swell.

Swelling is usually attributed to air or gas in the body and thus is defined as a cold condition. On the finca women usually wash clothes and dishes and bathe themselves in the stream, which is considered cold both in quality and actual temperature. Washing clothes in the stream can take a couple of hours. A woman should not cook too soon before or after washing in the river or after getting caught in the rain because of the temperature contrasts. The extent to which such restrictions are followed varies widely. They are more relevant if the mother is ill because of the disturbance of the hot-cold balance.

Siriaca says that a pregnant woman should not take Alka-Seltzer, aspirin, purgatives, or lemon juice because they are considered cold and may provoke a miscarriage. In the rainy season, women frequently get wet and thus cold, and may have pains. If a woman has pains, she should take a little black coffee with drops of *esencia maravillosa*. Or she can cook some leaves of *manzanilla* (chamomile) or *pimpinela* (anise).

Pregnant women should not exert much force or lift heavy objects such as water jugs and market baskets. Of particular concern is carrying heavy loads of coffee beans, which can weigh as much as one hundred pounds. As María said, "carrying too much is bad." Slipping or falling down can cause the child to change position to one side and thus make the birth difficult. Despite María's warnings, her clients continued carrying out their daily activities during pregnancy, including carrying heavy loads, washing clothes in the cold river, grinding corn, and sweeping the house because they felt they had to do these chores.

María advised women to take a rest for one or two hours after lunch (as she has been taught by the doctor) but said that afterward they should get up and exercise. She said sleeping too much is dangerous and will cause the woman's legs to swell and result in a difficult birth. For most women the problem is not getting enough sleep. The cases in which the woman might be considered to be sleeping too much may involve lack of energy due to anemia or because of toxemia, in which case her legs will have become swollen.

Laura had very swollen legs and was apathetic. María said that Laura ate a lot of salt and earth, slept a lot during the day, and was very careless. She scolded Laura and repeated her advice about not eating salt or clay. Laura was also very anemic, with a hematocrit of twenty-four, probably from iron deficiency, which could explain her tiredness and apathy. In general she and her family had a poor health and nutrition record. Three of her eight children had died, at two months, five months and one year old.

I asked Siriaca what does she do if a woman's legs are swollen. She said that she had one client, Juana, whose feet were very swollen. Juana was also very pale, which, according to Siriaca, was from anemia:

> I treated her with a bath from avocado leaves and boiled *hierba del cáncer*. She put her feet in the water and it lowered the swelling. The capability of the blood to nourish the body falls, and that's why it swells. This woman had gone to the doctor, and her husband bought her prenatal vitamins, which she is taking. This also helps. She is due at the end of this month and the swelling has lowered. (1996)

Some women also take iron supplements, such as *polvo de hierro* and *hierro ferros* from the pharmacy. However, one young pregnant woman said that the prenatal pills from the clinic, which contain iron, made her sick to her stomach, whereas the prenatal pills from the pharmacy do not. She attributed her upset stomach to the pills from the clinic being very hot, but it is possible that the vitamins from the pharmacy have less iron than those from the clinic.

During the prenatal exam, Siriaca checks the mother's eyes for signs of anemia, a new practice she has learned in the midwifery training sessions. If she finds evidence of anemia, she urges the woman to go to the prenatal clinic for iron pills. She also asks if the woman has had any headaches and checks to be sure that the hands and face aren't swollen.

> If the face, or the hands are swollen and the head aches, then it is considered an *alto riesgo* (high risk) birth. It is preeclampsia. If the baby is transverse, then it's high risk; if *viene de cadera* (it is seated), then it's high risk. Only if it is a *parto normal* (normal birth) will I attend it. (2010)

I asked Siriaca what causes the preeclampsia, the swelling. Siriaca said:

> Because of being too young or too old—under fifteen years old or more than thirty-five. Because of the blood. It is weak. The blood has more water, she doesn't have much blood. She is pale. If the hands or face are swollen and she has a headache, she should go right away to the hospital or health center. So for that reason there is the prenatal control. They have to see if it is a normal birth, if the child is good. Then there is no high risk. If there is, they have to talk to the woman, for that we have to examine the face, the hands. . . . If the face, the hands are swollen, then ask if the head hurts. If so, then it's a high risk. If it is a normal birth, then I will attend it. (2010)

Pregnancy cravings are common around the world and have been interpreted by anthropologists, nutritionists, and chemists in a variety of ways. One interpretation is that the substances a pregnant woman craves help her to cope with physiological changes during pregnancy, including nausea or spasms in the abdomen; another is that they satisfy some nutritional deficiency, especially of iron (McElroy and Townsend 2009; Bryant, DeWalt, Courtney, and Schwartz 2003; Young 2012). Yet another interpretation is that the mother unconsciously takes advantage of the opportunity to obtain special or status foods, or attention that she normally might not be able to get.

Pregnancy cravings, or *antojos*, are considered extremely important. If they are not satisfied, the woman may have a miscarriage. María attributed two of her own miscarriages to such unfulfilled cravings, one for deer meat and one for coconut milk water. One of them occurred when she was three months pregnant. María said:

> I was working, clearing the *milpa* to plant, and was very thirsty. I saw many coconut palms. I stayed looking at a coconut to drink the water. This craving did not leave. I came here to the house. I made a little of my *fresco* (cold drink) and drank it. But the craving did not leave me. Next day I was sick and miscarried. (1976)

The second miscarriage happened when María was two months pregnant: "I went to San Sebastian to buy corn. I saw deer meat there. I wanted a half-pound. But it was very expensive, and I didn't have money. Then I had strong cravings. The next day I hemorrhaged and miscarried." Several mothers attributed the cause of their miscarriages to such unfulfilled cravings. These are usually for fruit, special meats, cheese, greens, or something they had seen someplace but could not obtain.

Other cravings are a type of geophagia. Women crave a special kind of earth or clay locally called *tashkal* and clay tablets called *Pan del Señor*. These latter are made of kaolin and earth from Esquipulas. They are about two inches by one and a half inches and have a picture of Christ on them. Esquipulas is the site of the basilica of the Black Christ of Esquipulas, an important pilgrimage location that is famous for miraculous cures. According to Sera Young (2012:48), pregnant women are the tablets' main consumers because their special properties are related to fertility and birth. The tablets are also used as medicine for diarrhea. However, María said that the pregnant woman should not eat salt or earth, since these will "cut the blood" and make the woman swell, which will result in a difficult birth: "The child is purple when it is born, the water green, and the woman's placenta is black." María's concern was justified, but her reasons differed from those of the biomedical personnel, who worried because too much salt may cause water retention and edema, and the earth or clay may contain parasites. Also clay may bind iron from other foods and cause anemia. In contrast, Timothy Johns (1990) argues that clay may counter the effects of toxins found in some food plants.

Siriaca says that if the craving can't be fulfilled, then the woman should put a little salt in her mouth as a substitute. However, if the fetus is injured, a miscarriage can't be stopped: "There are some women with much pain and hemorrhaging. Then it is better that they go to the hospital. I take them to the hospital. There they take out the fetus" (1996).

The finca women explain these cravings in terms of the agency of the fetus, rather than that of the mother. The body's boundaries are considered permeable, and the baby's desires can influence the mother or the father, whose desires can affect each other. Thus a woman's husband may also experience cravings due to the baby's hunger. If these are not satisfied, his wife may have a miscarriage. For example, María was called by Victoria, who was three months pregnant and having pains. María went to examine and massage her. She asked her if she had any cravings. She said no. However, when the husband arrived home, they discovered that he had gone to the market and had cravings for tripe, but there was none left. María administered some medicine to Victoria for the pains. She then went to town, bought some meat, and gave the husband and wife each a piece.

Men on the finca also get other pregnancy symptoms. María said that some men have dreams, toothaches, or headaches; they don't want to work, they are lazy, and their hair is all messy because the woman is pregnant.

Men's pregnancy symptoms have been reported in many different societies. Carole Browner (1983) studied male pregnancy symptoms as reported by their female partners, and she interpreted them in terms of expressions of female dependency and insecurity, insufficient social support networks, and women's wishes that their partners would make a commitment to fatherhood. Women with loose-knit support networks expressed their insecurity by reporting more symptoms from their partners. In the above case from Finca San Luis, however, it was the male reporting the craving. Pregnancy symptoms expressed by the husband can be seen as a way in which he participates in the birth, claims the legitimacy of the father's role, or expresses support and commitment to the family.

PREVENTION OF MISCARRIAGE

Many of the various prescriptions and proscriptions are aimed at preventing miscarriages. María suggested drinking a remedy made from *seda pinto* mixed with the toasted earth from a wasp's nest to prevent a miscarriage. She also said that if a woman has much pain but it isn't time yet to deliver she should eat avocado. Then she should cut up three or four pits, boil them, add a little salt, and bathe from the heart downward. This will heat the stomach and the waist, the pains will stop, and she will feel better. One informant, Estela, who was having a lot of white discharge when she was seven months pregnant said she took nine pits of *cuajilote* to "disinfect" herself and avoid miscarriage.

Another remedy that María used to prevent a miscarriage was to raise the uterus externally by massage and apply a plaster made of egg white, mashed rue leaves, *pimienta de chapa*, and rum in a cloth on both the front and back of the abdominal area. Twenty years later, Siriaca mentioned that she gave the same remedy to one of her pregnant daughters who had begun to hemorrhage and have pains. In addition to putting on the plaster, she had her daughter drink a mixture of coconut water, wasp's nest, the heart of a *guisquil* (chayote squash), and a shoot of *cordoncillo* (*Piper auritum*). The bleeding and the pain stopped.

These remedies and practices illustrate both continuity and variations in the authoritative knowledge of María and Siriaca. They both use massage, plasters of egg whites and *pimiento de chapa*, and wasp's nests as a component in drinks, but they vary in some of the specific plants used in herbal remedies.

Eclipse

One of the most important restrictions for a pregnant woman is to avoid exposure to an eclipse, which is believed to cause cleft palate, harelip, anencephaly, other infant deformities, and stillbirths. Allegedly even if the baby is born alive, the baby will have difficulty breast-feeding, and will live only a few days. This belief existed among the pre-Columbian Mayans and Aztecs and is still very widespread in Mesoamerica.

The belief is based on an analogy between the moon and the fetus. The sun eats the moon during an eclipse, and a part of the fetus will similarly be eaten. According to George Foster, the sun eats the lip of the fetus, causing a child to be born with a harelip (1994:58). Foster argues that the beliefs about the eclipse have been interpreted in terms of humoral medicine and that humoral medicine incorporates pre-Hispanic beliefs and customs (1994:58, 186). The ancient belief is that an eclipse occurs when the sun and the moon fight. Fighting implies anger, which produces heat in human beings. Similarly an eclipse radiates a great heat that is life threatening and can cause a child to be born with a harelip or other deformity. In pre-Columbian times a woman put an obsidian blade in her bosom or waist, whereas metal is now used. Metal is considered cold, so to counteract the heat of an eclipse, the pregnant woman wears metal, such as hairpins or nails, in her waistband.

According to the reproductive histories collected from finca women, at least ten stillbirths or deaths within the first week or so after birth were attributed to eclipses. For example:

1. Regina said, "There was an eclipse the day the child was born. I went to wash in the river and as the eclipse is bad, it damaged the child, who began to cry a lot when born, and then died. Three hours after he died, blood came out from his ear. The eclipse blew up something inside the child's head."
2. Another baby was born with "eclipse," and she had her "head open. That is why she stayed alive only for thirteen days. They did not take her to the doctor."
3. "Sabina was born with a watery head, and her arms were like rags because of the eclipse."
4. "Amanda was born with her head all broken because of the eclipse."
5. Raquel was born dead. According to the midwife it was from the eclipse, but the mother didn't realize it.

Although this belief is associated with indigenous Maya culture, it has influenced the Ladino population as well. Two of the women who attributed their stillbirths to eclipses were higher-status Ladina women on the finca: the schoolteacher and the administrator's wife. The latter woman's baby was born at the hospital, but supposedly due to the eclipse, his head was divided into four parts. He was alive for only half an hour. One of María's daughters had a baby who was born with a harelip, and its head was watery; it died three days after it was born. She mentioned another baby boy who was born with a harelip and lived for eight days. Both of these deaths were attributed to an eclipse.

Corpses

Pregnant women should not go near a corpse, attend wakes or funerals, or visit cemeteries for fear of contact with the airs or emanations that come from a corpse. Otherwise they could contract the illness *hijillo*. Common symptoms of *hijillo* are swelling, diarrhea, vomiting, hair loss, stomachache and backache (Méndez Domínguez 1983:270). Sick people in general can get *hijillo*. According to Foster, in El Salvador *hijillo* refers to an emanation from a corpse; people bathe and change their clothing when they return home after attending a wake and ill people avoid wakes for fear of the *hijillo* exuded by the corpse (Foster 1994:72). María stated that if a woman gets *hijillo*, she should bathe with the herb *suelo con suelo*: "Cook nine twigs, throw in a little salt, a tablespoon of sugar. With this one bathes. It is very good. Now when this bath is ready, throw in an envelope of bicarbonate. With one, two, three treatments, one is cured."

Emotions

The body is supposed to be in a balance not only in terms of the qualities of hot and cold, but also emotionally. Strong emotions such as anger, fright, sadness, nerves, and anxiety are central to the etiology of illness and should be particularly avoided during pregnancy and the postnatal period. They can cause a miscarriage, early labor, a retained placenta, a cold, insufficient breast milk, or a sickly baby. On the finca the most commonly mentioned of these emotions was *enojo* or *cólera* (anger). Sometimes the anger is preceded by *susto* (fright), caused by physical abuse from a drunk or aggressive husband who causes the fetus or the mother to have the illness called fright, and the mother to then also have anger. This anger later causes the mother to miscarry or the baby to be stillborn or born prematurely.

Anger is not supposed to be expressed openly. It is thought to produce excess bile, and unless it is resolved, body functioning will be impaired. When a pregnant woman has *susto* or *enojo*, she should go to the midwife for herbal teas and massages to restore the body's equilibrium. According to María, "when one has some anger, take the stalk of an onion, the stalk of garlic, put it to cook in a pot, put in some rue, the heart of the orange plant, lime and anise; also throw in three coals. Then drink this. With this, one is cured" (1975). Siriaca recommends a tea of *pericón* (*Tagetes lucida*) for the sickness of anger.

Women describe strong emotions and the pregnancy complications they attribute to them in a variety of ways (Cosminsky 1977b):

1. Paula said a rage (*cólera*) caused her miscarriage, which was characterized by much pain and hemorrhaging. She sought help from a *curandero* on the finca, who gave her bitter coffee with lemon juice and clove, which caused the expulsion of the fetus.
2. Elena said her husband was going around with a lot of other women, drinking, and beating her. She thinks the fetus got *susto* from the fights with her husband and was born dead.
3. Juana had a big fright when a cow charged two of her daughters. Fortunately the girls escaped with only slight injuries, but she was in very bad shape and had a miscarriage, which she attributed to her fright.
4. Siriaca said one of her sisters suffers from anger because her husband beats her. He gets drunk and goes after her with a machete.

Anger can also be caused by children's behavior, especially the pregnancy of an unmarried young daughter, as in the following examples.

1. María was called to Finca Buena Vista to attend a woman who had gone into labor prematurely, which she attributed to anger. The woman had a fifteen-year-old daughter who had gone to fetch water and did not return: "She did not come, she did not come. How long ago it is since she went to get water." Her husband said the girl had gone to wash clothes. The mother went to see what she was doing. She met her talking to a twenty-five-year-old man who had a bad reputation. "He only likes to do bad deeds." She hit the daughter with a belt. When she came home, she hit her some more. Then she had more anger. This brought on the labor that night, and the baby was born prematurely, with a difficult labor and a lot of bleeding. (Maria, 1976)
2. Dominga attributed her gastritis to anger she developed when her daughter became pregnant from someone Dominga considered no good. Dominga warned her daughter that he would not care for her

or the baby. Dominga got angry and hit her. The person the daughter claimed was the father said it was not his and would not take her in. Dominga has to care for both her daughter and the baby, who are now living with her. (Siriaca, 2010)

According to Siriaca, there is more anger nowadays because men are drinking more. Unfortunately, data do not exist to document whether there is has been more drinking over the past thirty or so years, but drinking and domestic abuse have long been a problem on the plantation. Drinking was encouraged during the 1990s by the wife of the then-administrator, who had a store and would go out to the fields on the day before payday to sell alcohol to the workers. Some of these men would then become indebted to the store and have to work off their debts—a form of debt peonage. She later converted to evangelicalism and stopped.

The majority of cases of anger reflect the gender ideology of *machismo*; male superiority and the subordinate position of women, creating tense relations between the sexes and stressful family relationships. As an illness, anger reflects conflicting and unresolved social relationships, most commonly between mates or between parents and children (Finkler 1994:16). However, this does not address the question of why there is so much drinking.

Drinking can be an outlet for the stress and frustration that men experience in their work and their poor economic situation—stress that is deflected to their family members. There have been cases on the finca of males who have been so desperate that they committed suicide by drinking pesticide. Drunkenness has also resulted in male-male conflicts, including machete fights that have resulted in serious injuries and deaths.

Studies of alcohol drinking in Guatemala have usually been carried out in Mayan communities and have been linked to the effects of conquest, discrimination, exploitation, and Mayan religion and rituals. Abstinence has been linked to conversion to evangelical Protestantism, which prohibits use of alcohol (Garrard-Burnett 2000; Goldin and Metz 1991). Research on alcoholism needs to also be carried out in communities such as the fincas and the surrounding rural communities with mixed Maya and Ladino populations.

Anger can also result in or cause the illness *bilis*. It causes an overflow of bile, which has a hot quality, from the gall bladder. According to Foster, it floods the stomach with heat and produces "that most common of Mexican culture-bound illnesses, *bilis*, as well as diarrhea. . . . *Bilis* is a central concept in classical humoral pathology. Its local distinctiveness lies in being attributed to a strong emotional shock—particularly fright and anger" (Foster 1994:32, 79). Thus the term anger (*enojo*, *cólera*) can be used to designate an illness itself; the cause of certain symptoms, such as abdominal pains; or the cause of an illness, such as *bilis* or *nervios*. The Spanish term *cólera* reveals the humoral connection because yellow bile was referred to as *choler* and was hot and dry in Greek (Hippocratic) humoral medicine. One man said:

> When one has *bilis*, the eyes are yellow, the person swells and doesn't eat. If she takes a little soup, it gives her diarrhea so she doesn't eat. The legs swell. A greenish or yellowish liquid comes out from the gall bladder (*hiel*); . . . it comes from the cerebrum or brain. If a drop falls on a piece of skin, it breaks out there. If it isn't much, it remains purple. If it doesn't break out, it won't heal. Even if you go to a doctor it stays there. Always. If a drop falls on one, one can't move. One is rigid. One is alive but rigid. One just lies down. Here a woman died of the drop. Some blood showed up in between the fingers, the nails, the ears, and the drop in the nose, between the teeth, and the nails of the toes broke out. She became all purple. . . . When one is tired, the *bilis* comes strong.

María mentioned this remedy for *bilis*:

> You give them half an *octavo de guaro* (rum), the juice of one sweet orange, one sour orange, and a lemon. Strain it and put in bicarbonate and drink it. It lowers the swelling and collects the *bilis*. The next day do the same. A third day, before she goes to take coffee, give her the same. Some have a very big stomach and appear pregnant, but they don't have anything. It is *bilis*. (1978)

On the finca, anger can be considered an idiom of distress (Nichter 1981), a way of expressing moral outrage at the violation of norms on a social or interpersonal level, and a way of expressing one's powerlessness both within the family and within the larger political and economic system. The use of the category of anger on the finca is similar to that in Mexico, where anger is a central etiological explanation for sickness and is used to express the person's moral indignation and the accompanying suffering (Finkler 1994:20). According to Kaja Finkler, "Negative emotional discharge of anger is probably the most widely attributed generalized explanation for sickness" (1991:37). Horatio Fabrega and Peter Manning (1979) go even farther: "Anger is, in the Mexican view, the singularly most important source of illness" (cited by Finkler 1991:9).

Finkler suggests that anger is more than an "idiom of distress." Rather, it is a manifestation of what she calls "life's lesions": "the perceived adversities of existence, including inimical social relationships, and unresolved contradictions in which a human being is entrenched and which gnaw at the person's being. Such lesions become inscribed on the body and manifest in anguish, in generalized pain experienced in the entire body, and in non–life threatening symptomatologies of unspecified etiology" (1994:15–17).

In the local ethnomedical system, sufferers do not separate mind and body. Instead, they experience emotion and bodily sensations as continuous. Anger and other emotions become inscribed on the body and thus become embodied. The resulting illnesses are a metaphor for the moral violations and adverse social relationships experienced. The cases reported above center around physical abuse and neglect of women by their partners or conflict related to reproduction and child rearing, and around the problem of controlling the ensuing emotions, particularly anger (Low 1989:136). They reflect differential and unequal power in gender relationships, the problem in expressing negative emotions, and inability to fulfill social and cultural roles, particularly as related to responsibility and childbearing. However, whereas Finkler refers to non–life-threatening symptoms, often chronic gastrointestinal illnesses, we can also apply this concept to life-threatening or deadly situations, including miscarriages, stillbirths, neonatal deaths, and maternal deaths.

Anger is closely related to another illness: *nervios*, or nerves, which has been also discussed in the literature as an expression of social stress and personal distress, or as an "idiom of distress" (Low 1989; Davis 1989; Guarnaccia et al. 1996; Guarnaccia, De La Cancela and Carillo 1989; Guarnaccia and Farias 1988). "The illness (*nervios*) is the non-verbal language of the powerlessness" (Lock 1989:85). Setha Low reports that rage and anger were the primary cause of *nervios* in her study in urban Guatemala (1989). She argues that *nervios* reflects the "medicalization of distress": the body is used as a medium to express a social problem or conflict.

Although on the finca people sometimes attribute various symptoms to *nervios*, which is sometimes caused by anger, the use of the illness label *anger* (*un cólera* or *un enojo*) is much more common, even among the Ladinos on the finca. Low (1989) argues that *nervios*, a quasimedical term, is used primarily in an urban environment by Ladinos. The pattern of etiology and expression of illness, however, has not substantially changed. Illness is still attributed to anger and other strong emotions; only the label has been ladinoized: "*Nervios* is the ladino illness of choice, reaffirming an urban, upwardly mobile ladino identity" (Low 1989:133). It is a Ladino illness expression that, in contrast to *susto*, reinforces a person's Ladino identity, and becomes a culturally appropriate way to express anger. The rural context of the finca and the mixed ethnicity of the population may be factors influencing the differential usage of the term *nervios* versus *cólera* or *enojo*.

More recently, when I returned to Finca San Luis in the 1990s and 2000s, I heard the term *nervios* used more frequently. One case involved a woman who had been robbed on the dirt road off the finca and said that since then she had had *nervios*. In this case *nervios* seemed to refer to anxiety related to the fright (*susto*) she suffered in the robbery. In another case in 2013, the term *nervios* was used by a doctor in Retalhuleu when he diagnosed Elena with *presión* (high blood pressure). She had headaches, felt faint, and was very anxious. He told her that she had *nervios* from stress, which was also causing the high blood pressure. She suffers from anxiety and worry because of her poor economic situation and has chronic pains in her legs from arthritis, which causes her to have difficulty walking and working. The doctor prescribed pills for the high blood pressure, which she is suppose to take daily, and injections of Neo-Melubrina for the *nervios*. She takes these medications sporadically when she has some money to buy them.

In 2015 Elena's thirty-five-year-old daughter was suffering from severe abdominal pains and had not gotten her menstrual period for over a year. She was very worried and went to the same doctor in Retalhuleu. He sent her for blood tests and ultrasounds. His final diagnosis was gastritis, high blood pressure, and *nervios*. Unfortunately, after the expenses for the doctor, the ultrasounds, and the blood tests, she did not have the money to buy the injections that he prescribed. Ironically, *nervios*, which has been assumed to be a folk illness, is now being treated as a biomedical disease by the doctor, who comes from an urban Ladino background.

Anger is still much more often used on the finca as an illness category than *nervios*. Open anger is considered culturally inappropriate, and people try to control themselves. Illnesses such as *nervios* and anger are "culturally and religiously sanctioned suffering in a medicalized form" (Low 1989:136). For example, a husband spends money on alcohol, which usually translates to depriving his wife and children of necessities, including food. Meanwhile, the wife is supposed to be subordinate and maintain an outward emotional calm. Although it is the husband's behavior that provokes the wife's anger, she is to blame if something happens to the baby. Foster explains that the victim is then believed to cause her own illness by not controlling her emotions (1982:83); this reinforces the gender ideology of her subordinate status. At the same time, suffering or having anger is a culturally acceptable way of protesting or expressing her objection to her husband's violation of norms.

By going to the midwife for treatment, the pregnant woman is attempting to restore her bodily balance and save the baby and herself. The midwife, however, is also an agent of social control. She will treat the anger with massage and herbal teas or patent remedies, giving support to the woman, but the interpersonal conflict that led to the anger is not dealt with. If it is from a marital conflict or a drunk husband, the problem remains. As Low states, "Thus a medical discourse about cause, prognosis and treatment of the illness is created, rather than a political or economic discourse focusing on the social situations responsible for the distress" (Low 1989:132).

Anger can be viewed not only as a metaphor for powerlessness, but also loss of control in the context of social relations. Mary Douglas has suggested that bodily control is an expression of social control (1970:70). In this case, the woman herself is to blame for being angry and endangering her unborn child; her husband is not to blame for abusing her. She is the one who has lost control. The unborn child is endangered by the mother's anger and fright—by her lack of self-control. The woman is socially subordinated to her husband, who may lose self-control through drunkenness with relative impunity. These cultural definitions enlist the midwife as an agent of social control. By working to overcome the risk caused by a woman's emotions, she acquiesces to the prevailing definitions of social roles. Not only is an imbalance of emotions and social relations expressed in definitions of dangerous body states, but the crisis of a state such as threatened miscarriage is a stimulus for restoring normal social relations (Cosminsky 1982a:213).

Although the influence of Western European medicine—from

Hippocratic-Galenic traditions to the nineteenth century—is reflected in theories about the relation between anger and bile in the humoral hot-cold framework, and in theories about the relation of women's reproductive organs to their physiological, psychological, and emotional vulnerability, a second stream of influence stems from pre-Columbian Mayan medical beliefs that identify an excess of emotion or an emotional experience as a natural cause of illness. Women and children are thought to be weaker than men and thus more vulnerable to strong emotions like anger and fear, which can cause fright or other emotionally caused illness (Orellana 1987:30, 36; Low 1989:135). A third stream of influence is based on the inequality of gender relationships that is part of the *machismo/vergüenza* complex of Mediterranean and Spanish-American cultures. As Low (1989) points out, in the Catholic family model the husband and father is respected and obeyed while the wife and mother is humble and suffering, which reinforces this inequality.

EVIL EYE (*MAL DE OJO*; *OJO*)

On the finca, as elsewhere in Guatemala, the evil eye is an illness that is contracted only by infants and toddlers from four months to two years of age. A pregnant woman, being in a very hot state, can give a child the evil eye, which is considered a hot illness. Even though she herself is in a weak and vulnerable state, she may be a source of danger to others. The heat is transferred to the child through her gaze. This is unintentional, and she is usually unaware she has done this. Although in some places, evil eye has been associated with envy, this does not seem to be the case on the finca, unless presumably unconsciously. The symptoms include diarrhea, vomiting, fever, anorexia, crying a lot, having one eye that is bigger than the other, a foul odor, and sudden stretching or "jumping." Midwives and other healers diagnose and treat the illness.

The belief that pregnant and menstruating women can cause the evil eye reinforces gendered restrictions on females and supports the belief that they should stay at home. This is consistent with the sociocultural value of modesty because pregnancy and menstruation are conditions that should not be revealed openly. I have argued elsewhere in an analysis of the evil eye among the Maya in El Novillero, Santa Lucía Utatlán (Cosminsky 1976) that beliefs concerning the etiology of the evil eye support the value that the woman should stay at home because she is responsible for protecting her children by keeping them out of crowds. The same argument holds for the evil eye among the finca population.

URINARY TRACT INFECTION

Sometimes when a pregnant woman calls Siriaca for a massage because she is experiencing pain, the pain results from a urinary tract infection rather than from the pregnancy itself. In 2010 almost all of the women I visited with Siriaca had a urinary tract infection. Some of these cases were not only diagnosed by Siriaca but had also been diagnosed at the prenatal clinic.

I asked Siriaca if such infections were more frequent now; in my previous research people did not mention them as often. Siriaca said there were not as many cases before.

> I don't know why, but the weather is hotter now and the people drink a lot of Coke and Pepsi. This affects them a lot. They drink coffee. They don't drink *agua pura* (purified water). They eat a lot of chili, chili coban, which is very hot. It makes them sick. (*Le hace mal.*) That's why they get urinary infections. From the inflammation. It is worse in the summer, when it's very hot with a lot of sun. (2013)

Siriaca's explanatory model for urinary tract infection links it to the hot-cold principle in that the woman's condition is hotter than normal because of both the external factor of the weather and the internal factor of what she eats and drinks. For a urinary tract infection Siriaca prescribes a tea made from a mixture of fourteen herbs, including fenugreek, bark from *palo jiote* (*Bursera simaruba*; see Caceres 1996:296), bark of *cuajilote*, bark of *pancojuch*, *hoja de pescado*, *palo de la vida*, *flor de azúcar*, *salvia santa*, *ismut*, *violeta*, *hoja de arnica*, avocado pit or four *coquitos tiernos*, and *flor de volvo*. The patient should drink the tea before each meal and before going to bed for three days. The tea is supposed to be cooling to restore the balance in her body.

THE PRENATAL CLINIC

Midwives are told in the training classes and health centers to have their clients go to the prenatal clinic. All pregnant women are supposed to go, not only those with possible risk factors. They are examined, weighed, and told their expected due date. They may also receive iron pills and vitamin pills, or in some cases the prescriptions for them. Siriaca tells her clients that in the clinic the nurse or doctor will also listen to the fetus's heartbeat. Unfortunately the midwives do not have fetoscopes or stethoscopes. During a review session, the nurse told the midwives to listen to the fetus's heart with a stethoscope. One of the midwives informed her that they don't have any. The nurse said they would try to find out how much they cost and whether they could get some cheaply. I was surprised that the nurse did not know that the midwives don't have stethoscopes. They also lack fetoscopes even though they are simpler and can be easily constructed out of common objects (Klein, Miller, and Thomson 2009).

When some of the midwives told the nurse in one of the review sessions that the women refused to go to the prenatal clinic, the nurse responded that it was the midwives' own fault and that they should tell the patient they won't attend the birth or be responsible unless she goes to the prenatal clinic. The nurse said, "You should tell the patient she should go to the clinic because it is an *order* we are making" (Cosminsky 1982b).

This statement raises several issues. First, the nurse's statement reveals a complete lack of understanding of the economic realities on the finca and the possible problems of the woman's access to the clinic. To get to the clinic involves the cost for transportation; lost earnings because of time away from work, especially if it is during the coffee harvest season; and the cost in time involved in traveling long distances. When going to the clinic in San Felipe, people walk rather than ride because of the fare. However, the one- to two-hour walk involves crossing a rickety bridge over the Samalá River, which people perceive as dangerous. This bridge is often washed out during the rainy season, in which case they have to take the bus. They also believe that the *aire* (winds or breezes) they are exposed to from the river when they cross the bridge can make them sick. As for securing a ride to the clinic, the road is full of potholes and very bumpy, so women are concerned that the fetus may be harmed by the rough ride.

If a woman is several months pregnant or if she is not feeling well, the trip can be particularly arduous. It is also difficult to convince a woman to go if she does not perceive anything wrong with herself because pregnancy is regarded as a normal occurrence. Some of the midwives said that women aren't accustomed to going, and sometimes women have shame or *vergüenza* because they aren't supposed to advertise their pregnancy. Some women said they don't like to go because they are afraid that the doctor, who is male, is going to touch or feel them, a violation of the strong values related to both modesty and shame.

If a midwife says she won't attend the woman if she doesn't go to the prenatal clinic, the woman will just use another midwife. Furthermore, the midwife may believe that she will be punished by God if she refuses to help someone because a refusal is contrary to the sacred obligations of her role.

Incentives to visit the clinic have often been couched in economic terms. During the 1970s food supplements like powdered milk, flour, cornmeal, and oil were given out monthly to pregnant women and mothers with infants. In order to receive the food, the mother had to be registered for the prenatal clinic, as well as attend a nutrition class when the food was given out. This meant an additional trip because the food was not given out during the initial visit to the prenatal clinic but after the nutrition class on a different day. María said she got some of her patients to go to the prenatal clinic by telling them about the food benefits. One woman, Julia, went to receive the food from the *sanidad*, and the nurse said she wasn't registered. She had visited the prenatal clinic earlier and thought she was registered. They refused to give her anything. The lack of understanding of the reasons for nonattendance or nonregistration (if that was the case), or the clinic staff's failure to check the prenatal clinic records, seemed particularly insensitive considering the distance this woman had to travel. Such experiences have discouraged people from using the clinic.

In general, the nurses did not explain to the midwives why the prenatal visits were important. The review class would have been an excellent opportunity to do this. Instead, the tone communicated by the nurses was one of authority and threat. Their emphasis on attending the prenatal clinic reflected the hierarchical relationships and issues of control prevalent in the biomedical system; they did not offer explanations of the services offered by the clinic—such as administration of tetanus vaccinations—and of how those services would benefit the mother and child.

The authoritarian relationship reflected in the nurses' statements about the prenatal clinic is contrary to the traditional relationship between midwife and client. To María and to many midwives, the midwife's role is a sacred one based on a divine mandate or calling. It is a sin to refuse to help a woman. The midwife will be punished by God or some spiritual agent if she refuses. In addition, her role is a support-ive one, not a threatening one. The locus of decision making about whether to go to the prenatal clinic is primarily in the hands of the cli-ent and her family, not in the hands of the midwife. Biomedical per-sonnel need to have some understanding of this larger sociocultural context of the midwife's role (Cosminsky 1982b).

Some pregnant women do go to the prenatal clinic, especially if they are having problems. Julia, who had been having nausea and diz-ziness, went to the prenatal clinic four times. She did not say whether they gave her anything for this problem, but she continued to strug-gle with it even after the birth of the baby on June 25. The last time she went, on May 6, they were closed because the staff was out vacci-nating. The month before, she went because she had a toothache, and the public health clinic would pull teeth and charge only one quet-zal if you were in "prenatal control." Previously Julia had also gone to the clinic in San Cayetano and the private hospital in San Felipe be-cause of the dizziness. They had told her she was three months preg-nant. They prescribed Meprogesico and gave her several injections and pills, but these did not alleviate her discomfort. When she was four months pregnant she went to a doctor in the town of Mazatenango who prescribed Grunovit, which cost Q8.40 and did bring some relief. He also gave her a sample of Sermin pills, Hostaciclina (an antibiotic), and Neurastinol and Vitadoce (vitamins), but she did not say whether she had taken these.

Meanwhile, she was seeing María for her prenatal exams and mas-sages. Julia thus sought care from a public health clinic, a private Catholic clinic, a private physician, and the midwife. Prenatal care in-volves the same type of pluralistic health care that people use for other illnesses. María said:

> When they come to see me because they haven't gotten their period,
> I tell them they are pregnant, and they have to have prenatal control.
> They say they don't have money and "better I go with you to see me
> each month." I tell them fine but they have to buy the *prenatales* (vi-
> tamins). When I go to the pharmacy, they give me at twenty-five cen-
> tavos for the treatment, then I tell them if they give me the money I
> will bring the medicine. It costs me the fare. Then I check (*contro-
> lar*) them, each month. (1978)

Siriaca tells her clients (whom she calls *mis enfermas*) that they should go to the prenatal clinic, where they can get their tetanus vaccination to prevent neonatal tetanus in the infant—*mal de siete días* (the seven-day sickness), as it is locally called.

There used to be a hanging bridge over the Rio Samalá, which was passable in the dry season and enabled people to walk to San Felipe. However, today people have to go by bus to either health center. Occasionally, a mobile clinic comes to the finca to immunize children as part of the national immunization campaign. During these visits the mobile clinic also gives the tetanus vaccine to the women. Siriaca says that she brings women to get the vaccinations as well. She points out they wanted to vaccinate all women from fourteen to forty-five years old, whether or not they were pregnant. Many women protested and wanted to know why only the women had to get vaccinated and not also the men. Siriaca tried to explain the reason to the women.

By 2015, estimates were that 93 percent of pregnant women had at least one visit for antenatal care (UNICEF 2015). Recent estimates indicate that by 2013, 85 percent of pregnant women had received the tetanus vaccine (UNICEF 2015). This percentage includes the urban population, which has much greater access to prenatal care than the rural population. There are still many women, especially in rural areas, who do not receive the tetanus vaccine.

One of the problems faced by some of the mothers who go for prenatal care is that they are told to get lab tests, blood tests, and (more recently) fetal ultrasounds, all of which they have to pay for, often through a private doctor, and that cost more than they can afford. For example, one young pregnant woman, Francisca, had swollen feet and thought she also might have a urinary infection. She went to the prenatal clinic, where they told her she had high blood pressure. She had to get lab tests done and see the doctor before they would give her any medication or advice. This meant she would have to pay the fare for another trip to town, then pay for the tests, the doctor's visit, and the medication. The lab tests cost Q250 (over $34), and the doctor costs Q125 ($16). The doctor said that she did not have an infection, but she should drink purified water, eat greens, and avoid drinking gaseous sodas. At the prenatal clinic they also told her she should get a sonogram, although the baby seemed to be fine. This meant another trip to town, plus the Q250 cost of the sonogram. The private doctor she went to at the time of the lab tests asked her if she wanted to take the sonogram, but she said she did not have the money. The personnel at the clinic and health centers seem to have no idea of the economic situation and the practical difficulties of transportation for many of their patients.

The increase in the use of ultrasounds is a prime example of the technological aspect of medicalization and how it changes the discourse around pregnancy. Although this procedure is taken for granted as a necessary part of prenatal care in the United States, and this might be the case in Guatemala City, as it is in many other societies, it has not been so in rural Guatemala. Eugenia Georges (2008, 1996) has analyzed the increasing use of fetal ultrasound in Rhodes, Greece, from the viewpoints of mothers and doctors, and shows how it can both increase the mother's anxiety, as well as help allay her anxiety and provide pleasure. This increases her dependence on the biomedical system and augments the authority of the doctor. Similarly for the finca women, the ultrasound can be a double-edged sword. Because it is recommended primarily in cases where the nurse in the prenatal clinic thinks there might be a potential problem (which, from the biomedical view, exists for any pregnancy), and because it often leads to a recommendation for a caesarean delivery, the ultrasound may increase the mother's anxiety by emphasizing possible problems. A recommendation that she have an ultrasound pressures her to choose between finding the means to get the ultrasound or to continuing being anxious. On the other hand, if the ultrasound shows that there is no problem, then the mother's anxiety may be allayed. Either way, the increasing use of the ultrasound is linked to a discourse of risk that is increasingly being used in prenatal exams and in the midwifery review sessions.

Whereas the prenatal clinic only concerns the physical aspects of the pregnancy, prenatal care as perceived by both mothers and midwives involves spiritual, emotional, and social care as well as physical care. The mind and body are not regarded as separate, and neither are spiritual and emotional characteristics. Prenatal care may also involve rituals for spiritual protection. María usually lit a candle on her altar and said a prayer for clients. Some finca women go to a spiritist to ask for protection for themselves and their baby.

INJECTIONS

A major concern of the health system is the availability of injections and their use and misuse by the midwife, which is also a result of medicalization. Prenatally these are usually vitamin injections. María did not give injections of any kind, but Siriaca learned to give injections as part of the health promoter course she took, and she does so at the request of her clients. One woman asked Siriaca about injections of *cuerpo amarillo* ("yellow body," or progesterone), and about how many she should have. Siriaca said that *cuerpo amarillo* is used when there is a miscarriage or abortion to *amazisar* (fill up or harden) the uterus. However, progesterone is also used to decrease the chances of a miscarriage. The woman was worried because with the last baby, when she had eight days left she didn't feel any movement. She went to the hospital, and the baby was born dead. That's why she wanted the injections for this pregnancy. Siriaca told her to take only three injections of progesterone but recommended injections of vitamin B complex and liver extract to give her strength and to sustain the baby. Siriaca would inject a cubic centimeter of liver extract and a cubic centimeter of B complex.

Although the main concern of biomedical personnel is not prenatal injections but the use of oxytocin injections by the midwife during delivery, the level of hygiene involved in injection use is questionable. Siriaca uses disposable needles, but said she was told she could use them twice if she boils them. She does boil them, but it is not clear whether she boils them for a sufficient amount of time or whether other midwives boil them sufficiently or at all. The reuse of needles can result in the spread of hepatitis, HIV, and other infections. Ironically, injections represent a case in which midwives and their patients have accepted the use of medical technology, but with possible negative as well as positive consequences.

EMERGENCY PLANS

A recent emphasis by the World Health Organization and Guatemalan medical personnel is that the mother-to-be, her family, and the midwife should make an emergency plan for obstetrical emergencies. The midwives have been given a chart called a *plan de emergencia* for this purpose. The plan involves the pregnant woman learning the signs of various complications, figuring out how to save the cash she would need if she had to pay to get to the hospital for an emergency, and deciding how she would get such transport. If a complication does occur or the mother or baby dies, and the midwife has not made such a plan with the family, she is legally liable and can be accused of negligent practice or lose her license (Hallowell 2012, 2014).

Although well intentioned, the policy ignores the reality that some women cannot afford emergency transportation to the hospital or even obtain such transport, especially at night. The requirement related to emergency plans is linked to the growing discourse of risk and the emphasis on the midwife and mother recognizing various risk signs. Elizabeth Hallowell argues that these plans form a "technology of emergency." She suggests that the plans are a tool not only for biomedical management of the pregnant body but also "for managing the socialities and temporalities of caregiving and shifting modes of reproductive governance" (Hallowell 2012:10). Furthermore, she argues that such emergency plans "position biomedical birth as the only possible outcome of moral action" (2014).

CONCLUSION

María and Siriaca have been able to maintain a degree of autonomy with respect to prenatal care because they provide a service that is outside the realm of biomedicine and is not provided by the prenatal clinic, but is perceived as important by the women they serve: the *sobada*, or massage. The massage is used by midwives primarily to estimate the due date, align the fetus, and make both the fetus and mother more comfortable; it is also used to treat pains during pregnancy and to prevent miscarriage. The pains experienced by pregnant women may be attributed to an imbalance of hot and cold resulting from some type of strain, a fall, or anger or another strong emotion—causes that are not recognized by the biomedical system.

At the cognitive level of medicalization, Siriaca, as María had earlier, continues to attribute causation of problems with a pregnancy, like pains, bleeding, and potential miscarriages, to hot-cold imbalance or to strong emotions such as anger. The biomedical system, on the other hand, views prenatal problems in term of risk. Pregnancy in itself is perceived as a risk, and certain conditions and characteristics are viewed as high-risk—*alto riesgo*—such as a first pregnancy, a previous cesarean operation, being over thirty-five years of age, preeclampsia, and malposition of the baby. Midwives whose clients have these characteristics are supposed to refer them to the hospital. Whereas María did not use a discourse about risk, Siriaca does now. She is also pressured by the doctor and the health and legal system not to attend births of new mothers or to attend women who have had a previous cesarean delivery; if she does so, she may lose her license. In this way the discourse about risk also entails control of the midwife and the mother-to-be.

Shared ethnomedical beliefs are one way the midwife maintains her role. Her knowledge concerning diagnosis and treatment—usually with massage, plasters, and herbal remedies—are not recognized by the biomedical system. However, medicalization of even traditional practices is beginning to occur. Medicalization has also had an impact in areas of practice such as nutritional advice, recommendation of vitamin and mineral supplements or other pharmaceuticals, examining the eyes for signs of anemia, and encouraging mothers to go to the clinic or health center for biomedical prenatal care.

In 2013 Siriaca no longer warmed the oil or pomade on her hands before the massage because the doctor had suggested that the pregnant woman has her own heat and that the temperature contrast on Siriaca's hands when she washes them in cold water after the massage can cause arthritis. The way Siriaca obeys the doctor's recommendation in this practice reinforces the hierarchical relationship between the doctor and midwife, thus also reinforcing his authority over both the midwife and the pregnant woman. Fortunately, the process has not reached the extreme that it did in Costa Rica, where the massage itself was banned and the midwife could be charged with a crime if she performed a massage (Jenkins 2001). Midwives in Guatemala have also been told repeatedly in training courses and review sessions not to use herbs, not because they may not be effective but because they may be too effective: they may cause uterine contractions or other effects.

The midwife is told to recommend that women go to the clinic or hospital not only for certain risks, such as malposition of the baby or carrying twins, but for regular prenatal care. One of the problems in getting women to go to the prenatal clinic is that clinic personnel do not explain to midwives the procedures followed at the clinic and the benefits of the clinic prenatal exam, so midwives are not necessarily able to communicate these procedures and benefits to the mothers. Another problem is that clinic personnel communicate information to the midwives in a condescending manner, explicitly assuming the superiority of the clinic over the midwife and the pregnant women. This attitude is also a reflection of the hierarchical nature of the medicalization process. The hierarchical order in which the nurse tells the midwife to tell the mother what to do—or even threatens the mother with consequences if she doesn't do something—is against the social and spiritual relationship of the midwife and her client. The midwife perceives pregnancy and birth as spiritual, and she prays for spiritual protection for her client and for divine assistance with the birth. Both María and Siriaca have experienced what they interpret as various signs of their divine calling, which increases their clients' confidence in them, as well as their own confidence in their midwife roles.

The recent pressure for women on the finca to have an ultrasound is an example of the technological level of medicalization of childbirth. In this case the technology is also being used to replace an aspect of the midwife's role— estimation of the size, position, and due date of the fetus, via the midwife's measurement by hand. In this way technology is being used to increase the control of childbirth by medical personnel and correspondingly the dependence of the pregnant woman on the sonogram technology and the doctor. If a woman is told she should have an ultrasound because of possible complications or risks, her anxiety increases, especially if she cannot afford the ultrasound but feels the pressure to get it. The only way for her to allay that anxiety and be reassured is to get the ultrasound, even if she has to borrow money to do so. The ultrasound is thus relevant not only at the technological level of medicalization, but also at the interactional and control levels. The woman interacts directly with the machine when she views the sonogram image, which can change and intensify her sense of reality of the fetus (Georges 1996:165). Both the machine and the information it produces are controlled by the doctor or other biomedical personnel, as is what they choose to interpret and reveal to the woman about the sonogram.

Denial of access to technology is another form of control. This is illustrated by the failure to provide the midwives simple and basic technology such as fetoscopes, stethoscopes, and blood pressure monitors.

The biomedical personnel's attitudes of condescension toward and denigration of the midwives' and mothers' knowledge, beliefs, and practices as part of the medicalization process also reflect class and gender relations. Both the nurses and doctors are of a higher class and are more educated than the pregnant women, their family members, and the midwives, who are usually rural and poor, and some of whom are Mayan as well. The nurses are primarily female, but all or most of the doctors are male. Although more female physicians are being trained, to my knowledge all the physicians in the National Hospital in Retalhuleu and the local health clinics and centers were male, in addition to being of a higher class than patients from the finca. They were usually not OB/GYNs but were more general practitioners. Their negative attitudes are reinforced by class and gender stratification, which are manifested in the medicalization process and are also evidenced in the contestation over control of women's bodies, which continues during the birth. I analyze those attitudes in the next chapter, on the management of labor and delivery.

Most births on Finca San Luis and in the surrounding area occur at home, attended by a *comadrona*. Before the 1990s María attended the majority of these. Since then, especially after María's death in 1997, her daughter Siriaca has attended many of them. During this time the pressures of medicalization on the *comadronas* have increased, partly due to policy changes at the World Health Organization and to new restrictions by the state and the biomedical system, resulting in attenuation of midwives' role and a decrease in the number of births they attend. In this chapter I compare the impact of medicalization on María's and Siriaca's management of labor and delivery, beginning with a birth attended by María.

CHRONOLOGY OF A BIRTH WITH MARÍA

When I arrived at María's house one morning in 1976, I found that she had been called to Pancha's house in Buena Vista during the night because Pancha had gone into labor. María had instructed one of her daughters to bring me, so we walked together to Pancha's house, about an hour away. For the next several hours I observed María and participated with her as she attended Pancha's birth.

8:45 a.m.: When we arrived, Pancha had not yet delivered. The pains had started during the night. She was dressed and had her head tied in a scarf to prevent it from getting cold. When she felt pain, she bent over a table. María put one hand on the left side of Pancha's abdomen and one on her rear and rubbed downward until the pain passed.

8:55 a.m.: María put a plastic sheet on the bed and Pancha lay on top, covered with a bedspread. When each contraction came, one about every five minutes, María pushed gently downward with her hand on Pancha's abdomen until the contraction passed, then asked me to do the same while she while she watched for the crowning of the baby's head. At this point the amniotic sac had not broken yet.

9:55 a.m.: María gave Pancha two white capsules called *cápsulas de la Señora* that she had gotten from the pharmacy. Pancha swallowed them and drank a tea of clove, cinnamon, and *pimpinela* (*Poterium sanguisorba*) to quicken the labor and lessen the pain.

10:00 a.m.: María gave Pancha some olive oil to drink *para ensuavacer los labores* (to soften the labor pains).

10:05 a.m.: María tied a white cloth sash around Pancha, above her abdomen.

10:15 a.m.: Pancha was having trouble pushing in the horizontal position, so María had her try squatting, holding on to a rope that was hung over the rafters, but she wasn't strong enough to hold the position.

10:35 a.m.: María suggested Pancha try kneeling and holding on to a chair for support, which María had me hold as well, so Pancha could exert force. María put a canvas sack on the ground and a slip on top of that for Pancha to kneel on. She knelt down and María squatted behind her, pushing downward on her back and telling her to push down with each contraction.

"*Ay, ay*! I am going to die! I cannot stand it! I am going to die!" cried Pancha as she knelt and tried to push out the baby with each contraction, while she pushed against the chair I was holding for support. "Pray to the Virgin Mary to help you instead of crying," said María as she held her from behind, massaging and pushing downward on Pancha's abdomen and on her backside from the waist down. With each contraction, María told her to push hard: "*bajo, duro.*" She told her, "The remedy is in your hands." María said she scolds a woman if she makes a lot of noise and talks about dying. She told Pancha to stop thinking of dying, to have courage and to realize that she is doing something of great value: "You must ask God to help you give birth." María explains, "In the end, the women pay attention to me and do not make noise when the baby comes" (Cosminsky 1977b, 2001a:346).

11:15 a.m.: Pancha had been kneeling and pushing for about a half hour when the baby was born. María caught the child in her hands from behind. With one hand under the baby's head, María carefully eased him out.

The baby looked purple, but then he began to cry and get red. María put him down on a white cloth and covered him while waiting for the placenta to descend. Pancha was still kneeling. María kept telling her to push hard and to put her two fingers in her mouth so she would choke and her muscles would contract. The placenta came out after about five minutes. María rubbed Pancha's stomach lightly. Then Pancha got up and lay down on the bed while María attended to the baby. She gave Pancha *café amargo* (bitter coffee) with *esencia maravillosa* and rum to help heat her body, which was now in a cold state after the birth. María helped Pancha change her slip and clothes, which were bloody.

A chicken was killed and chicken soup prepared, which is supposed to give strength, warmth, and nourishment to the mother. A couple of hours after the birth, chicken soup and tortillas were served to everyone, including Pancha, María, and myself. María made the tortillas and lunch because there wasn't anyone else to do the preparation. One of the neighbors girls helped bring water. María had sent for one of her own daughters and a granddaughter, who was also Pancha's niece, but they came after lunch. María's granddaughter would stay and help Pancha. María would visit her the next day to check on her and the baby, and on the day after, she would bathe the mother and the child. The importance of the social aspects of birth at the finca are reinforced when kinship and neighbor ties are mobilized during birth. These are a form of social capital.

Pancha's husband worked on another plantation. He asked if he could get off work because of the birth and was permitted to leave. He arrived at the house and took care of their son, whom María chased out of the house. Usually the husband would help support his wife, and Pancha's husband might have done so if I had not been there. Instead, he helped by taking the boy outside, and I assisted María with supporting Pancha. He returned at about 2:00 p.m.

2:30 p.m.: María and I went to wash the dirty clothes from the birth in the river. When we returned from washing the clothes, she changed Pancha's clothes again and washed Pancha's nipples. She checked the baby and cleaned him, then put him to Pancha's breast. The baby nursed briefly. Then we said our goodbyes and left.

During the birth of Pancha's baby, María exerted both her personal authority and her authoritative knowledge through massage and physical contact with the mother. This knowledge is experiential and embodied in her hands. She knew that the kneeling position is easier for some women in delivery, even though she had been taught in a biomedical midwifery training course to use the horizontal position. María provided both physical and psychological support by urging Pancha to pray, and she distracted her from focusing on her physical pain (Cosminsky 1977b, 2001a).

Birth gains religious significance through the midwife. María emphasized the sacredness of birth not only by telling Pancha to pray, but also by praying herself. "At the time that the woman is giving birth, I have to pray a little. I have to ask the invisible midwives, the spirits, the invisible doctors that they help in the moment that the woman is giving birth" (1976).[1] This knowledge and experience is devalued by the hegemonic biomedical obstetrical system in its claim as the only possessor of authoritative knowledge.

The midwife is usually called to the home of the pregnant woman by her husband or a relative when she goes into labor. The husband is expected to be present if he is living at home "so he will know what the woman goes through" and he is expected to help support the woman. If he is working in the fields he is sent for. In Pancha's case, the husband was present but had taken their young son outside to keep him occupied because children should not be present at a birth. Instead, I was asked to help support Pancha. If I hadn't been there, her husband probably would have been holding her or the chair to support her.

The midwife is on call twenty-four hours a day. Sometimes when she is called, it is not yet time or the woman is experiencing false labor. Siriaca mentions this problem, especially for *primíparas*—women who are having their first child—and for women who live a distance from the finca. She was called ten times for one client in the village of San Juan.

Last Sunday they came to get me at 6:00 in the afternoon. I said I had just gone there two days before when they called me. I told them if they can find a car I will go, but I will not go by foot. I was very tired going the last time. If they come in a car, I will go. It is useless because she is not going to give birth today because I just saw her and it is not yet time. Then he got a car here on the finca, a taxi. Then I said to the taxi driver that he should wait a little while I examine the woman and then he takes me back. I went to examine her, and she still has not delivered, and they have not yet come to call me. The taxi driver covered Q20. . . . I didn't pay because each week (every eight days) they want me to come there, but they do not give me the fare. I pay Q1 from here to above. For that reason I told the husband, "You are an older man. This is your second wife and you have seen how a baby is born. Do not send for me when she is not with labor pains. I came to examine her and my duty is to come each month, but every eight days, every two days, I do not have that much for the fare." Then he told me, "Don't worry. I will not send for you until I see that it is serious. Then I will send to call you." Now they won't be bothering you every little while. I told him that perhaps it is the effect of the moon. When there is the waning of the moon, or a quarter waning or a quarter increasing (waxing), women begin to have pains.

Even though Siriaca was annoyed at this family for calling her so often, especially without helping her with the cost of transportation, she negotiated their paying the fare, then offered the husband a reason why the wife may have felt some pains even though she wasn't due yet. More recently, in August 2011, a young woman pregnant with her first child was concerned a couple of weeks before her due date because the baby was being very active and kicking a lot and she was having pains in her hips. Both her mother and Siriaca told her the cause was the effect of the moon—either a full moon or a new moon—and that she shouldn't worry (Siriaca, personal communication).

LABOR AND DELIVERY

In the above vignette, Pancha tried various delivery positions. First she bent over, holding onto the table, while María massaged her to ease the pains. María had her lie down on the bed and asked me to help push downward on the fundus each time a contraction came until it passed, while she watched for the baby's head. Pancha was having trouble pushing in the horizontal position, so María had her try different positions: first squatting, holding on to a rope, and then kneeling, holding on to a chair for support, which María had me hold as well. María squatted behind her, telling her to push down with each contraction. After Pancha was in a kneeling position for about thirty minutes, María carefully eased the baby out. The baby began to cry. She then put him down on a white cloth, covered him, and waited for the placenta to descend (figure 5.1).

María tried to have Pancha use the supine or horizontal position that she had been taught in the training course because it would be easier for her to see the birth. Biomedical personnel also consider lying on a bed to be more hygienic. María said the doctor told her, "You should not have the woman kneel, only lying down. You have to put a plastic sheet, well cleaned, and a cloth or blanket like a shawl. Then get a rag or cloth. But the people here, they want to lie down. Lying down is better." Most women that I spoke to, however, said they prefer kneeling, that it is easier for them.

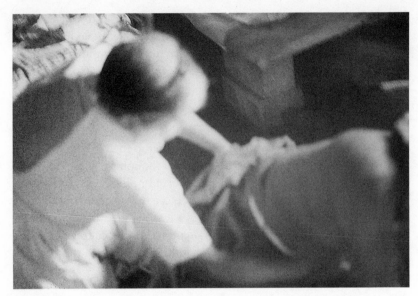

FIGURE 5.1. *Woman using kneeling position for delivery with María (1978).*

María and the mother were able to negotiate the best delivery position for the mother and baby. Although María first tried to exercise her authority by having the mother lie down, she allowed the mother to be the focus of her attention and use the position she found most comfortable. In fact, she ended up suggesting that Pancha kneel, which is the most commonly used birthing position in rural Guatemala.

In a normal delivery, María saw her job as mainly to catch or guide the child. She believed it was the job of the woman to facilitate delivery of the baby, as reflected in her saying, "The remedy is in your hands." This statement relieves the midwife from blame if something unfortunate happens. It also epitomizes one of the differences between a midwife-attended birth in the home and one that occurs in the hospital. In the hospital the woman plays a passive role; she has no agency, control, or authority. She is delivered, and the doctor has control of the birth. The woman's loss of control is even more extreme when the delivery is done by cesarean section.

Siriaca, in contrast to her mother, says that the patient has to deliver lying down in the supine or horizontal position, or semireclining and supported by her husband or another person, instead of using the customary position of kneeling or squatting during delivery. She says this is because they might get tired in that position and faint or fall at the time of delivery. Also, if the mother is on a bed, she can rest after the delivery, rather than having to get up again. Siriaca says that it is uncomfortable for the woman to kneel and push in that position and that it can sometimes result in a hernia. Thus she insists lying down is better for the mother and the baby.

Even if the woman wants to use a kneeling position, Siriaca will not let her. She says that she lets the woman walk around during labor, and when she sees that it is time, she tells the mother to lie down to rest. According to Siriaca they obey her. Siriaca tells the mother to grab her knees, but if the mother cannot, she tells the husband or other helper to go behind the woman and help hold her and lift her up while Siriaca stays by the feet. The woman can then put her arms back up around her husband's neck to exert force while she pushes from a semireclining position. Siriaca also says that the doctor told her that if you want the baby to live, it is better to use the lying down position. This is a very powerful statement because the doctor is saying that the midwife can cause the baby's death if she doesn't use the horizontal delivery position.

Use of the supine position is a clear example of the biomedicalization of birth. Siriaca is following the biomedical practice taught in the training course and in this way differs from her mother. Siriaca takes a more authoritarian position toward her patients than her mother did, which also may be a result of the medicalization process. María, as shown in Pancha's case, would let the patient try out different positions for the birth and use whichever one the patient preferred, even though María would encourage her to lie down as she had been taught in the course. In this manner María acted as a cultural broker, encouraging the position favored by biomedicine but presenting alternatives to that position. She also allowed women agency and control within the birthing process, permitting them to make choices concerning the delivery position, including the locally accepted kneeling position, whereas Siriaca, following biomedical practice, does not give women a choice.

Many investigators have suggested that the horizontal position is less desirable or more disadvantageous for the woman than the traditional vertical delivery position of kneeling, half-sitting, or squatting (Haire 1975; Jordan 1993:207-8; Klein, Miller, and Thomson 2009:200; Thilagavathy 2012). Roberto Caldeyro-Barcia states, "Except for being hanged by the feet, the supine position is the worst conceivable position for labor and delivery" (quoted in Arms 1975:83). Gelis (1991:130) writes, "We now know that this position is the worst possible, because it causes compression of the big abdominal veins (aorta and lower vena cava) by the pregnant uterus, which increases fetal distress and is a factor in hypotension and hemorrhage in the mother." He also asserts:

> We now know that intra-abdominal pressure depends largely on the woman's position in the final phase of labour, and that the various vertical positions do most to help the expulsion. Thus our knowledge of physiological mechanisms assures us that the physical techniques of labor used in past times were effective. (Gelis 1991:133)

Gelis is writing about France, where, as in the United States, the vertical position has now been completely replaced by the horizontal one as the birthing position advocated by doctors, whereas in many parts of the world, including Guatemala, women are still using vertical positions and resisting biomedical pressure to use a horizontal position during delivery. However, some women and midwives like Siriaca have been persuaded by biomedical personnel to use the horizontal position.

The supine position is one part of a cultural complex developed in a Western context of gender ideology and medical technology. It reflects the values of efficiency, the obstetrician's convenience and dominance, and physical and chemical interference with labor. Historically the horizontal position for delivery was related to physicians' concepts of women's frailty and was used during labor as well as delivery to prevent exhaustion. Ironically, however, it can contribute to longer labor (Murphy-Lawless 1998). A horizontal position can make delivery harder for the woman and promote the use of chemical and technological interference.[2] Pushing against the perineum rather than assisting the baby down the birth canal can also lead to tearing of the perineal tissues. To prevent this, some midwives and doctors perform an episiotomy, cutting the perineum.[3] In a rural household without hospital resources and facilities, the horizontal delivery position may promote a more difficult and anxiety-provoking birth. A potentially harmful modern practice is being advocated at the expense of a beneficial traditional one.

About her methods, Siriaca says she has learned most of them from her mother:

When a contraction comes, I massage. When it comes each min-
ute, the woman has to breathe deeply, to have oxygen. When a
woman says "No aguanto, no aguanto" (I can't endure it), I tell her,
"Respira, respira profundo" (Breathe, breathe deeply). Then I show
her how to do it. If she is sitting, breathe. If she is walking, breathe.
My mother showed me how. She said that before they didn't have
this method. Then when the contractions began, the midwife would
tell her to push, the woman became weak, and when it was time, she
couldn't push. This happened to my mother. She was sick for three
days. The midwife was telling her to push. She couldn't take it. Then
the owner of the Finca Buena Vista, where she was living then, gave
her the car to go to the hospital. That was the seventh child of my
mother. It is useless to push before it is time. She showed me how
to know the position by touch. If you feel something hard, round,
it is the head, and if you feel something soft, then it is the buttocks.
She showed me how to practice well. Because before, many pregnant women died because the midwives had them push too early.
At times the child was born tired because when it was pushed it was
not yet time; it gets knocked hard and is born dying or retarded.
That's why there are some children that can't learn to read.

Pushing too early is a problem also mentioned by Brigitte Jordan in
her discussion of Yucatecan Mayan birth (1993:38).
    When I asked Siriaca how many hours one should wait before it
is considered a problem delivery, Siriaca said that normally the birth
takes six to eight hours. "If it is more than eight hours, say twelve
hours, and it doesn't advance, then one should go to the hospital.
There they will give her *suero* (serum) and an injection." María, on the
other hand, viewed the labor of each woman according to that individual's characteristics and situation. She evaluated how the labor was
progressing, not just how long it took. If she thought there was a problem with the labor, then she referred the woman to the hospital. The
setting of a time limit for normal versus abnormal delivery applies to
almost every phase of the birth process and is based on assumed universal standards. This standardization is a part of the medicalization
process.
    Sometimes Siriaca is called early for a birth:

I go to examine the woman. She has begun to dilate, but it isn't
time, it will take the whole day. Then the family says to stay because

of the time and expense of the trip. After lunch, around 3:00, the woman has more pain. I examine her, "It is still lacking, my daughter, not yet time. You have to wait, you have to breathe deeply." Around 6:00 or 7:00, contractions begin. If it is a female baby, it is slower because the woman has a contraction, then not another for an hour, then the baby is crowning and the pain stops, then in a while another contraction, until a dilation of ten. With a male baby, the pain keeps coming, one contraction, another, another, the baby is born faster.

During labor the midwife may give the woman herbal teas. María gave Pancha a tea made with cloves, cinnamon, and *pimpinela* "to give her strength and lessen the pain." Sometimes she added oregano, nine leaves of poinsettias, and nine avocado leaves or twenty drops of *esencia maravillosa*. She also gave Pancha a little cooking oil to drink "to soften the pains." In addition, she gave her *cápsulas de la Señora* to quicken labor because she felt Pancha had been having a long labor. At other times, María has used *Cápsulas Materlan*. About an hour and minutes after taking the capsules, Pancha gave birth.

During the delivery Siriaca uses disposable gloves that she gets from the health center. María did not use them. The use of such gloves is being promoted for hygienic purposes not only to prevent infection of the mother, but also because of the risk of contracting HIV and hepatitis. Although there have been no cases of HIV/AIDS reported from the finca itself, there were some cases in 2010 in the adjacent *aldea*, including that of at least one former finca resident. Although some midwives don't like to use gloves because they consider it harder to handle the baby with them, Siriaca has adopted the practice.

PLACENTA AND CORD

While Pancha was still kneeling and waiting for the placenta to be expelled, María told her to put two fingers in her mouth so she would gag, causing muscle contractions to aid in the expulsion of the placenta. After the placenta came, María examined it to be sure it had all been expelled. Pancha then got up and lay down on the bed, covered with blankets, while María tended to the baby. María said that if the placenta has not come yet, one looks where the point of it is or where the "ball" is, because if it is big, then the placenta is ready to come. Then she would press down toward the placenta to encourage it to be delivered. María knew that a retained placenta could result in death and thus tried various means to expel it.

> When the baby comes, I clean the face, eyes, and mouth and clamp the cord. I massage the mother, and the placenta comes in three or four minutes. If it is five to ten minutes and the placenta doesn't come, I give the mother a little salt and three spoons of water to drink. If the placenta still doesn't come, then I put the baby to nurse. It should come. If it still doesn't come and it is more than fifteen minutes, I tell the husband to help her get up and urinate. When she urinates, the placenta should come. If it still doesn't come, she has to go to the hospital. She shouldn't wait more than twenty minutes because it may be far and you have to calculate the time. If not, she may die.

María tied the cord with a white strip of cloth in two places, one about an inch away from the cord's attachment to the baby, and the other about six inches farther up, and cut the cord in between with scissors that had been soaking in a bowl of boiled water. She put alcohol on the scissors and put alcohol and merthiolate on the cord stump to disinfect the cord, as she had been taught in the course. Then she cauterized the end of the cord with a candle flame, which is the more traditional practice. She then sprinkled a white powder from the pharmacy called *licopodio* (lycopodium) on the cord and wrapped a white cloth around the cord and bound it. At other times she used talcum powder (Cosminsky 1977b).

Siriaca treats the cord in the same manner, combining the methods she has learned from her mother. However, in addition, she takes care to put a cloth under the cord to be sure no melted candle wax drips on the baby. She continues to use the candle even though doctors tell the midwives they should not do so because wax might drip and burn the baby. Siriaca says she continues to use it because it makes the umbilicus smaller, leaves it dry, and prevents bleeding. She has adapted the practice to meet the doctor's criticism by using a cloth to protect the infant. She also uses the alcohol, merthiolate, talcum powder, and *licopodio*, combining practices while maintaining her authoritative knowledge (Cosminsky 2001a). In 2013 she said she had stopped using *licopodio* powder on the cord.

María and Siriaca both wait until the placenta emerges before cutting the cord. They believe that if the cord is cut before the placenta is expelled both mother and child might die. The body is conceived of as a tube in which organs can be displaced and move up or down. Thus the midwives believe that the placenta might rise up inside the woman, choke her, and kill her. María gave me specific examples of this having occurred in cases treated by another midwife. Siriaca explains to me in almost the same words her mother had used twenty years earlier that the doctor has clamps that he uses when he cuts the cord, and these prevent the placenta from rising up in the body, so he can cut the cord first. The midwives do not have these clamps and do not want to be responsible for endangering the mother and child. Thus Siriaca was continuing a practice used by her mother.

Both María and Siriaca exercise their agency and use their authoritative knowledge in the face of a conflicting practice used by the biomedical system. If the placenta is retained and the cord must be cut, the cord is tied to the woman's leg so the placenta will not rise until it is expelled or the woman is taken to the hospital. This same belief and practice was reported to be common in France (Gelis 1991). However, when I returned in 2000, Siriaca had a clamp that the doctor had given her and was now cutting the cord immediately after delivery.

The local practice of waiting to cut the cord is condemned in the medical midwifery training programs. One nurse said that while waiting for the placenta and delaying cutting the cord, the midwife may neglect the baby. However, she did not provide any examples, and whether or how often such inattention occurs is unknown. This is another example of biomedical personnel assuming that biomedical practice is best and that whatever the midwife is doing is wrong and needs to be changed.

Ruben Grajeda, Rafael Escamilla, and Kathryn Dewey (1997) report that research has demonstrated the beneficial effect of waiting until the cord stops pulsing before cutting because it maximizes the amount of oxygen and iron going through the cord to the baby. Ryan McAdams (2014) similarly argues that delayed cord clamping decreases iron-deficient anemia and increases iron stores in neonates. P. Van Rheeman (2011) and Mary Esther Malloy (2013) also promote delayed cord clamping and support the conclusion that there is no benefit from and more evidence of harm in immediate cord clamping and cutting. Susan Klein, Suellen Miller, and Fiona Thomson write: "Some people wait until the placenta is born before cutting the cord. This is a healthy custom" (2009:214).

María related a case in which the baby was having difficulties after a long delivery, so she squeezed the cord, pushing the blood toward the baby, which she said saved the baby's life. However, the process of medicalization entails pressure by biomedical personnel to get rid of traditional childbirth practices such as this one. They are to be replaced by modern medical practices that are assumed to be scientific and safer, but are not necessarily so. This is also an example of a time lag in biomedical learning: what is being taught in Guatemala as modern medicine is now outdated according to more recent findings.

Even the World Health Organization says that waiting to cut the cord may be beneficial. One WHO report (1998) supports the practice of late clamping or cutting of the cord in cases such as home deliveries, where there is a tradition of late clamping and waiting until the cord stops pulsing or the placenta had been expelled, and where there has not been active interference in the delivery. Such interference often occurs in the hospital, in which case early clamping may be necessary because of active management of the birth. The report says that one of the benefits of late cord cutting may be to help prevent anemia in the infant. It also mentions that no negative effects of late cord cutting have been found. At the 2013 Women Deliver conference in Kuala Lumpur, a famous midwife from Bali acted out a birth, insisting that the midwife wait to cut the cord. She then rose to her feet and addressed the audience. She lifted up two plastic water bottles, one full of red liquid, the other one-third full, in a dramatic demonstration of how much mineral- and oxygen-rich placental blood the baby fails to receive when the cord is cut before it stops pulsing (Macdonald, Pascali Bonaro, and Davis-Floyd 2014).

One of the practices the WHO report mentions is the use of dusting powders: "Several studies have shown that dusting powders promote rapid healing of the umbilical stump and early separation time. Dusting powders formulated with talc, starch or alum and zinc oxide have been shown to promote faster healing of the stump than powders containing hexachlorophene. Zinc oxide with its astringent properties is probably important in promoting drying and healing of the stump" (World Health Organization 1998). This information directly contradicts Goldman and Glei (2003), who have called the use of dusting powders a harmful practice, on the basis of earlier WHO recommendations. They object to putting a substance on the cord regardless of what that substance is. In measures of quality of care midwives have been marked down for using dusting powders on the cord. This confusion also highlights the complexity of trying to classify practices as harmful, beneficial, or harmless. The assessment may differ according to which criteria are used as the basis of classification and what the latest evidence is.

The burning of the cord leaves it dry and sterile and is thus beneficial, especially in an area where it is hard to be aseptic. The practice also prevents neonatal tetanus. Nancie Gonzales and Moises Behar (1966) point out that in certain regions of Guatemala, tetanus neonatorum is rare because of the practice of cauterizing the cord. Ironically, the midwives, including María had been taught to use alcohol, merthiolate, talcum powder, or *licopodio* in the earlier biomedical training courses, and they had dutifully followed the practice. However, in the review session I observed in 2013 the midwives were told not to put anything on the cord except alcohol. They are now told not to follow a practice that they had been previously taught by biomedical personnel.

María combined biomedical and indigenous methods in her postnatal care of the placenta and cord, a double precaution against neonatal tetanus, or what is locally called *mal de siete días* (illness of seven days). María rubbed the baby in an upward direction with oil of rue, first over the head, then over the body, and made a cross over its head while saying a prayer. She said that she did this to prevent the *mal de siete días*. When I asked her about this illness, she said it was caused by infection of the umbilicus, which she had been taught in the course. Nevertheless, she also took the traditional ritual precautions. María sacralized the procedure by using the rue oil, making the sign of the cross, and saying a prayer. If oil was unavailable, she said, she cleaned the baby with cotton soaked in alcohol and mineral oil.

Siriaca recognizes that the *mal de siete días* is from tetanus, an infection of the cord. Today the prenatal clinic and a mobile clinic give tetanus vaccines to pregnant women. Siriaca encourages her clients to receive the tetanus vaccine, which was unavailable in the clinic during the 1970s. However, she still continues to cauterize the cord because, she says, it leaves it dry and clean, which is beneficial since some women still don't receive the tetanus vaccine. Thus she combines the traditional and biomedical practices.

María examined the cord for various signs. Like with many Mayan midwives (Rogoff 2011: 157, 201), María considered it to be sacred knowledge that the knots or bumps signify how many children the woman will have and the interval between births. Round lumps signify girls and long ones males. If the cord is short or smooth the mother will not have any more children. Also, if one strips the cord, then the woman will not have more children.

Siriaca, on the other hand, is skeptical about this belief and questions it on the basis of both her own experience and a doctor's opinion. She says that when she had her sixth and last child, María, who delivered that baby, pointed out that according to the cord, she would have six more children. Siriaca and her husband were very upset, wondering how they would manage with more children. Fortunately, she said, she did not have any more despite the fact that she did not use birth control. She also asked the doctor about the cord, and he said these signs were not true, confirming her own conclusion and overriding her mother's knowledge.

Gelis (1991:161) reports the same belief for Western Europe, tracing it back to the medieval Arab doctors Avicenna and Rhazes:

> The umbilical cord was also considered to be a good indicator of the couple's future fertility: the knots in it were counted carefully, for they were believed to represent the number of children which the woman had still to bear. "And if there is no knot, she will have no more and if there is a great distance between the said knots, the woman also will put a good interval between one pregnancy and the next; and if the distance is small, she will put scarcely any interval." Finally, if the knots in the cord are black or red, "She would have as many boys; and if they are white, as many girls."

Presumably the belief in these signs in the umbilical cord were brought to the New World with the Spanish and were incorporated over the years into the local ethnomedical system. Barbara Rogoff reports that Chona, a midwife in San Pedro, also reads signs in the umbilical cord (2011:201).

The placenta is considered to have a special relationship to the child and is referred to as the companion or sibling of the baby.[4] Proper disposal of the placenta is necessary. The husband is supposed to put the cord and the placenta in a bag, which is burned, and he buries the ashes. If a dog or animal digs up the placenta, harm may come to the child. The stump of the cord should be saved and put in a covered jar after it falls off. Some people throw it away; others tie it in a tree if it is a male baby so he will be able to climb trees when he gets older; if the baby is a female, the cord is put under the hearth so she will do her household duties.

María said that some people use the cord in a remedy for barren women. To become pregnant, the woman can cook a piece of the dried cord with clove, cinnamon, cumin, oregano, *pimienta de cas-*

tillo, and *balsamito de aire*, plus two *octavos* of rum and some white honey. This mixture is put in a bottle, and the woman should drink a cup each morning until the bottle is finished. If the woman has intercourse, she will not get her next period because she will be pregnant. However, María said she didn't use the cord in this mixture because she thought of the cord as dirty. She had no confidence in this use of the umbilical cord, only in the herbs (Cosminsky 1977b).

After the baby was taken care of and the placenta was out, María massaged the abdominal area of the mother to help her uterus return to normal. First she rubbed olive oil on her hands and heated them over the coals. Then she massaged so the blood would leave. She pushed from below the abdomen upward, then kneaded the abdomen. After this, a *faja* (binder) was put on the woman.

Both María and Siriaca did this and regarded it as necessary to prevent *descompostura* (prolapsed or fallen uterus). The uterus is raised externally, and a wide sash is tied around the lower abdominal area below the woman's navel. This is to close the bones, which are believed to have opened for the birth, and to put the uterus back in its normal place and support it there. Then the woman can walk or work and nothing will happen to her. If a woman delivers in the hospital, she usually will not put on a binder afterward. However, if a woman has pain, she may call the midwife to apply the binder, which is usually preceded by a massage. For example, when Siriaca was in Guatemala City visiting one of her daughters and thus unavailable, one woman back home was attended by another midwife and another delivered in the hospital. Both of these women requested postnatal massages and the placing of the binder by Siriaca when she returned, reflecting both their confidence in her and the continuation of these ethno-obstetric practices.

María took the mucus from the mouth and nose of the baby with a syringe. She had been taught to use the syringe in her training course years before and it was part of her midwifery kit from WHO.[5] She said she put eyedrops in the infant's eyes, although I did not observe her doing anything to infants' eyes. She then swaddled the baby tightly in several layers of cloth, making sure its arms were down by its side, and put a hat on its head. The baby must be kept warm and not exposed to the winds and cold, since a newborn baby is in a cold and very vulnerable state. Swaddling is considered necessary for the proper development of the child. After the swaddling, María made the sign of the cross over the baby again. She then weighed the swaddled baby with a portable hook scale and announced the weight. This included the several layers of swaddling, so it was not known what the actual weight of the baby was. Many of the newborns in the area have low birth weights, below five pounds.

WASHING CLOTHES

In the case of Pancha presented at the beginning of the chapter, María washed Pancha's bloodstained clothes in the river. Pancha had given birth fully dressed. María changed Pancha's clothes and made sure she was warmly covered. Sometimes one of her daughters or granddaughters went with her to assist with drawing water, cooking, and washing the clothes. Although washing the clothes is part of the midwife's role in various parts of Guatemala, María said that she does it as a favor only if the woman has no other female relatives to help her.

This practice was hotly debated in one of the midwifery review sessions I attended with María. The nurse said that the midwife should neither wash clothes nor help prepare meals nor give medicine. The only thing she should do is assist with the birth. According to the nurse, if the midwife does such chores, she should charge extra. However, some of the midwives complained that untrained midwives were performing such tasks and charging less, thus undercutting them. The nurse who gave these instructions lacked an understanding of the traditional role midwives play in the social support system by providing attention, assistance, and postpartum care. The nurse defined the midwife's role according to the biomedical model: as strictly obstetrical.

Pressure from the biomedical system has had an impact on Siriaca's practice. She stresses that she does not wash the clothes. She does not consider that as part of her duties: "The only thing that I do is give the attention to the birth, and I do not wash one piece of clothing. Before, the midwives had to wash for eight days. They still do that in San Marcos."

BIRTH COMPLICATIONS

Most of María's assistance with difficult labors was in the form of either massages or teas, but she also said prayers and performed rituals. María knew first hand the importance of rituals and prayer during birth. In one case in which hard labor had continued for one day and one night and the mother was trembling and couldn't give birth, María passed candles over the woman and burned incense while praying, asking the *Santa Tierra* (Holy Earth), *Nuestro Señor* (Our Lord) and the invisible midwives to help. Shortly after these prayers, the baby came.

Retained Placenta

María understood firsthand how a retained placenta could affect a mother. One of her own children was born dead, and her placenta was not completely expelled. She almost died then:

> The placenta came but not all of it. It brought a piece (membrane) about six inches wide with a thing like a *boleadora* (lariat with balls). Then the next day when I woke up, I felt something. *Ay*, what is this that I have? I sent everyone outside. I stayed alone. I went to a corner to see. It was hanging down. Then I began to pull, to pull with force, a piece came. The rest came. Then I was frightened. I said now I am going to die. Then I began to cry, I am going to die alone. It came out green. For a while I had fever, a strong fever. I vomited. . . . I was praying. I am about to die. One woman here went to the priest. She said that there is a sick person you have to visit. Señora María is in her house, she is seriously *su vida*. The priest came. I never saw him. They told me afterward that the priest arrived, many people arrived. He went to pray. I didn't feel anything. He told me that I was purple all around my mouth. My fingernails were purple. Just by a little I was going to die. There is something they call spiritism. Then the spirits said that I should make a *lavado* (douche) of Zonité and permanganate. They sell it in the pharmacy. The Zonité is in a little bottle, which is prepared with water. They gave me a douche of Zonité. After, they made me a douche of permanganate. Then they gave me a purgative to drink. Then they looked for a little of leaves of Santa María. They threw sufficient leaves of Santa María, and a few coals from the fire, wrapped in a cloth. Then they gave me a good knock (punch) in the stomach, hard, hard, downward, downward. In a little while, the bleeding came, pure black and some big pieces that had stayed came. It was green, green. With this, I got better. If not, I would have died. The spirit that came was a female. She would come in the house, and would make her talk or consultation. This is what the big altar is for. (1974)

María's experience with such cases made her very aware of the dangers of a retained placenta and reinforced the importance of the sacralization of birth. In the first case, María prayed, performed a ritual, and communicated with the spirits of dead midwives, which she credited for a successful birth. In the latter, the spirit was the source of the treatment that María acknowledged cured her and saved her life. It is not clear whether she was unconscious when she didn't see the priest, delirious from the fever, or in a trance when she saw and heard the spirit, or a spiritist possessed by a spirit, perform a cure for her. The spirit's prescription gave the medicine from the pharmacy a sacred nature. The medicine became sacralized. In this healing, María was using both pluralistic medicine and pluralistic religion. Just as there is no conflict in using different medical resources, María saw no conflict in being both Catholic and a spiritist (although the Catholic church sees a conflict). It is not clear whether the priest was called to pray for María's healing or to administer the last rites because people thought María was dying. In either case, both the ritual and the sacralized medicine were perceived as essential by the attending people, as well as by María.

María related the following case of hard labor, in which the mother retained the placenta.

> I had gone to Retalhuleu. Since no one came to advise me that someone was ready to give birth I didn't have to worry. When I came back, a man was standing waiting. He said, "They sent me to call you to see Veronica because she is very sick. She began to be have pains last night but the husband didn't want to come to you because he was afraid he was going to lose his way." He said, "I am going to work first, and when I come from work, I will call the *Señora* [María]." Meanwhile, this morning the girl went to wash a little clothing, went to the fields to look for *yerba mora*, said she was going to get water to cook the greens and going to get her corn dough because it was early, like 9 a.m. Thus she arranged her grinding stone, washed it, took out the dough when the pain came. Then she sat there and the baby was born in the pure dirt. From that comes the pure sicknesses, from that is where comes the cancers, tumors. Then she said, "*Ay María,*" and I said, "*Ay Veronica. What are you doing?*" At the same time, the baby choked, and Mario came out running to call the mother. From there they went to call the mother-in-law who was working far. And they were struggling to get the

placenta out and didn't remember to come to call me. It was good that they didn't come because I wasn't home. Then they became tired and left, when suddenly she fainted and fell. . . .

They laid her down. Then when I arrived, I spoke to her. She was very pale. I said, "Why did you not send for me earlier?" But Veronica left her mouth open and couldn't speak. "*Jesús María Santísima* (Holy Jesus, Mary), this woman is going to die. But if she dies, I am not responsible," I said. "I have just come. Why did you not call me when she began to be sick? You can know what you have done, to tie the cord of the placenta," and it was black, black as pure charcoal. Then I began to touch her there. . . . I came and cut the baby's cord, tied it, and sent it to be wrapped.

I wrapped the baby myself. The baby was alive but very cold. Then I picked up the baby. . . . Veronica was stretched out. Now she is going to die, and they all began to cry. "Now don't cry because all of you that are here should have gone to call me." . . .

Then I put on a thin glove, and I pulled and I pulled and I took it out. When it came it was pure black, and I grabbed it and it became pieces. Then I picked up the girl and said, "Veronica, Veronica." She said, "Where am I." I said, "You are in your house." I dressed her and said to her mother-in-law and her mother that they help me, and we put her in the bed, and I gave her a little tea with *esencia maravillosa*, nothing more. And with this her color came back. In a while I asked to give her a little black coffee with *esencia maravillosa*. The next day, I went to give her a douche to get rid of anything remaining inside and now she is good. The douche was only boiled water. If it is very inflamed then I give a douche of Zonité.

In this case, both the mother and the baby lived. María related a different case of retained placenta in which the woman died:

The woman was delivered by a different midwife, someone from the *aldea*. The baby came with the cord around its neck, so the midwife pulled it and cut the cord. She was cleaning the baby, and the placenta stayed loose. She didn't tie it. You need to prepare the cord before cutting, calculating where you are going to tie and cut it. . . . The thread is long because you tie it on the leg while you attend to the baby. Then go see if the placenta hasn't come yet. You feel where the ball is. If it is big, then it is ready. Then press down toward below for it to come, but you don't want to exert force. In this case the midwife didn't look or see because the girl began with what looked like seizures. The husband asked the midwife what happened. She said the placenta went up. She told him he had better look for a car. By the time he returned, she had died. She choked. Blood came out of her mouth, her nose. The midwife should have looked and if it didn't want to come, she should have pushed and when it is nearer little by little it is going to come.

A retained placenta is believed to also be caused by strong emotions, such as anger. One pregnant woman, Celestina, got angry in the afternoon. That night she began to be sick. The child was born around 3:00 a.m. María said she had been massaging her so that the placenta would come, but it did not come. She took her to the hospital around 6:00 a.m. The nurses there could not take it out. They had to call the doctor. He did a vaginal operation, and with that he cured her.

Malpresentation

Both María and Siriaca would tell their clients to go to the hospital if there is a malpresentation, such as a breech, transverse or foot presentation. However, sometimes the family or the client would refuse to go. María said "I tell them, I can't do it here. But they say, 'I won't go. If I die, I die here.'" María proudly gave various examples of successful deliveries in cases of malpresentation, including those in which she did external versions, gradually turning the baby with outside manual maneuvers. One woman who had a breech presentation refused to go to the hospital, saying that she would not be able to stand the rough ride and would die on the way. María described how she delivered that baby: "When the sac breaks and I see it sitting, I put a lot of alcohol and a little oil, then little by little I go to see. I put my fingers here to one side to take out a foot, and then the other side for the other foot, and put together the two feet. Now the baby comes standing. I tell the woman to push harder. The shoulders are difficult. Then it passes and it is big."

In contrast, Siriaca says that if a baby comes with a malpresentation, she will not attend the birth. She will accompany the woman to the hospital, but the family has to look for a car. "In the hospital they congratulate me because they say I do not put my hands inside the woman. I only attend the birth when the head comes first. Also, when those that are having their first baby cannot, I bring them to the hospital, because it is very dangerous" Siriaca explains (1996). Nevertheless, she does describe a case of foot presentation in which she delivered the baby. She says that when they came to get her at 5:00 a.m., "I told them to bring her to the hospital because the baby is coming bad, and look for a car because the husband did not want his wife to go to the hospital. He was afraid. I lifted the hips of the baby up, and then the baby was born. Now the little girl is big."

Death

The complex relationship of the midwife and the medical personnel was highlighted in two cases in which deaths occurred (Cosminsky 2001a:363–364). The first case was that of an unmarried woman who had had two teeth extracted and then began bleeding for three days. Her family had not sought any medical help for the bleeding; nor had they called Siriaca when she was hemorrhaging or at any time during the pregnancy. The girl said her parents were very angry with her for having become pregnant and scorned her.

On the fourth day, the bleeding had stopped, and she went into labor. When the woman went into labor, her mother and father refused to call the midwife, just as they had done during the pregnancy. They didn't want to pay for the midwife's services because they were angry with her, a single woman, for having become pregnant. They said she could deliver in the hospital, assuming that it was free, and be taken there by the *bomberos* (firefighters who serve as ambulance drivers). Another woman was going to go to the hospital with the pregnant woman, but asked Siriaca to see her first. When Siriaca arrived, she seemed okay. The bleeding had stopped, and the baby and placenta had already come. Siriaca cut, cauterized, and dressed the cord, and bathed the baby. The woman said that she felt better and that she did not need to go to the hospital. About five and a half hours later, she felt thirsty and asked for a Coca-Cola. Then she got a severe pain in her stomach. The next morning her mother and father were out picking coffee. Someone came to get Siriaca because the woman was still having stomach pain. She suggested they give the woman some *pericón* tea for the stomachache, but she was screaming from the pain. Siriaca said they should get a car to take her immediately to the hospital. Her uncle and cousins tried to get a car and couldn't find one. Finally the firefighters came and took her in their vehicle. On the way to the hospital, she died, and they returned to the finca.

Siriaca said she went to the doctor to tell him what had happened in this case. Siriaca had not been called by the woman's family during the time she was hemorrhaging; nor had they arranged with her to attend the woman during her pregnancy. By the time they called her to attend the birth, the woman had stopped bleeding. The doctor assured her that the death was not her fault, but had occurred because the mother had lost so much blood before the birth. He calculated how much blood she had probably lost with all the hemorrhaging and excused Siriaca from any blame.

Single mothers sometimes have hospital deliveries because they and their families worry about possible gossip if the midwife delivers the baby and because they don't want to spend the money on a midwife. This situation shows a lack of social support for the mother and a lack of agency on the part of both the mother and the midwife. The risks faced by a young, unmarried mother are not solely because of her age, but also because she lacks the social and material capital necessary for support and assistance for the delivery.

The second case involved a young woman whose husband had beaten her while he was drunk (Cosminsky 2012:93). This caused her to "have anger" and to go into labor earlier than expected. The girl's mother gave her hot chocolate with egg because she thought her daughter was cold. However, the young woman was in a very hot state because both anger and being in labor are hot, and she had not yet delivered. Chocolate is believed to also have a hot quality, so consuming it increased the young woman's hot state to a dangerous degree. Also she had had a cesarean section with her previous child. The family called Siriaca at 3:00 a.m.

Siriaca told them she was not going to attend the birth because of the prior cesarean and told the family that they should call an ambulance to take the woman to the hospital. The midwives are told that they should refer women who have had previous cesareans to the hospital for subsequent births, rather than trying to facilitate a vaginal birth. However, the expectant mother felt a terrible pain after drinking the chocolate, her stomach swelled, and within ten minutes she died with the baby still inside. The baby also died. The family threatened Siriaca, saying it was her fault. Siriaca went to the director of the health center and told him the story. He said it was not her fault but was the fault of the husband, who had hit the woman, causing her to have anger so her labor started early.

It is important to note that these stories are Siriaca's recollections or interpretations as she told them to me. I do not know what the doctor actually said at the time. Both of these cases involved family conflicts that were beyond Siriaca's control. However, Siriaca's negotiations with the doctor to validate her actions and her position show her increasing dependence on him and the consequent undermining of her own confidence. The doctor's validation and support becomes a double-edged sword, enhancing her status and authority on the one hand, while simultaneously decreasing her autonomy. Contestation occurs for control not only of birth but also of death (Murphy-Lawless 1998).

HOSPITAL DELIVERIES

The above two cases highlight the realities of the lack of transportation and difficult access to the hospital for finca women. Although midwives are taught to refer women who have certain risk factors to the hospital, it is often difficult for them to get there even if they want to go. Some women are afraid to go to the hospital because they do not want to have a cesarean. In addition, whether to have a hospital delivery is not only the midwife's decision; the mother and other family members can make decisions that override those of the midwife. Often the mother herself has little say, and it is her husband and mother-in-law or her own parents who make the decisions concerning her delivery. If a midwife will be used, they may choose the specific midwife, or they may decide whether or not she will go to the hospital. If a death occurs, regardless of what the doctor considers the cause of death in physiological terms, its cause has roots in the social realm: a lack of social capital in the form of social support can also be considered a factor.

A number of factors affect people's decisions about whether to go to the hospital for delivery, even in an emergency: access, transportation, cost, fear of surgery, cultural differences, visitor restrictions, being scolded or humiliated, and worrying about children left at home (Berry 2009, 2010). The nearest public hospital is in Retalhuleu, about twelve kilometers away. A private hospital in San Felipe, Hilario Galindo (also called San Cayetano), was also used in the 1970s but was closed for several years due to local politics and economic factors. It has since reopened, but it is harder to get to via public transportation and is more expensive than the national hospital. Its newly furnished, modern maternity ward had few patients when I visited in 2010, possibly because it had only recently reopened.

Access to transportation for emergencies, especially at night, can be very difficult. María was once attending a delivery in which there were twins. However, the placenta came first, and the baby was *sentado* (breech). She took the mother to the hospital. María said that the finca administrator at that time (1975) would make a car available for emergencies. Before the car, María said, in such a case she would push the placenta back in, and then the baby would come out. But "since there is a car here, I do not want the responsibility," she explained. However, that administrator died in 1979. More recently, although the finca has a car, they rarely use it to take people to the hospital. Siriaca laments, "You can be dying in the corridor and they won't give the car."

Although a few more buses are available now than in the 1970s, the road to the hospital is very bumpy, and several people expressed concern that the ride might provoke delivery or more complications. At nighttime or in an emergency, a car or taxi must be obtained, which is usually problematic. One or two families on the finca have old cars that can be hired for a cost if they are available. It can cost ten dollars to get to the hospital in a taxi, which could be several days pay. In the above cases, when there was difficulty finding a car, the women were taken to the hospital by the *bomberos*, or firefighters from the nearest town whose vehicle serves as the ambulance.

On my return to the finca in 2010, there were many more taxis in the *aldea* San Luis, making the trip from the finca to the hospital in Retalhuleu more feasible, but also more expensive. In addition, many people had cell phones, so it was easier to call a taxi. However, there has been a surge in crime in the area near the finca, and people are very reluctant to go out on that road at night. This fear further militates against going to the hospital during the night and increases the demand for the midwife to deliver in the home.

The public hospital is overcrowded, unsanitary, and understaffed. Women may end up giving birth alone in the hospital either because of the lack of staff, the inattentiveness of the staff, or their own modesty or shame, known as *vergüenza*, which is an extremely important value among finca women (Paul 1975:452).

One woman, Margarita, had been sick with tuberculosis, and her previous birth had been difficult. She was pregnant again and had been encouraged in the prenatal clinic to get sterilized with a tubal ligation after delivery because of the danger to her, the baby, and future pregnancies. She and her husband agreed that she would deliver in the hospital so she could get her tubes tied. When the time came, she went to the hospital at 11:00 p.m. There she gave birth by herself at 3:00 a.m., and the baby was born dead. The nurse had not come to check on her or to see how much she was dilated. She did not have her tubes tied at that time. She said she didn't call the nurse because she had *vergüenza*. The sense of shame in this case would have come from exposing her private parts before strangers, especially if there was a male doctor. This example not only reflects the depth of the traditional value of modesty and shame, it also raises serious questions about the quality of care and lack of attention given at the hospital.

I went to visit Margarita at that time. The maternity section of the hospital was very hot, with no fans. Everyone was sweating. There were thirty beds, about two feet apart. Margarita was very thirsty. People depend on relatives and visitors to bring them food, drink, and other items. My co-investigator, Mary Scrimshaw, and I went and bought some sodas for Margarita. She was concerned about having to bathe in cold water at the hospital and hoped it would not make her swell. The nurse told her that the cold was good for her breasts, which were sore with excess milk because the baby had died. This is contrary to the hot-cold principle, according to which one would apply heat to the mother because the mother is in a cold state after the delivery.

In another case, Juana went to the hospital on a Tuesday night because she was having *dolor de corazón* (heart pain). They gave her three liters of *suero* (IV bags of serum) on Wednesday and Thursday. Friday at 4:30 p.m. she began to have labor pains, and at 6:00 p.m. the baby was born. She gave birth by herself under the sheets, saying she had *vergüenza*. "When the doctor took account, the baby was already born. They scolded me that I should have told them when the pains began. They said I could have died." She said she didn't make any noise when she was in labor or when she was pushing:

> When the baby came the other women in the room yelled, "Doctor, doctor, a woman has given birth," and the doctors ran to see me. The doctors were there when the placenta came. The doctors scolded me and asked me why I didn't tell them. I said it was my *herencia* [heritage], my *costumbre* [custom]. That I felt ashamed or embarrassed that they see me. Sunday they gave me leave from the hospital.

I was told about another case twenty years later by a mother who went to the hospital because Siriaca wasn't around when the time for delivery came. She stayed in the hospital for two days. She said that the nurses didn't pay attention or listen to anyone. They told her she still had some time when she said she was experiencing labor pains. The baby was born in the bed, then they finally took notice of the mother because of the baby's crying. She didn't go to the delivery room because the baby was already born. The doctor scolded the nurses for not paying attention.

These incidents raise questions about the level of care and attention given to poor women at Guatemalan hospitals. Such incidents also may have consequences for future deliveries of mothers from the finca. A midwife might refer a woman to the hospital for some complication, and the mother may be reluctant to go because she has heard about these situations or has experienced them herself.

The lack of attention by hospital staff was reinforced by the experience of Siriaca's daughter. She was going to deliver at the hospital instead of having her mother attend her because she wanted to get a tubal ligation. However, she went into labor on New Year's Eve and got to the hospital at 1:00 a.m. The staff had been having a party, and according to Siriaca's daughter the nurses were drunk. No one came to see her until 6:00 a.m., by which time the baby had been born. She did not have her tubes tied then. In 2010 she went to the private hospital Hilario Galindo in San Felipe, which was providing a special service in November for women who wanted to have tubal ligations. A group of volunteer doctors from outside Guatemala would be performing them. However, on my return in 2013, I learned that she had had another child because when she went to the hospital to be examined before she could get her tubes tied, she found out she was pregnant.[6]

Despite their misgivings, women have delivered at the hospital for various reasons: referral by the midwife for an emergency, complication, or illness; referral by the midwife for having a condition considered high risk, such as malpresentation, having a first child, being under sixteen or over thirty-five years of age, having had a previous cesarian; referral by the prenatal clinic because of malpresentation or because her pelvis is considered as too narrow; wanting to get a tubal ligation; the midwife being unavailable when she started labor or when she called; or voluntarily wanting to come to the hospital to give birth.

Jacinta went into labor, and her father went to get María. Unfortunately, María was not there, having been called to attend a birth on another finca. Jacinta said, "it was better they took me to the hospital"; she gave birth there and stayed for two days. One of the problems she mentioned was the food. She said things had gone okay in the hospital but it wasn't the same as in the home, where you are taken care of and you don't eat cold things: "It is not like cooking here at home. In the hospital they give one everything, cold foods, even beans and all that." She said she did not eat it: "Since one is not used to eating just anything, one feels embarrassed."

Another mother, Margarita, said she did not get much to eat in the hospital, only soup with chicken or beef and one tortilla. More recently another mother said she was given fish, beans, a cold drink, two pieces of bread, and no tortillas. These are all considered cold foods, which women are not supposed to eat postpartum because of their cold state. Relatives have to bring extras. Lucía, another mother, also said that there's more care at home. She referred specifically to covering one's head, covering the baby's head, putting on a sweater, and eating chicken soup, which are protective measures for both the mother and the baby to avoid cold. Of particular concern was having to take cold baths or showers in the hospital at 6:00 a.m. According to the women from the finca, it causes the milk to stop flowing or to become cold, which will make the baby sick. Flora, a young mother who had just delivered her first child, said the other women in the hospital told her just to bathe the lower part of her body, so the milk wouldn't be affected. The air in the hospital, however, is very hot with no ventilation.

Isolation from family and the strangeness of the hospital surroundings can be a source of anxiety and concern for the mother. For example, in the hospital no attempt is made to accommodate people's beliefs about the need to restore the humoral balance of the new mother by avoiding cold and applying heat or eating hot-quality foods. This failure is perceived by the finca women to increase the mother's vulnerability to illness. Another problem is that if someone intends to deliver in the hospital, they are supposed to bring with them two disposable diapers, sanitary napkins, towels, soap, and a Gillette (a new razor blade). This may cause financial difficulty. If the hospital delivery is because of an emergency, the mother may not have these items because things like diapers are not need needed for a home delivery.

On the other hand, women were previously concerned that they must leave the hospital in two or three days, whereas the usual confinement period in the house is eight days. Now, partly due to hospital overcrowding, mothers leave in one day unless they have had a cesarean or some other complication such as an infection, in which case they stay for three days. Some of the issues about diet and hospital conditions are not as much of an issue as they had been because the stay is much shorter.

The restriction placed on midwives that seemed to affect Siriaca the most was the one concerning *primíparas*, or first-time mothers. Siriaca mentions several times that the doctor forbids midwives to deliver first-borns. If they do, the midwives can lose their kit, license, and right to work. She can see the expectant women prenatally, but she tells them they have to go to the hospital for delivery. According to Siriaca, "If the woman says no, that she has to give birth in the house, I tell her, 'I will examine you here, but I can't attend.' If she wants me to accompany her, by all means I will do so. She is afraid because the nurses are very rough; they hit the patients ("muy bravo, le pega"). The midwife is not allowed to go into the hospital in Retalhuleu with the woman. This isn't the case in some other parts of the country, such as Sololá, where the midwife can enter the national hospital with her client. When Siriaca goes with the woman, the doctor asks them why they've come to the hospital, and she explains that it is because it is the woman's first baby.

When a woman arrives, the nurse examines her, and if it isn't time yet to deliver, the nurse makes the woman wait outside until she is fully dilated. Soraya Fleisher (2006:66) mentions similar problems that women have in the national hospital in Antigua: they are examined when they arrive and then told they must come back later when they are fully dilated because the hospital does not have the capacity to attend everyone who comes. To go home and return is impossible for most women, so they wait in the halls, in the waiting area, or outside.

Another factor that influences reluctance to deliver in the hospital is the disrespectful and condescending attitudes of the nurses and doctors, and their rude treatment of mothers and midwives. Siriaca mentions one such example. She brought in a woman at 11:00 p.m. after a long labor. The nurse scolded her, "Why didn't you bring her during the day? At night they stay awake and one is tired." She then said angrily, "Leave her there." Siriaca says the poor girl was so upset she began to cry. Such behavior on behalf of the hospital staff does not encourage midwives to refer people to deliver in the hospital or mothers to voluntarily go to the hospital. I have observed this type of condescension and scolding behavior toward patients at times when I brought people to or visited them at the hospital.

On the other hand, not everyone from the finca has negative attitudes toward the hospital. Some expressed appreciation. For example, one woman said she preferred going to the hospital because she got away from her kids and her responsibilities, and she got more rest in the hospital than at home. Another woman said she preferred the privacy of the hospital because on the finca the houses are close together; neighbors hear and know everything, and they gossip. Some of the women who went to the hospital for their first birth said that they had been well attended to, but expressed concern over the cold showers and food. A few of the women who voluntarily delivered at the hospital were Ladinas of a higher socioeconomic group, such as the finca schoolteacher, and they associated the hospital with modernity, status, and safety. They may also have been treated better by the hospital staff and may not have encountered the same problems as the average finca worker or peasant.

CESAREAN DELIVERIES

According to the Pan American Health Organization (PAHO 1999), 25 percent of all births in Guatemala were by cesarean section. Surprisingly, the most recent figure provided by UNICEF (2015) for Guatemala, for 2009–2013, is 16.3 percent. This figure suggests that there has been a decline in the cesarean rate. However, it may indicate a gross underreporting of cesareans. With more restrictions on midwife deliveries and thus an increase in hospital births, one would expect an increase in cesarean deliveries. Although I don't have rates for the National Hospital in Retalhuleu, a recent study of over five hundred women from twelve rural finca communities carried out in the Trifinio area, at the intersection of the departments of San Marcos, Quetzaltenango, and Retalhuleu, found a cesarean rate of 30 percent in October 2015, an increase from 27 percent in 2014. The cesarean rate reported by the public hospital is around 40 percent of their births (Gretchen Heinrichs, personal communication, 2015).

Another study was carried out in the Chimaltenango region, where new obstetrical and neonatal wings had been opened in the Chimaltenango Hospital in 2011 and 2012, respectively. Quality of care and the presence of qualified health personnel or skilled birth attendants improved during that time period. The authors write that "85 percent of midwives in the Chimaltenango region report one month or less of formal training, 60 percent are illiterate, and fewer than one-fourth report using a stethoscope for heart rate auscultation" (Garces et al. 2015:2). As is the case in Retalhuleu, the midwives have neither been trained in the use of a stethoscope nor given one, yet they, not the Ministry of Health or the training programs, are blamed for this deficiency. "Cesarean section rates increased from 13.3 percent to 24.3 percent from 2010 to 2013" (Garces et al. 2015:7), which the authors argue contributed to a decline in stillbirths and neonatal and perinatal mortality. Furthermore, they suggest that because there was not a similar decrease in mortality in deliveries with traditional birth attendants, "consideration should be given to a policy of phasing out home births with TBAs" (Garces et al. 2015:7). However, no comparable improvement was made during this four-year time period with respect to the training of local midwives. In addition, although the authors attribute the increase in cesareans and decline in mortality rates to the expansion of obstetrical and neonatal hospital facilities and personnel in Chimaltenango, there is no consideration of the likelihood of such an expansion of obstetrical and neonatal hospital facilities and personnel to other parts of the country.

Jennifer Houston (2001) reported that the cesarean rate at one of the hospitals in Guatemala City was 40 percent, and she recently said that reports have indicated an increase (personal communication). The WHO recommends that cesareans should never exceed 15 percent, even in high-risk populations. A cesarean operation entails a considerable expense for the patient. Siriaca says that her sister-in-law was charged Q320 (US$53). In addition, one has to pay for a car or taxi to and from the hospital. Cesareans also involve a longer recovery period and increased chance of infection, which may constitute an added burden for the mother and her family (Cosminsky 2001a:369). From the biomedical perspective, a cesarean is a solution to risk presented by birth complications, such as malpresentation or prolonged labor. In contrast, the view of several of the women on the finca is that the operation itself is a risk because it may result in a variety of problems. They perceive such surgery as possibly causing complications with recovery, including infections, and problems with future pregnancies.

I asked María in 1996 if there were more cesareans because there are more problems associated with births. María said yes. I asked her why. She said "because of the moon," or "They don't take care. They delay. They carry a lot of wood. A pregnant woman shouldn't carry wood. Just carry a little. They can slip, and then the baby changes position. One woman in El Tambor was carrying a bag of coffee. It was harvest time. She got caught in a heavy rain, slipped and fell with the coffee. When she gave birth, the child was born dead."

Siriaca also says that there are more cesareans nowadays than before. She told me the story of one of her daughters, who almost had a C-section. Siriaca left for Guatemalan City because one of her daughters lives and works there and was going to be giving birth in the hospital. Her daughter had gone to the clinic because she had felt some pain. First the staff said there were no numbers left and she would have to come back another day. (Most public health clinics and health centers in Guatemala have a first come, first served policy and only see a limited number of patients. Patients are given a number when they arrive and are seen in numerical order). Then someone who was already on line, gave Siriaca's daughter their number. When she went in, they examined her. One doctor had told her he thought the baby was transverse and she would have to have a cesarean. Another doctor thought the baby might even be dead. Siriaca says that as they were taking her daughter to the delivery room, she prayed very hard. Her daughter started to have contractions, and the baby started to come. Just as they were getting ready to operate, one doctor said "Wait, the baby is coming," and it came out in a normal vaginal birth. Siriaca believes that God answered her prayers—that because of her faith in God the baby came out normally.

Nicole Berry (2008, 2010) points out in her studies of Sololá that many women think that a cesarean delivery will affect future pregnancies. This idea partly derives from the usage of the term *operación* for both a cesarean delivery and a tubal ligation. Such ideas may be reinforced by medical personnel, as in the warning given to a new seventeen-year-old mother on the finca who had a cesarean delivery with her first child. She was told that she had to have the C-section because her pelvis was too small or narrow and that she should not have any more children because it would be too "risky." For a young, newly married woman, this message can be devastating, with psychological implications as well as implications for her relations with her husband and in-laws. She has since vaginally delivered two more children at the hospital.

Some possible factors contributing to the increase in C-sections include more referrals by midwives for complications, acquisition of new technology, doctors at the hospital in favor of doing the operation, financial gains, the perception that cesareans are an essential aspect of modern obstetrics, and doctors and residents performing them to gain more experience. This last factor was mentioned by various informants. A cesarean takes birth completely out of the hands of the mother and midwife, even more so than a vaginal hospital birth, and places it completely in the hands of the doctor. Neither the midwife nor the mother has agency in this situation; they are instead clearly subordinated to the doctor (Cosminsky 2001a:369).

DISCUSSION

In this section, I apply the model proposed by George Lowis and Peter McCaffery (2000) to analyze the impact of medicalization on the birth beliefs and practices of María and Siriaca affecting management of labor and delivery. At the technological level, medicalization ranges from the use of simple technology such as disposable gloves; pincers to clamp the cord before cutting it; a new, sterile razor blade or scissors that have been boiled to cut the cord; and pharmaceuticals, including medications and injections—to the most complex, such as ultrasounds and surgery, perhaps the most pervasive and controversial change.

During births Siriaca uses disposable gloves that she obtains from the health center or buys from the pharmacy, although many midwives don't use them. Gloves both prevent infection of the mother and protect the midwife from infections such as HIV and hepatitis.

Both María and Siriaca waited until the placenta was expelled before cutting the cord, mentioning that they didn't have clamps as the doctors do, and thus if they cut the cord first, the placenta might rise in the body and choke the woman. However, by 2010 Siriaca had been given clamps by the doctor and was cutting the cord first. This change in the timing of cutting and the treatment of the cord reflects medicalization. After the cord is cut, usually with a razor blade (supposedly new) or with scissors that have been boiled, both María and Siriaca cauterized the cord with a candle flame, and then they put alcohol, merthiolate, and talcum powder or *licopodio* on the cord, combining the medical practices they have been taught with the traditional use of the candle.

An example of medicalization at the low-tech level is the use of a scale to weigh the baby. María carefully weighed the baby on a spring scale that she had been given in the training course, but after she had swaddled the newborn in several layers of clothes and blankets. Thus children's weights may have been recorded as greater than they actually were; finca babies tend to have low birth weights. These weights are recorded by the midwife and given to the health center or vital registry, along with the names of the children whose births she has attended. When midwives are given technology but lack complete instructions on how to use it, incorrect data may be reported and passed on to the Department of Statistics or other government offices. This illustrates a possibly significant problem of incomplete technology transference.

Both María and Siriaca used a syringe to take mucus from the newborn's throat and nose and put *colirio agirol* drops in its eyes, again a manifestation of medicalization. Neither María nor Siriaca used oxytocin injections, like Pitocin, to speed up labor or during the postpartum period. This is a major controversial issue and is an area in which medicalization has had a major impact. Although oxytocin injections are used routinely in the hospital, midwives who use them are regarded as participating in a dangerous practice because of the timing of the injections and the possible negative consequences of overdoses. Siriaca has been trained in a health promoter program to give injections, and she gives antibiotic and vitamin injections to those who request them. She uses disposable needles.

They both used pharmaceuticals such as *Cápsulas Materlan*, which are vitamins, and *cápsulas de la Señora*, which induce labor. Siriaca continues to use traditional teas and other herbal remedies to calm pains during labor. In addition to remedies she learned from her mother, Siriaca has learned others from a course she took from a nongovernmental organization. She is a very strong proponent of *medicina natural* (natural medicine), or *la naturaleza* (nature), and exerts her agency and knowledge through her recommendations for administrations of herbal teas and baths.

The use of cesarean surgery has rapidly increased and affects women's fear of a hospital delivery.[7] Episiotomies are also of concern. When mothers refer to an *operación*, it is sometimes not clear whether they are referring to an episiotomy or to a C-section. One mother who went to the hospital because it was her first child and who had had a normal vaginal delivery said that she had inflammation and pain where they cut her vaginally. They had given her pills to take but she didn't know if they were for pain or antibiotics for infection. Such statements reflect the lack of communication or understanding between medical personnel and the patient.

At the conceptual medicalization level, concepts of time, including standardization of the time of labor, the time it takes to fully dilate, and the time expected for the expulsion of the placenta, have had a big impact on both midwives and mothers. Whether labor is prolonged depends on what is considered long. According to Klein, Miller, and Thomson (2009), one day and one night is considered long, whereas Siriaca says she had been told in the training course that twelve to fifteen hours is considered long, regardless of the mother's rate of dilation or the timing and intensity of her labor pains. Throughout the birthing process, it is the time that the biomedical profession has determined to be normal, presumably on the basis of statistical averages, that determines the time frame to be followed, instead of the individual mother's natural bodily processes. According to hospital personnel, the variation that exists in the timing of labor and delivery according to the specific biological, psychological, and emotional states of a woman is irrelevant.

In the hospital there is pressure for a delivery to be completed within or at a certain time. Siriaca gives the example that the nurses were annoyed and yelled at her and a patient whom she brought at night because they prefer deliveries during the day. Yet they will blame the midwife if she does not refer a possible problematic birth to the hospital.

Another concept that forms part of medicalization both in the prenatal stage and during labor and birth is risk. Birth conditions viewed by biomedicine as high risk include malposition and prolonged labor, both of which may result in a cesarean section. As Lowis and McCaffery point out, "Ultimately, the question of who has the power to successfully define risk—the woman, the midwife or the physician—is of paramount concern" (2000:27). The power to define risk is also an example of the control aspect of medicalization.

Medicalization at the interactional level occurs primarily through hospital deliveries and the increasing restrictions being placed on the midwives. This also relates to the control level. At the finca birth is usually a social event occurring at home with other relatives present—usually the husband or partner and the mother or mother-in law or both, and possibly other female relatives. A close, supportive, and emotional relationship exists with the midwife, who has been treating the woman prenatally and is often present throughout the labor.

In contrast, the hospital is an unfamiliar place with unfamiliar people. The woman is alone, surrounded by strangers with whom she has no ties and who are in a hierarchical relationship to her. With the midwife there is continuity of care through the different stages of pregnancy, birth, and postnatal care, but at the hospital the staff is different from that of the prenatal clinic the mother might have attended. The midwife is not allowed in with the woman when she goes to the hospital in Retalhuleu, even if she has referred her there. This differs in the various national hospitals; the hospital in Sololá allows midwives in with their clients and is trying ways of integrating them into hospital programs (Berry 2010). The lack of interaction between midwives and hospital staff, as well as between the staff and the patient, is part of the medicalization process. This lack of interaction is starkly illustrated in cases in which the woman delivers the baby by herself in the hospital because of the lack of attention from hospital staff.

The interactional level is closely linked to the control level in the hierarchical relationship between the midwife and the doctor. The midwife is increasingly under the authority and control of the physician, whose social authority is backed by the state through the Ministry of Health. Siriaca's use of the phrase "the doctor forbids it" regarding the policy about attending *primíparas* is revealing, as is the risk that she will lose her license to practice if she does attend *primíparas*.

Siriaca is increasingly under the authority and control of physicians. The increased insistence that certain women deliver in the hospital and restrictions on whom the midwife can and cannot attend reflects the attenuation of the midwife's role. The doctor's authority is also revealed in the two cases in which the mother died and Siriaca went to the doctor to explain what had happened, after which he absolved her of any blame. She sought his validation because he had the authority to validate her behavior and protect her; at the same time this validation reinforces her subordinate position vis-à-vis the doctor and undermines her own authority. Such instances epitomize the transfer of power from the midwife to the doctor. The redefinition of birth at the conceptual level as dangerous and the consequent perception of the midwife as also dangerous involves the control level of medicalization by enhancing the doctor's cultural and social authority.

Another area of control is manifested in the use of herbal remedies. In 2013 Siriaca said that the doctors had forbidden the use of herbs, especially *pimpinela* because they say it causes contractions to be too strong and can thus cause brain damage. The midwives were also warned during the midwifery review session I observed in 2013 about using *pimpinela*. The plant is used by the midwives in Santa Lucía Utatlán and in other parts of Guatemala as well (Proechel 2005).

TABLE 5.1. MANAGEMENT OF LABOR AND DELIVERY

	María	*Siriaca (1996)*	*Siriaca (2010)*
Delivery position	Prefers horizontal but also lets mother use kneeling or vertical position	Horizontal on bed	Horizontal on bed
Labor time	No specified time, but don't push too early; goes by progress of labor	12–15 hours; if longer, refer to hospital	12–15 hours; if longer, refer to hospital
To ease pain and give strength	Herbal teas	Herbal teas	Herbal teas
Disposable rubber gloves	Doesn't use them	Uses them during delivery	Uses them during delivery
Placenta and cord	Waits for placenta to be expelled before cutting cord	Same	May cut cord before placenta is expelled and uses clamps on cord before cutting
Treatment of cord	Cut with boiled scissors; put alcohol, merthiolate, on cord; cauterize with candle flame; sprinkle talcum powder and *licopodio* powder on it; wrap a white cloth around it and bind it	Same	Same but use cloth under cord when cauterizing so candle doesn't drip on baby
Prevention of tetanus (*mal de siete días*)	Above treatment of cord, plus rub baby with oil of rue, making a cross over its head while saying a prayer	Tells client to get tetanus vaccine at prenatal clinic	Same
Signs in cord	Believes knots or lumps in cord predict number and sex of future children	Doesn't believe in these signs	Same
Disposal of cord	Stump saved; if male, tie it in a tree; if female, put it under the hearth	Depends on the family	Depends on the family

(continued)

TABLE 5.1. (*CONTINUED*)

	María	*Siriaca (1996)*	*Siriaca (2010)*
Disposal of placenta	Family decides	Family decides	Family decides
Massage	Rubs olive oil on hands, massages abdominal area	Same	Massages but does not warm hands
Sash	Puts abdominal binder on	Same	Same
Swaddling of baby	Wraps baby in several layers and hat to keep warm because it is believed baby is in cold state	Same	Same
Wrapping of mother	Covers mother in scarf, sweater, and blankets to keep her warm	Same	Same

In this framework of medicalization, the control level is implicitly related to the gender and status level. Lewis and McCaffery state, "There is no question but that any discussion of the medicalization of childbirth must consider the displacement of the midwife as the principal childbirth attendant. Displacement is synonymous with loss of control by the midwife over the childbirth process—such authority now being transferred to the obstetrician and hospital" (2000:28). However, it is not only the midwife who loses control to the doctor, who in Guatemala is almost always male; the mother and her female relatives lose control as well. In the biomedical model, science and technology are seen as the solution to what are defined as risk factors in childbirth, and sociocultural and ritual factors are seen as irrelevant or a barrier to successful childbirth. According to Lewis and McCaffery, "Most writers agree that the transition from control by lay women to control by medically trained men in industrialized society is one of the most crucial changes that has occurred in the management of childbirth over the last one hundred years" (2000:29).

We see this dominance of the male doctor over the female midwife being repeated now in Guatemala as it occurred earlier in the United

States and other industrialized countries. One can question whether this is the most appropriate and beneficial model of childbirth, especially in rural areas. To what degree does female-to-female support, socially, tactilely, ritually, and medically, help allay anxiety and promote an easier birth?

SUMMARY

This chapter has examined various elements of the birthing event, including delivery position, management of labor, physical contact via the massage, and appeals to God through prayer and rituals. It has shown how different elements of the birth process are being medicalized through alterations in the midwife's practices and through other changes associated with hospital births.

The next chapter discusses the continuities and changes in postpartum care of the new mother and newborn baby as practiced by the midwives María and Siriaca. These include massage, herbal bath, examination of the newborn, and infant feeding. I then apply Lowis and McCaffery's model to analyze the medicalization of the associated beliefs and practices.

During the time after the birth, referred to as the postpartum or post-natal period, the mother and the infant are perceived as highly vulnerable. The length of this period varies culturally. On the finca, a week or eight days is considered the dangerous period, during which the mother's activities are restricted and the baby is susceptible to getting an infected umbilicus or neonatal tetanus (locally referred to as *mal de siete días* or seven-day sickness) and during which the midwife visits on the second or third day and the eighth day to examine and bathe mother and infant.

In the case of Pancha's delivery, described in the previous chapter, María returned the day after the birth to check the baby, change the dressing on the cord, and massage Pancha. She rubbed her hands in warmed oil, then lifted Pancha's legs and massaged them toward the body, and pushed upward from the abdomen. She explained that this makes the blood leave, and it returns the uterus to its normal size and position. She then refastened the *faja* (abdominal sash) to close the bones and keep the uterus in place. While the water for the herbal bath was being prepared, María checked the umbilicus of the baby, put more alcohol on it, placed a clean piece of gauze or cloth over it, and redressed it, then reswaddled the baby. The baby was nursing on demand, almost every half hour.

In contrast, in Santa Lucía Utatlán, this period of restriction and vulnerability is twenty days, during which the midwife visits three to five times to examine the mother, massage her, and give her a sweat bath, and examines and bathes the infant as well.[1]

BEHAVIORAL RESTRICTIONS

After the birth, the mother spends as much time as she can in bed, well covered with a sweater, a head scarf, and blankets, usually in a corner of the room, to keep warm. Both she and the baby are considered to be in a cold state and therefore *muy delicados* (dangerously weak or very frail) and susceptible to cold and *aire* (wind). The baby is swaddled and its head is covered with a hat. Many of the prescriptions and proscriptions, including behavioral and dietary restrictions, are aimed at keeping both warm.

According to Siriaca, the woman is supposed to stay in bed for only three days: the day she gives birth; the second day, when she may still be experiencing some pains; and the third day, when she is bathed. Then she can get up to walk and to eat, sometimes to help to make tortillas or cook. At the eighth day she leaves the bed, but she still cannot sweep. She can do other housework, however, such as wash clothes and diapers. She cannot wash sheets, so she must look for someone to wash them. Washing in the river is dangerous not only because it is strenuous but also because it is cold. According to María (Cosminsky 1977b), the new mother shouldn't carry water until the fifteenth day and must not wash in the river until after twenty days. If a woman does heavy work or washes clothes in the river, she will become *desmanda* (sick) and may suffer from *descompostura* (a fallen uterus) because she hasn't healed completely. The cold water will also make her milk cold and thus make the baby sick.

The mother must abstain from sex for forty days, and she should not enter the church during the same amount of time. This period is referred to as *la cuarentena* and derives from the Spanish belief that the woman is ritually unclean after birth because she still might have some bleeding. Thus the period of confinement is not only for her own and that of the child, but to prevent contamination of others (Foster 1960:119). According to George Foster, in Tzintzuntzán, Mexico, most of the care during the *cuarentena* was to maintain and restore heat in the mother's body (1994:66).

In the past when women delivered in the hospital, they stayed three days. Now, they leave the next day. According to Siriaca:

> When they leave in a car on a bad road, the bruises from the car ruin their legs. In the house, after delivering, the next day they can stretch their feet and they should follow their *dieta*, and only get up to do their washings [douche]. But in the hospital, when they come, worse here than the road below, see how bad it is, the bouncing and the poor woman who comes on it. Thus many prefer the house to the hospital because the house costs less, whereas if they go there they have to pay a car and the women suffer. And they can have postpartum problems because of the rough ride from the hospital.

DIETARY RESTRICTIONS: *LA DIETA*

The new mother is supposed to follow a variety of dietary and be-havioral restrictions, which are referred to as *la dieta*, especially for the lying-in period of eight days. Dietary proscriptions and prescrip-tions are emphasized in the postpartum period more than during the pregnancy because of the perceived effect of the food on breast milk. "Cold" foods will cut the milk, making it less abundant as well as cold and thin, so the objective is to give the milk a warm quality. Thus the mother must avoid cold foods, including beans, cheese, pork, cabbage, eggs, and cold greens such as *yerba mora* (*Solanum americanum*). She should not drink plain water, *frescos*, sodas, or *torpollitos* (ices). In-stead the mother should consume "hot" foods and liquids, including coffee, atole, and greens such as *chipilín* (*Crotalaria longirostrata*) and *kishtan* (*Solanum* sp.).

María said that on the first day after the birth, the woman should eat lightly, having toasted bread or tortilla and chicken soup. She should not eat the chicken itself because it is too strong, or *alimento*, for the weak mother. *Alimento* means especially nourishing (Cosmin-sky 1977a). According to one woman, she cannot eat the meat of a young chicken because it is strong, but she can eat that of an older one because it is not as strong. The strong-weak distinction is another important dimension of the ethnomedical system. Both children and newly delivered mothers are in a weak condition and thus vulnerable or susceptible to various illnesses, and their strength has to be built up. However, as in the hot-cold principle, too great a contrast can also make a person sick. Thus a weak person can't have anything consid-ered too strong. Restrictions hold for the eight-day confinement pe-riod. After that, the women can eat most foods.

HERBAL BATH

One of the most important aspects of postpartum care is the herbal bath the midwife gives to the recently delivered woman. This herbal bath performs the same functions as the sweat baths used in many in-digenous communities in Guatemala, especially in the highlands (Cos-minsky 1982a). In Santa Lucía Utatlán, one of the K'iche' terms for a midwife is *ajtuj* or "person or owner of the sweat bath." As one mid-wife said, "the sweat bath is my medicine." Beginning on the third day after the birth, the midwife gives between three to five sweat baths until the twentieth day, which marks the end of the restriction period. The midwife takes the woman into the sweat bath, bathes her using the herb *chilka*, and massages her. Some midwives let the woman take the sweat bath by herself and massage her afterward in the house.

The herbs used in the bath by María are of a hot quality because the woman is in a cold state after the birth. Both she and the baby are vulnerable to cold illnesses and her body must be heated to restore the bodily balance. The herbs are *Santa María* (*Piper* sp.), *guaruma* (*Cecropia peltata*), *ciguapate* (*Pluchea odorata*), and *siquinai* (*Vernonia* sp). According to María, the use of these hot herbs also prevents the woman from getting a fever. María gave patients these baths on the third day and the eighth day. Until she has this bath, certain activities are restricted. She is not supposed to heat water or make tortillas, and she is supposed to stay in bed. If the bath is delayed for some reason, the mother may become concerned and anxious because of the quality of the milk and the restrictions on her activities. The bath is supposed to warm and lower the milk and increase the flow. In one case, after the first bath had been delayed, María made the mother squeeze out some of the milk first, saying that the milk would still be cold because the herbs had not yet taken effect. Also hot milk is said to be thicker than cold milk. Milk of a cold and thin quality can make the baby sick. The bath is regarded as critical, both to free the woman from some of the restrictions on her activities and to maintain the proper quality of her milk.

Siriaca similarly gives two baths. She explains:

> If the baby is born in the morning, I tell the mother, her mother-in-law, or someone who is there to heat some water and make a *lavado* (vaginal wash, or douche), and also the same on the next day. On the third day I bathe them and they continue with their douche, and in another three days I bathe them and leave them *entregado* (delivered). By then, the cord has fallen off and the woman is finished. After the cord falls off and is well closed I leave her *entregado*. The last bath marks the end of the mother's seclusion and the end of the midwife's duties.

Both María and Siriaca bathed the mother the same way (figures 6.1 and 6.2). The woman is undressed except for her slip. Modesty dictates that the lower part of the body be covered. The mother's hair and head are washed first, with water in which onion stalks have been boiled so she won't get a headache, and then covered with a scarf to keep it warm. Then the midwife puts a handful of the herbs from

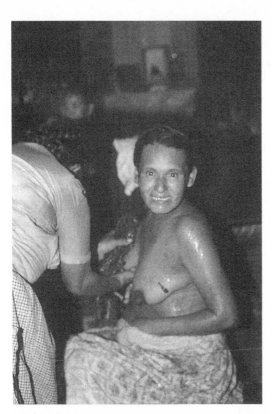

FIGURE 6.1.
María giving postpartum herbal bath (1978).

FIGURE 6.2.
Siriaca giving postpartum herbal bath (2000).

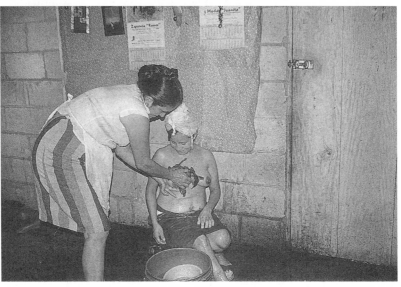

the bath water on the stool or bench that the woman is sitting on and inside her slip in front of the vaginal opening. She then takes a handful of these herbs and massages the woman's breasts, beats her shoulders with the leaves' backs, then presses the herbs against her knees and massages her legs, rubbing upward and punching the bottom of the feet. Then she places leaves underneath her feet. The vagina, the knees, and the feet are regarded as potential points of entry of *aire* (wind or cold) and thus must be heated. Then she pours the bath water over the woman.

After the bath, the midwife massages the woman and ties the abdominal binder below the abdomen. Extra cloths are placed between the mother's legs to absorb any bleeding; María said it is not good if the children see the blood. Then María gave the mother a tea made from all hot herbs, *comino* (cumin), lavender, oregano, and three cloves, and some rum for stomachache.

In the words of one woman, the bath was *sabrosa* (delicious). Even though it was hot, the women whose baths I observed seemed to enjoy them and feel better after them.

According to Siriaca, by 2013 some women no longer wanted the herbs in the water. They say they just want the bath because they get a rash from the herbs. In such cases, Siriaca says, she accommodates them and just gives them a plain, herbless bath.

> If they want just water, I make it only with water; if they want with herbs, I make it with herbs. I don't force them because day to day one has to change. . . . For a young woman, even with just a plain bath with warm water, it helps lower the milk, but at times, when there is a woman that has had several children, the milk doesn't come down and then bathing her with the herbs, the milk comes in.

In these latter cases, she tries to convince the mother to have the herbal bath. Thus the midwife may negotiate with the mother in trying to give her an herbal bath, exerting her authoritative knowledge.

Regarding this changing practice, Siriaca seems to be more flexible than she is in the case of the delivery position, where she insists that women adopt the horizontal position. Concerning the postpartum bath, Siriaca represents the traditional practice of using herbs, and the mother prefers the newer one of using plain water; with the delivery position, Siriaca represents the newer practice of delivering in a horizontal position while some mothers request the older kneeling or squatting position. Women who have a plain bath may not receive the purported beneficial effects of the herbs but do receive its cleansing and relaxing effects, as well as the physical and emotional support of being the center of the midwife's attention.

The midwife washes the baby after she bathes the mother. She checks the umbilicus to see that it is not infected, and puts a new dressing on it. María said that at fifteen days, the mother is supposed to take the child to the health center for an examination. They will give the mother a card on which is written the health of the child. According to María, most of the finca mothers would go because she told them to take the child there and because they got worried if the child was sick.

If a woman has delivered in the hospital, she may choose not to have the bath or the postpartum massage or use the binder. Nor does she follow the *dieta*, or dietary restrictions. One mother, Julia, after delivering in the hospital, did not call María, did not have the binder, did not have the traditional bath, and bathed in cold water. She did not have much breast milk and believed it was because she did not have the postpartum bath. However, another woman who had delivered in the hospital did the bath herself. She asked her mother-in-law, who was the other midwife on the finca but had rarely practiced since the 1970s, for the names of the herbs for the bath. One of her sons looked for them, and the woman bathed herself. Yet another woman, Marina, had pain in her uterus, and it hurt when she urinated. María said it was inflamed and was going to fall. The baby had been born in the hospital and thus the mother did not have on the abdominal binder. María massaged her abdominal area upward with *aceite de almendra* (almond oil), *aceite nervina* and *agua florida*. These are bought in the pharmacy. Then she tied the abdominal binder on her.

Siriaca mentioned another more recent change in 2010. The doctor told her not to use the herbs and not to use hot water, saying she should use only warm water. Because of the increase in hospital deliveries due to restrictions on whom the midwife is permitted to attend, Siriaca now gives postpartum baths to those who request them even if they have delivered in the hospital, and she charges them separately for these baths.

People believe that the milk flow is affected not only by the hot-cold quality of the bath water and diet but also by the emotions of the mother. A lactating mother should avoid getting angry, frightened, or very sad because such strong emotions can make the mother ill and will affect her milk by either making the milk cold or cutting the milk flow, thus making the baby sick. Jacinta said she had a problem with a lack of breast milk, which she believed was caused by sadness because of the death of her mother. Due to the intense sadness she felt, her milk left her, and she was giving the baby diluted formula in a bottle. Unfortunately, by the time I returned the following year, in 1979, the baby had died.

FALLEN OR PROLAPSED UTERUS
(*CAIDA DE MATRIZ, DESCOMPOSTURA*)

If a woman does not follow the restrictions on her activity and does things such as lifting heavy objects too early, she may suffer from *descompostura* (a prolapsed uterus), also called *caida de matriz* (fallen womb). According to Siriaca, this condition may also be caused by failure to wear the postpartum abdominal binder. It can also occur in circumstances not associated with birth, from some type of strain on weakened muscles. *Descompostura* can cause stomach pains during menstruation, a white discharge, bleeding, tiredness, diarrhea, lack of appetite, waist pains, and leg pains.

Both María and Siriaca mentioned several cases of *descompostura* they had treated and said this is one of the commonest problems women have. It is treated by a combination of massage, putting on an abdominal binder, and drinking teas. In one case María cleaned the woman with boiled water, massaged her, heated her stomach, and then pushed up the uterus inside with a cloth on which she had put some cooking oil. She then put on a binder. She told the husband to take some milky sap from the *amate, matapalo, sangretera, palo amarillo, pantan, pinion,* and *ule* (rubber) trees, mix them together, and apply the mixture to the woman as a plaster.

In one case of *descompostura* that I observed, the woman still had pains one and a half months after she had given birth. To ease the pains and treat the prolapsed uterus, María massaged her legs, rubbing the thighs upward and the calves back toward the body, for stretched or distended nerves. She also hit the soles of the feet. She kneaded the stomach by pushing upward, then put on the binder to keep the uterus in place. She believed that if the uterus stayed out it could become cancerous. She made a tea from oregano, lavender, cumin, clove, cinnamon, *salvia santa, pimienta de castilla, balsamito de aire* (a half ounce of each), then mixed in a half bottle of white honey and a quarter of a bottle of rum. The woman is supposed to drink a cup every morning

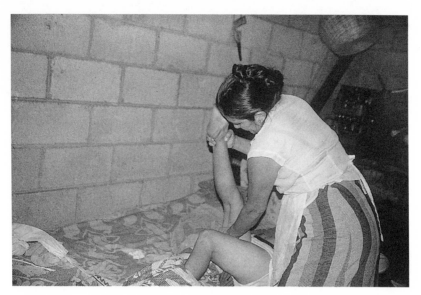

FIGURE 6.3. *Siriaca massages woman's legs (2000).*

until the bottle is finished, which is about eight days. This collects the *aire* (air) or cold that is in the uterus. Then the uterus rises up, because the *aire* in the uterus is what causes it to fall.

This treatment is based on restoring the hot-cold balance. The condition is a cold one, so one needs to get rid of or displace the *aire*, which is cold. The massage heats the body, and the tea is made up of hot substances. Siriaca has continued this practice and does the same massage of the abdomen and the legs and uses the binder (figure 6.3). Like María, she believes that if the uterus stays out it may become cancerous.

Treatment of *descompostura* illustrates a combination of the humoral principle and the displacement principle. The body is understood to be a tube in which bodily parts can move up or down. Either the strain or *aire* has displaced the uterus, causing it to fall. There are also cases where the uterus has come out, and there is no bleeding nor diarrhea. María said:

> I ask for a little boiled water and wash the vaginal area with some cotton, dry it well, and then put a little oil and then grab the part from the uterus to the vagina with the cloth and then I push until it enters. When it has entered, I put my hand a little bit inside for it to raise a little bit, then from the outside I take the part from below

upwards, feeling where the ball of the uterus is, and I raise it more. Then I put a lot of cloths there and put the binder on, well bounded. Then it will be adjusted and stay well. Now it won't fall. But I have to do it more than once. I have to go the day after the next and then I will see how it is. Usually four treatments are needed. Then I recommend that they do not lift something heavy and that they begin to walk little by little. They should not wash clothes because washing clothes needs a lot of force and they should not sweep. It is not good for a recently delivered woman to sweep. It causes the stomach to hurt, it loosens (slips) and hemorrhages, and the cure becomes more expensive. It is not good to have much bleeding because the blood will finish. Then the person becomes very weak, appears *desvalido* (helpless). One has to be careful. This is what I do. That's why people come to look for me. Many people know that I know how to cure this *descompostura*.

INFANT FEEDING: BREAST-FEEDING AND BOTTLE-FEEDING

Initial breast-feeding is almost universal on the plantation. However, supplemental bottle-feeding became increasingly common, especially during the late 1970s. The time when breast-feeding is initiated varies. Some women begin nursing within the first few hours of the birth. However, others feel that the colostrum, or *nueva leche* (new milk), is bad for the baby. They call it *shuka* (dirty) and say they do not have any milk until the third day. Both María and Siriaca followed what they were taught in the training course and had the woman breast-feed shortly after the birth. They said that they told women to give the baby the colostrum because it is nutritious; it has vitamins, protein, and antibodies; and it acts as a purgative and helps develop the baby's gastrointestinal system and is thus good for the baby. As this instance indicates, the area of infant feeding is a highly contested one.

Mothers and midwives are feeling the pressures of both medicalization and commoditization with regard to infant feeding (van Esterik 1989). The midwife has to decide in which aspects she is going to support changes according to biomedical practice and in which aspects she will continue the existing practices. For example, María tried to promote a change in the practice of withholding colostrum from the baby on the basis of new knowledge she gained in the training course. However, she disregarded the nurses' admonition to tell the mothers to breastfeed every three hours. This is very unrealistic in a population that does not have watches and feeds babies on demand. The mother usually carries the baby on her back in a shawl, and breast-feeding is often used as a pacifier whenever the baby starts to cry. In addition to being impractical, scheduled feeding is medically and scientifically unsound and can be more harmful than demand feeding. The frequency of feeding promotes breast milk production by stimulating the hormone prolactin. Thus a more harmful practice of scheduled feeding, which is also related to bottle-feeding, was being pushed by the biomedical personnel to substitute for the more beneficial and situationally appropriate practice of demand feeding.

During the 1970s doctors frequently promoted bottle-feeding, placing more pressure on the midwives and mothers who supported or continued breast-feeding, often out of pragmatic experience. Several doctors and nurses in Retalhuleu promoted bottle-feeding and thus contributed to the decline of breast-feeding. Sometimes this began in the hospital after delivery if the mother was sick or had difficulty in nursing. Other times, it was when the baby was sick and the mother took it to the doctor, who told the mother she should stop breast-feeding because the mother's milk was making the baby sick. This recommendation may reflect the negative and condescending attitude that some doctors tend to have toward poor peasants, both Ladino and Indian.

By the late 1970s, bottle-feeding had become commonplace on the finca. In the summer of 1979, I interviewed a sample of thirty-six mothers with children under two years old concerning feeding and weaning practices. In addition, I employed formal eliciting techniques using paired comparisons to study mothers' perceptions of breast milk, breast milk alternatives, and weaning foods, in order to assess how these alternatives were differentiated and how they entered into the mothers' decisions about what to feed their babies. All the infants in the sample had been initially breast-fed, except one, in which the mother had been ill and had delivered at the hospital, where bottle-feeding began.

Supplementation—introduction of other foods—usually begins between four and six months. Breast-feeding continues during this period, and weaning is often completed by nineteen months, although it may continue to two or more years. It is important to distinguish between bottle-feeding, in which a number of milk alternatives or supplements are used, and the use of the commercial formula. One of the most striking aspects of bottle feeding on the Guatemalan plantation is the early introduction of boiled water with sugar. This was the item most frequently given in the bottle.

In a sample of thirty-six mothers, sixteen gave boiled water with sugar to the infant, usually three or four times a day, and one or two times a night. Six others had used the bottle in the past, but had stopped using it. Other ingredients that were put in the bottle were coffee, with four teaspoons of sugar or *panela* (dark unrefined sugar), and about one liter of water. However, *panela*, which is hot, is thought to make the coffee too hot for an infant. If milk was available, that might be added to the coffee. Other items that were given in a bottle were *Harina de San Vicente* (a mixture of thirteen grains or cereals that is bought in the store and used for malnourished children, people with anemia, elderly people, and convalescents), *maizena* (corn starch), and *leche de polvo* (powdered milk) from the clinic or church or CARE program,[2] *leche de bote* (canned milk, meaning commercial formula such as Nan, Lactogen, Nido, or Cerelac), atole (a thin gruel made from corn dough), and on rare occasions Incaparina, a high-protein food.

Cow's milk is also occasionally given in a baby bottle. According to María, cow's milk is stronger that human milk. It is usually mixed with and equal amount of water, one spoon of salt, and one spoon of sugar. If it is given alone, it is believed that the baby will get a rash. Cow's milk is also considered *pesado* (heavy) and will give the baby diarrhea.

A striking characteristic of bottle-feeding is the age at which the bottle is first introduced (table 6.1). Of the women who were bottle-feeding, all except two were using the bottle by fifteen days. This is a striking difference from the babies in a study done by Lilian Izurieta and Laura Beth Larson-Brown in eastern Guatemala, where all the children who were receiving the bottle began to receive it after six months of age (Izurieta 1995:255). The first item used in bottle-feeding is usually boiled water with sugar, and gradually other items are put in the bottle. This early usage, especially of boiled sugar water, is related to several factors. One is the negative attitude toward colostrum. Most of the women thought it was bad for the baby, and traditionally after the birth the baby is given water with anise and sugar with a spoon, until the mother's milk comes in, usually on the third day, although the midwife says she advises them to nurse after three hours and tells them that the colostrum is good for the baby. The mothers

TABLE 6.1. AGE OF BABY
WHEN HE/SHE FIRST USED
BOTTLE OF WATER

Age	No.
At birth	5
2–7 days	4
8–15 days	5
15–28 days	1
7 months	1

feel it is easier with the bottle than with a spoon, especially at night. The amount of water given in the bottle is more than that given by spoon. They start with an ounce and increase to two ounces, then to four ounces.

In one specific case a three-month-old infant was being given two ounces of sugar water four times a day and twice at night. The mother mixed four spoons of sugar with one liter of water. She started at birth with one spoon of sugar to two ounces of water. María said, "It refreshes or cools the stomach, so it won't be hot. It is *puro alimento* (pure nutrition)."

Another factor contributing to bottle-feeding is insufficient milk syndrome. Several of the finca women said they began giving the bottle because they didn't have enough milk. Yet early feeding with sugar water will lessen the child's sucking and appetite for breast milk, leading to a decreasing supply from the mother. Some of the mothers specified that they did not have enough milk because of fright, anger, or sadness, a conclusion related to beliefs about strong emotions in causing illness. Siriaca says that the baby gets colic from nursing when the mother is angry. This happened with her last child: "I got angry (*incomodo*), and he nursed and got the colic." Both she and the baby drank a tea from orange leaf and rue, with *esencia maravillosa*. Anita Chary and colleagues (Chary, Dasgupta, Messmer, and Rohloff 2011:176) report similar cases of women attributing lactational failure or insufficient or inadequate milk to sadness, shock, and anger. They argue that the loss of breast milk "legitimates public conversation with other women about male behavior" (177). However, such cases also invoke mother blame because the mother's excessive emotions are considered the cause of her insufficient or poor quality ("thin") milk (179). A woman may also use the insufficiency of her milk as a means to obtain resources, such as vitamins, money, or formula, from a health worker or her spouse (179).

Another factor some women thought might have caused them not to have enough milk was having taken antibiotic injections during pregnancy or right after giving birth. One young woman who was working in Guatemala said her son was born there in the hospital by cesarean section because he was transverse. Her legs were swollen, and she had hemorrhaged. She had taken penicillin, which she believed cut the blood and thus the milk. In 2011 her younger sister, who was on the finca, was pregnant with her first child and developed a urinary tract infection. At the prenatal exam in the clinic, they told her to go to the doctor, who prescribed antibiotics. After she gave birth in the hospital, she had trouble breast-feeding and attributed it to the antibiotics having cut the supply of milk. Siriaca gave her herbal teas to help stimulate milk flow, but to no avail.

Other mothers said they did not have *puntas* (nipples) and thus started giving the bottle. I asked María about the problem of being unable to nurse because of inverted nipples. She explained it in terms of the traditional framework of hot and cold: the padding in the bras that the young girls wear was *muy caliente* (very hot) and caused the *puntas* to turn inward. Others said they give the bottle to help. It fills the baby and keeps it quiet, and it allows another caretaker, like a sibling or grandmother, to feed the baby while the mother works—picking coffee, going to the market, and so on (figure 6.4). Another mother said she had a breast infection when the baby was fifteen days old and started to use the bottle then, and two other mothers were sick in the hospital when the baby was given the bottle.

The impact of early use of the bottle and sugar water is not known. It can be hypothesized that it will lessen the child's sucking and appetite for breast milk and lead to a decline in the production of breast milk. This would, in turn, lead to earlier supplementation or substitution with other food items, with earlier weaning and earlier malnutrition because of insufficiently nutritious weaning foods. Research needs to be done in this area.

The water to be used in bottles is boiled partly because of beliefs that boiling changes the quality of crude water, which is cold and dangerous and parasite-ridden and thus could make the child sick. Boil-

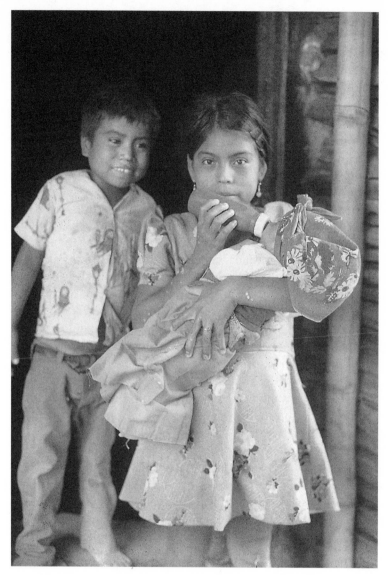

FIGURE 6.4. *Sibling helps to feed baby with bottle (1979).*

ing makes the water hotter, but not hot. People also believe that boiled water is *puro alimento*, or nutritious, which crude water is not. The sugar is also thought to be nutritious (Cosminsky 1975, 1977a). This belief is strengthened by the fortification of Guatemalan sugar with vitamin A. Some say sugar is added because the baby won't drink plain water. Sugar is also considered cool compared to *panela*, or brown sugar, which is hot.

Water that is boiled for bottles is left open, usually to cool, and sometimes put in a thermos for the rest of the day. The thermos, the bottle, and the bottle's nipple, however, may be contaminated and dirty. It is not boiled, but left lying around. One woman said she washed the inside if cockroaches got in it. The bottles are usually plastic, which is hard to clean by simple washing, and the water used for washing is possibly contaminated. Although people consider sugar nutritious, unfortunately it is not. It can prevent the baby from breast-feeding by filling its stomach with empty calories.

The problems with formula use have been well documented and discussed in the literature (van Esterik 1989, Cunningham 1995, Stuart-Macadam and Dettwyler 1995). These include contamination of the water used to make the formula, contamination of the bottle, and over dilution of the formula. When other foods are used and they are made thinner or more diluted so they can flow through the bottle, this reduces the nutritional value of the food. "Malnutrition acts synergistically with the microbial burden to weaken the bottle-fed infant" (Cunningham 1995:244). Furthermore, Cunningham states that among infants the mortality risk of bottle-feeding is at least ten times higher than the risk for breast-fed infants (244). On the finca bottle-feeding is promoting earlier and more extensive use of substances such as sugar water and coffee as milk substitutes. These are nutritionless, or empty, calories and may interfere with successful early breast-feeding.

The use of milk alternatives and supplements is influenced by the perceived quality as well as quantity of breast milk. Guatemalan mothers are concerned about the quality of their milk; they would claim that the baby wasn't nursing or was sick because their milk was no good, too cold, too thin, and so on. Foods that are said to reduce both the quantity and quality of milk are considered cold foods and should be avoided during lactation because they decrease the quantity of the milk or dilute it as well as make it cold. For example, water makes the milk thin, sparse, and bad. To ensure that her milk is the right quality, the mother should eat food that is considered hot, and on the third day after the birth she should receive a postnatal bath during which the breasts are massaged with hot herbs. This is said to stimulate the flow and heat the milk. In some villages in the highlands, as in Santa Lucía Utatlán, a sweat bath is given after the birth. The mother's body and breasts are massaged within the sweat bath to both stimulate the milk flow and heat the milk (Cosminsky 1982a).

Mothers and midwives were asked if there were any foods or medicines to stimulate the flow of milk or to increase the quantity. Mothers frequently mentioned *atól de masa* (drink or gruel made from corn dough) because it is *pesado* (heavy), stimulates the flow of milk, and increases the quantity. It thus makes the milk come out thick, which fills up the baby. María said the new mother should drink soup, hot coffee, and atole, which heat the milk as well as thicken it. The mother should not drink water, because the milk will become thin (*ralo*).

Both María and Siriaca mentioned certain herbs that help lower the mother's milk. Lavender (*alhucema*) is put in a little bit of fire, and a clean cloth is placed over the smoke to heat the breasts and lungs of the nursing woman. Another plant used is *quequexte* (*Xanthosoma robustum*), whose veins contain a white liquid. It is cooked and made into a *caldo* (broth) that the mother drinks. The mother also eats the herb. *Cáscara de cangrejo* (crab shell), a powder bought from the pharmacy and made into a drink, is also used. According to Siriaca, *suchela* is a paste made out of the pit or seed of the *zapote* and *cacao* (someone else said it was made from sesame), and mixed with *atól de masa* and drunk.

María and Siriaca play an important role in encouraging and supporting the mother's breast-feeding of the new infant. The advice and information they impart is within the context of the larger local ethnomedical system that uses concepts of hot and cold, weak and strong, and heavy or thick and thin. However, they also are channels that spread new information from the biomedical system, such as the reasons it is important for the mother to give the baby the colostrum, and new practices, such as stimulating the nipples during the prenatal period to prepare them for the baby's nursing. Siriaca promotes breast-feeding by showing the woman during the prenatal exam how to stimulate her nipples so that they will have *puntas* and won't hurt when the baby nurses.

Interviews from more recent fieldwork, in 2000 and 2013, indicate that there was less bottle-feeding with infant formula and milk substitutes on the finca than before. Some said that this was due to the price of infant formula and the poor economic situation on the finca. However, it also may reflect a change in physicians' and nurses' attitude toward breast-feeding, which is being supported by the WHO breast-feeding policy. This policy in turn influenced the Ministry of Health and new physicians in Guatemala. However, bottles with boiled sugar water are still commonly used by finca mothers.

In 2013, the medical system strongly encouraged breast-feeding. I observed a monthly review session for the midwives, which was run by a nurse, a doctor, and a nutritionist who was the guest speaker. The midwives were told that the mothers should have skin-to-skin contact with the baby immediately after the birth to help them breast-feed and that breast-feeding helps the uterus go back to normal. The nurse had a model of a breast so she could show how to encourage the baby to nurse by placing the baby's stomach on the mother's stomach and the baby's face directly in from of the breast. She stressed that the baby should be fed breast milk exclusively for six months without supplements and went over the benefits of exclusively breast-feeding the baby. She emphasized that nursing should be guided by the baby, not by a schedule. According to the nurse, the baby should breast-feed often to promote good production of milk. She also said that the midwives should teach the mothers to learn the signs of the baby's hunger, which include the baby crying and it passing its hand to its mouth.

Ironically, the nurse giving these instructions did not acknowledge or seem to recognize that feeding on demand is the normal practice of the finca mothers. She also did not know that midwives had been told in past training sessions to advise scheduled feeding every three hours, which was not only against their practice but also unrealistic and impractical for mothers. Now it is medically recognized that on-demand feeding is scientifically better for the infant. Thus there have been extensive changes in the medical personnel's knowledge and attitudes about breast-feeding, which have affected what they are teaching the midwives and mothers and what they are doing in the hospitals. Previously in the hospital they would give the newborn infant a bottle with boiled sugar water, which might have gotten the child accustomed to the bottle instead of the breast nipple; they might also have given formula to the baby and free samples of formula to the mother, thus encouraging bottle-feeding of the baby.

Although the nutritionist giving the talk recognized the importance of the midwife in helping and supporting the mother to breast-feed and said that the midwives should consider the emotional needs of the mother, she stressed that they should not use massages or herbs. But the massages and herbs may help relax the mother and stimulate milk flow. The nutritionist and nurse thus promote the control aspect of the medicalization process by ordering the midwife not to continue the practices she uses to stimulate milk flow. They thereby exert their authority over her whether she follows their orders or continues her own methods of treating breast-feeding problems.

This 2013 review session stressed the importance of six months of exclusive breast-feeding.[3] In practice, supplementary feeding begins much earlier, and breast-feeding continues much later. The doctor present mentioned that the president of Guatemala has started a new thousand-day program called Hambre Cero, for children six months to two years old. A cereal called Vitacereal, made from corn flour, soy flour, and various micronutrients, is being distributed as a supplementary food through health centers and schools. It comes in a bag, and the mother mixes it with boiled water and gives two glasses or bowls a day to the baby. The doctor and nurse at the review session showed the bag to the midwives and passed it around. The instructions on the bag were written in Spanish, and although there were some illustrations, the accompanying instructions were not very clear.[4] Because they told the midwives they should promote this cereal to the mothers, it would have been helpful if they had demonstrated how to prepare it. In addition, contamination of the water may be another problem if it is not cooked long enough.

One of the major problems with foods that have to be mixed with water is that of dilution. If too much water is used, the child will not get the proper nutrition. According to the World Food Program, Vitacereal is distributed to pregnant and nursing mothers as well as to children from six months to three years of age and is designed to increase weight. Unfortunately, no mention of this broader use for mothers was made at the midwifery session; they only discussed its use for children six months to two years. This was a lost opportunity; the use of Vitacereal by pregnant and nursing women could be very beneficial. When the presenters stressed the importance of exclusively breast-feeding for six months, they did not acknowledge the fact that many of the mothers are malnourished and that breast-feeding might be an additional strain on their body. As Chary and her colleagues state, the WHO policy of exclusively breast-feeding for six months "is symptomatic of a larger inability to address the true root causes of maternal-child morbidity" (Chary, Dasgupta, Messmer, and Rohloff 2011:182).

Although Vitacereal was introduced in Guatemala in 2008 and distributed through health centers in some of the indigenous areas, it faced funding problems in 2009. These were supposedly resolved, and in 2013 the product was being publicized more heavily throughout the country as part of the national strategy to reduce chronic undernutrition. However, the government has been "unable" to pay providers, and supposedly a large amount of the product was rotting in a warehouse. In 2015 the government was promoting a different cereal mixture called Mi Comidita, which is also being distributed by the World Food Program and Catholic Relief Services through health centers, primarily in the department of Totonicapán. Mi Comidita is being distributed with a small bowl with measurements for complementary feeding. Catholic Relief Services is using the bowl to stress the importance of preparing it in the form of a thick puree. The switch was made to prevent people from preparing it in the form of a thinner *atol*, which was a problem with Vitacereal. Unfortunately, one of the pictures in the illustrated preparation instructions shows a rather liquidy form of the mixture being poured from a pot (Elena Hurtado, personal communication, 2015).

While the aim of such programs is admirable, the problem is their financial sustainability. Other problems may also arise concerning the addition of water. If the water is not boiled sufficiently, diarrhea from an infectious disease and contamination may result. If the mixture is diluted, the supplement will not contain the proper amount of nutrients. Both these factors could contribute to further malnutrition. In addition, if the supplement contains milk, gastrointestinal problems, including diarrhea, could arise from lactose intolerance.

CONCLUSION

The midwife's role does not end with the birth but continues during the postpartum period and involves monitoring both the mother and the newborn child. As in the prenatal and birth stages, the hot-cold principle conceptually underlies and links many of the beliefs and practices of the midwives and mothers. Medicalization often involves violation of the hot-cold principle, especially with regard to the postnatal bath.

Biomedical personnel condemn the sweat bath, arguing that the heat can be too strong and debilitate the woman. However, in the local biology, the woman is in a cold state after birth, and the sweat bath not only cleanses her, but also heats her. Especially important is that the heat stimulates milk flow and makes the quality of the milk hot— or prevents it from being cold, which would make the baby sick. The herbal bath used on the finca serves the same function of heating the body and the milk. The herbs are of a hot quality, and the water is hot in temperature. The bath also prevents diseases caused by *aire* or cold, which can enter the body at weak points such as the knees and the vagina. Since 2010 the doctor has told Siriaca that she should not use the herbs and that she should use only warm water, not hot. She now gives women a choice as to how they want the bath: with herbs or without, hot or warm. However, this undermines the cultural logic of the hot-cold principle and the authoritative knowledge of the midwife and increases control by the doctor.

One of the main complaints women had about the hospital was that the water to wash or shower with was cold, and the food served was often items classified as of cold quality, contradicting the hot-cold principle. At the technological level of medicalization, hospital delivery results in abandonment of the use of the abdominal binder that the midwife puts on the mother after home delivery. According to the midwife, without the binder the uterus might not return to its proper size and in place, and this may result in the condition of fallen womb, or *descompostura*.

Medicalization is also evident in bottle-feeding, as is commoditization. In some cases bottle-feeding begins in the hospital, where the infant is given sugar water in a bottle shortly after delivery. One of the main problems in the use of the bottle is the lack of knowledge or resources to keep the water and the bottle clean and free of contamination. In addition are problems of dilution in the use of commercial formula. In such cases, medicalization in the form of bottle-feeding may cause diarrheal diseases or malnutrition.

The postnatal massage and bath reinforce both social and physical interaction between the midwife and the mother. In contrast, there is no biomedical postnatal exam of the mother unless there are complications. The mother is supposed to take the baby to the clinic for a checkup and to receive vaccinations. However, most mothers do this only if the baby is sick. Periodically a mobile clinic comes to the finca to give vaccinations.

At the gender level, during the postpartum visits both María and Siriaca give nutritional advice involving both proscriptions and prescriptions to strengthen the mother, who is in a weak and cold state, and to stimulate the flow of milk (table 6.2). They also advise the woman about restrictions on her activity to prevent a prolapsed uterus, which they treat by massage, applying plasters, using an abdominal binder,

TABLE 6.2. POSTPARTUM CARE

	María	Siriaca 1996	Siriaca 2010
Bath, third and fifth day	Herbs, hot water	Herbs, hot water	Herbs if woman wants them; warm water
Massage	Massage while giving bath	Same	Same
Emotions	Mother should avoid strong emotions that will cut milk flow	Same	Same
Restore hot-cold balance	Advises mother to eat hot foods and avoid cold ones	Same	Same
Wash mother's clothes	Washes clothes if mother doesn't have help	Does not wash mother's clothes	Does not wash mother's clothes
Treat fallen uterus, pain	Uses massage, herbal plasters, abdominal binder; makes herbal teas	Same	Same
Breast-feeding	Encourages mother to give the baby colostrum and begin breast-feeding immediately, treats breast-feeding problems with herbal teas	Same	Same

and administering herbal teas. Biomedical personnel are constantly telling the midwives not to use herbs, thus denigrating their knowledge of how to treat these female conditions.

Curing illnesses of both the mother and the infant extended María's and Siriaca's role in the postpartum period and beyond. This continuity of care is a striking contrast to the biomedical system, where specialization has resulted in a discontinuity of care between obstetricians dealing with the mother and pediatricians treating the infant, although in rural Guatemala this is not the case because of the lack of doctors. The multiple roles of midwives as healers are linked to their knowledge of plants, largely in the secular realm, but also to their spiritual characteristics, which lie in the sacred realm. Both the sacred nature of care and the physical postnatal care of mother and child by midwives persist despite the pressures of medical personnel to limit the midwives' role to attending the birth without also recognizing their importance prenatally and postnatally. The midwife's multiple roles, especially her healing role, are the subject of the next chapter.

*It is up to God, but I would like him not to send me so
many children.*

JUANA, FINCA MOTHER, 1978

Midwives often combine midwifery with other kinds of healing roles, as Brad Huber and Alan Sandstrom (2001) have described. Both María and Siriaca are examples of such healers. They not only treat a variety of women's reproductive problems directly related to pregnancy and birth, but also address other female conditions and needs, such as *descompostura*, urinary tract infections, *detención*, amenorrhea, infertility, miscarriage, abortion, and contraception. Women consult midwives when their adolescent daughters have not reached menarche or have missed their period for a few months, or when they themselves have missed their period. Several of the herbs employed are emmenagogues, which are used to bring on one's menses and may also be used as abortifacients. Mothers are concerned about their own and their daughters' future fertility, as well as other illnesses of both men and children. Midwives treat worms, diarrhea, respiratory infections, and other common children's illnesses, and they are also called on to diagnose and treat nonbiomedical, or "folk" illnesses, such as the evil eye, fallen fontanel, *pujido*, *chipez* or *chipil* (jealousy), and *susto* (fright), which are not recognized by the biomedical system. Many of the cures combine over-the-counter remedies, such as Alka Seltzer, pharmaceuticals, and herbs.

MARÍA AS SPIRITIST, *AJQ'IJ* (SHAMAN), AND *CURANDERA* (HEALER)

In addition to being a midwife, María was also a spiritist (*espiritista*) and a shaman, or daykeeper (K'iche': *ajq'ij*). These are two very different types of religious specialists, although both are involved with healing. A spiritist goes into trance and becomes possessed by a spirit; a daykeeper uses the Mayan 260 day ritual calendar, or *tzolkin*, and divining seeds to diagnose and treat illnesses and other problems. María became a religious specialist and healer as a result of treatment she received when she was very ill by the same healer who revealed her calling as a midwife. He diagnosed her illnesses at various times as being related to these two divine callings. He said that if she did not accept these positions, she would not recover from her illnesses. Thus she apprenticed with him first to become a spiritist, and later to become an *ajq'ij*.

María had two different altars: a large one in her living room with several statues and pictures of Mary, Jesus, and various saints on it, where she did her spiritist consultations, during which she became possessed by a spirit who divined the causes of the problem that the client asked about. She would also light a candle and pray for the protection of a pregnant or recently delivered woman before and after she went to visit one of her clients. María explained that she did not work much as a spiritist when she became older and was busier with her midwifery work because going into and out of trances was very tiring, and she was concerned that the fatigue might interfere with her effectiveness if someone called her for a birth after she had come out of trance.

María also had a smaller altar made of cane and thatch behind her house. On it were two wooden crosses; pictures of saints, including San Simón Tadeo and San Pascual; and a small statue of Maximón (San Simón). María laid out her divining seeds (*tz'ite*) and counted them out according to the Mayan ritual calendar to divine the answer to a question or the cause of a problem posed by a client who came for a consultation.

SIRIACA AS INJECTIONIST, *CURANDERA*, HERBALIST

Siriaca has eagerly expanded her role as a healer by taking additional courses whenever she can. These include information and practices in both the biomedical domain and the local ethnomedical ones. She attended a training course to become a health promoter, in which she learned to administer injections. She received a certificate and is now a health promoter, but she doesn't practice officially as one. However, she does give injections if someone has bought them in the pharmacy and needs them to be administered. These are primarily vitamin injections. She does not give oxytocin or other injections during labor. She also has a tremendous knowledge of herbal remedies. Many of these she learned from her mother. However, she has expanded her knowledge in this area of the *naturaleza* through a course she attended that was given by the NGO ASECSA (Asociación de Servicios Comunitario de Salud).

DETENCIÓN AND INFERTILITY

The average age of onset of menstruation for finca girls was fourteen, according to María. This was supported by a survey of the reproductive histories of seventy-seven women, whose median age at menarche was fourteen years. However, this figure may be problematic methodologically because it was based on the women's recollections, often after many years. Women might round their actual age at menarche to what they think is the average number.

One women's condition that midwives treat is *detención*: delayed menstruation or when a nonpregnant woman does not get her period. In the highlands, people tended to use the phrase *la regla no baja* (her menstruation doesn't come down) or *no tiene su costumbre* (*custom*, in English, is a euphemism for menstrual period). According to María, only unmarried girls get *detención*. Thus if someone comes to the midwife who hadn't menstruated, the midwife must first determine if the woman is pregnant. She examines her and says if the abdomen is high and is very hard, then it is *detención*. If the woman is pregnant, the abdomen is lower and the breasts are bigger, with darker nipples. In addition to an enlarged, swollen stomach, other symptoms of pregnancy include wheezing and difficulty breathing when walking.

If María decided that her client was pregnant, she would not give her anything to induce abortion because she considered it a sin, and she said that the health center forbade it. On the other hand, if she had diagnosed *detención*, she would treat it. María would give the woman a firm massage and make her drink a tea of boiled *salvia santa* (*Lippia dulcis*) leaves with oregano, white honey, rum, and *esencia maravillosa*. After drinking the tea for nine days, the woman was expected to get her menses. *Midwives* in the highland town of Santa Lucía Utatlán also used *salvia* to treat *detención*.

Siriaca also says that she insists on examining women who say they have *detención* to see if they are pregnant. She mentions examples very similar to those given by her mother twenty years earlier, such as the following:

A girl came to me because she had not gotten her period. She insisted that she did not have a boyfriend and was not pregnant. She was afraid her brothers would beat her up if she was. I spoke to the girl's mother to tell her she was pregnant. Finally, the girl said there was a man who was fixing the road who had spoken to her from the other side of the river, but that was all. Unfortunately, the baby was born dead, maybe because the girl had taken so many medicines from different people trying to abort it.

Other remedies are used as emmenagogues to bring on one's menstrual period. These include a tea made from three sprigs of *artemisa* (*Artemisia mexicana*), and another tea made from mustard leaves (*Brassica nigra*), pink honey from the pharmacy, and the root of *escorcionera* (eryngo; *Eryngium carlinae*). The latter plant was also used in Verapaz to regulate menstruation (Orellana 1987:137). According to José Ignacio Aguilar Girón (1966:350), *escorcionera* is a strong emmenagogue and may also cause abortion. *Artemisa* may be used if a woman is getting her period every fifteen or twenty days to regulate it to once a month.

Sanguinaria or *botoncillo* (bloodwort; *Gomphrena dispersa)* is another plant that María used as an emmenagogue. Nine flowers are taken in a tea for nine days. Use of *sanguinaria*, also called *sangranita*, has also been reported in Costa Rica, where a tea made from boiling dried leaves and stalks are used to "bring down the period" (Low and Newman 1985:154).

All the herbs used as emmenagogues or abortifacients or for infertility are of a hot quality. All the herbs that have oxytocic properties are also classified as hot. Therefore, if a woman were pregnant, a hot condition, and wanted to have an abortion, she would be given these herbs because they would make her excessively hot and possibly induce an abortion. On the other hand, if a woman had been infertile and wanted children, she would be given remedies to heat her uterus, which would bring on her menstrual period.

Carole Browner and Bernard Ortiz de Montellano point out in their study of herbal emmenagogues used by women in Colombia and Mexico that cases of menstrual delay may be due to various conditions, some needing a hot remedy and others a cold one. All the remedies for amenorrhea or delayed menstruation, including avocado pit, are characterized as irritating. To be effective, the remedy must have an irritating quality (1986:42).

The midwife may also attribute delayed menstruation to a condition called *falta de sangre* (lack of blood). This term may indicate anemia, which is a problem among women on the plantation, especially during pregnancy. Iron pills are often prescribed by the clinic. On the finca, because blood is considered to have a hot quality, lack of blood would be a cold condition treatable with heating substances. Lack of blood also causes *debilidad* (weakness), in which case the patient needs to take fortifying substances. Thus another dimension of the bodily balance system is the strong/weak principle. Lack of blood is not only cold, it also causes weakness, whereas sufficient blood is needed for a healthy or balanced body.

Delayed menstruation may also indicate fertility problems. María said that to treat delayed menstruation, she cooked a piece of dried umbilical cord with *pimiento de castillo*, clove, cinnamon, cumin, oregano, *balsamito de aire*, and two *octavos* of rum. This mixture would be put in a bottle, and the woman would drink a cup each morning until it was finished. Her period would begin soon, and pregnancy would occur in the next month. María said that she stopped using this remedy because she considered the dried umbilical cord dirty. That attitude may reflect the influence of medicalization on her ideas about cleanliness.

Infertility may also be attributed to a cold womb, so warming remedies are administered to the affected woman. Victoria, a married woman still childless after twelve years of marriage, came to see Siriaca. She was very unhappy and thin because her abusive husband beat her for not having any children. Siriaca gave her a massage, then a remedy of *balsamito de aire* boiled with oregano and sweetened with honey to drink before each meal. These are some of the same ingredients in María's remedy, but without the dried umbilical cord. The next time the woman came in, she said her period was coming. She was told that if she did not menstruate again in the next two months, she could be pregnant or just delayed. She became pregnant and gave birth to twins.

According to Siriaca, infertility may also be caused by the womb having been turned around so it won't hold the child. She adjusts the womb by massage so it is normal, then gives the woman a bottle of a remedy with white honey. Six or eight months later the woman is pregnant.

In Santa Lucía Utatlán and many other Mayan communities, especially in the highlands, the *temascal*, or sweat bath, may be used to warm the womb and treat infertility. One of the midwives said:

The sweat bath is my medicine. Because *la matriz* (the womb) is cold, it doesn't want to receive the liquid from the man. Place her in the sweat bath. Put the fire below her, two times: on the first day when her period comes and on the third day, give her a sweat bath, blow it, and heat the womb. The next month, her period won't come and she will be pregnant.

Both María and Siriaca are arbiters of moral values and agents of social control in their role as midwives. They reinforce the norms of society, including the role of motherhood and the value placed on children, by preventing abortions, gossiping about and passing on news from case histories, and treating menstrual problems and possible infertility with emmenagogues and other remedies. However, as Amy Willats (1995) states, "the midwife also has 'social permission' to induce menstruation by diagnosing *detención*." She "can interpret and manipulate the physiological concept of delayed menstruation because of its ambiguity: abortion is a sin, but inducing menstruation is social and culturally acceptable" (Cosminsky 2001c:267).

During the 1970s and early 1980s, the World Health Organization (WHO) and other international organizations were promoting the development of programs focused on primary health care and community health to meet basic health needs in developing countries. As part of these programs, they were interested in training and using traditional midwives, and training traditional healers as health promoters. There was also an increased interest in these healers' knowledge of herbal medicine, especially herbs used in various aspects of fertility regulation. WHO identified research in fertility regulation as a priority area and set up the Task Force on Acceptability of Fertility Regulating Methods in 1972. After that, the Indigenous Fertility Regulating Methods projects were established, and the Task Force on Indigenous Plants for Fertility Regulation was set up[1] (Newman 1985b).

FAMILY PLANNING AND CONTRACEPTION

Family planning programs and the use of modern contraceptives involve almost every aspect of medicalization. As part of the emphasis on primary health care, midwifery training programs expanded to include family planning. WHO and the Pan American Health Organization (PAHO) held a conference in 1972 in Geneva on the training and use of traditional midwives for family planning (Velimirovic and Velimirovic 1978; Velimirovic and Velimirovic 1981). Although most training programs have tried to limit or attenuate the role of the traditional midwife by changing her practices, family planning is one area in which her role has expanded. Several countries developed training programs for midwives that included family planning with the support of WHO, PAHO, USAID, the Population Council and various NGOs (Peng, Keovichit, and MacIntyre 1974; Verderese and Turnbull 1975). Carol McClain (1981) has reviewed some of these early programs, their underlying ethnocentric assumptions, and the problems they faced, and has made a series of policy recommendations aimed at increasing the effectiveness of such family planning programs.

Renewed interest in family planning in Guatemala is related to the WHO Millennium Development Goal Number 5, which calls for a reduction in maternal mortality and for universal access to reproductive health care. One central component of both of these goals is access to contraceptives, which is assumed to empower men and women to make their own reproductive choices. Contraceptive use reduces maternal mortality by helping women to delay, space, and limit pregnancies, reducing the health risks of frequent and numerous pregnancies and of complications from unsafe abortions due to unintended pregnancies (USAID 2013).

The Guatemalan fertility rate is the highest in Latin America, with an average of 3.6 children per woman, having dropped from 4.3 (PAHO 2012); it also has the second lowest average age of mothers at first birth in Latin America, which can have serious negative consequences for both maternal and child health and mortality (World Bank 2004:113). These figures hide ethnic and rural-urban differences. On the finca, many women have had ten or more births. Guatemala also has the lowest contraceptive use in Latin America, with wide disparity among ethnic groups. The figures from the Fifth National Maternal and Infant Health Survey, 2008–2009, report a contraceptive prevalence of 40 percent among indigenous women and 63 percent among nonindigenous women (MSPAS 2010).

One study using data from the Guatemala Demographic and Health Survey and the 1997 Providers Census carried out in four highland departments found that only 11.7 percent of women in the sample used a modern contraceptive method, reflecting lower usage among Indian and rural populations (Seiber et al. 2005). The official figures for the use of contraceptives in Guatemala as a whole were 15 percent in 1978, 21 percent in 1985, and 54 percent in 2009 (United States, Global Health Initiative 2010, PAHO 2012), indicating a gradual increase. Multiple factors contribute to the low contraceptive use, including inaccessibility, unavailability, lack of economic resources for health care, and sociocultural factors such as attitudinal barriers and the Mayan genocide of the 1980s (Ward, Bertrand, and Puac 1992; Warren et al. 1987).

Given the emphasis in the literature on sociocultural barriers or constraints to the use of modern contraception, I was intrigued when I visited the finca in 1974 and heard several women say, "When is the doctor coming? It is time for my injection," or "It is time for my pill." Even a few husbands asked where the doctor was because it was time for their wives' "treatment." Although some women, both in Santa Lucía and on the finca, said that the number of children born to them is "up to God" and that "abortion is a sin," they requested emmenagogues and abortifacients, and they would ask me about acquiring contraceptives. People may express fatalistic notions about regulating reproduction, but they are not rigid in regard to their own reproductive decisions.

A family planning program existed on the plantation from 1971 to 1974. It was run by a private physician who was a friend of the *finquero* and was paid by him. The physician held a monthly health clinic that included a family planning program.[2] The program ended in 1975 when the doctor stopped holding the clinic. After he left, it was harder for those who wanted it to obtain contraception. The doctor continued to hold a clinic at a nearby plantation, and a few women would go there to receive contraceptive injections.

In the beginning the doctor at the finca distributed contraceptive pills at a cost of fifteen cents per month per woman. In the middle of 1972, he also began giving injections of Depo-Provera, which last for three months and cost one dollar. Despite the higher cost, people preferred the injections to the pills because of the convenience. The doctor did not perform any gynecological exams. Not having an exam, which is considered a dangerous practice from a medical point of view, was an incentive for the women because in order to receive contraceptives from the public health clinic or Aprofam they needed to have an exam, about which several women expressed anxiety, fear, and shame. Some women expressed concern because they did not get their period with the injection, although the doctor said he explained the possibility of having amenorrhea or breakthrough bleeding but did not discuss other possible side effects. He did not discuss other contraceptive methods such as condoms or IUDs with the women. He also tended to minimize female patients' complaints, condescendingly attributing them to overreactions.

One problem some women experienced might have been a consequence of ambiguity: women did not know whether their amenorrhea was caused by the injection or by pregnancy. In contrast, a few women who had IUDs experienced heavy bleeding, and this blood loss was of more concern than not menstruating. This difference in emphasis might reflect the traditional belief that the body has a limited amount of nonrenewable blood, and its loss causes a body to be weak and cold and thus susceptible to various illnesses.

Some women also expressed misconceptions about the way the oral contraceptives work, which related to their concepts about the body. They perceived the body as a tube, and according to one woman, when women take the pills, they pile up and form an obstruction that blocks the entrance of the semen or sperm. When the woman goes to the doctor for an exam, he washes out the piled-up pills. The nurse and the family planning center tried to explain that the pills are dissolved like food; they demonstrated by dissolving a pill in water and explained that it is the same in the stomach. By contrast, the women believe that the injection, like other injections, goes straight to the bloodstream, so they believe that it is more a effective as well as more convenient form of birth control. In addition, it is easier to get injections, and they are easier to conceal if a woman and her husband disagree concerning contraception. The women also had a general preference for injections over other pharmaceuticals. One woman said that people liked the pills and injections but wanted someone to explain how they worked.

The doctor hired a young Ladina girl of seventeen years of age from the finca to help distribute the contraceptive pills and to keep records about program participants. She was single, without children, and she had been to school and was literate. Some women expressed ambivalent attitudes about her, saying that she was too young and didn't have the correct knowledge about the pills. According to them, she also did not have any experience with childbirth since she was single and did not have any children. She had been sent for a brief training program, but several informants didn't know that and believed that she didn't have any special training to compensate for her youth and inexperience. To the community at large her status in these respects made her one of the least acceptable people to the play this role in the program, whereas to the *finquero* and the doctor, because of her ethnicity, education, and relative socioeconomic status she was one of the most acceptable choices.

According to the records the doctor had kept earlier, forty-five women participated in the finca program, although twenty-three of these had stopped contraceptive use or dropped out of the program by December 1974. In addition, fifteen stopped when the doctor was no longer coming to the finca because the contraceptives were no longer easily accessible. Several of these women and their husbands expressed concern about stopping and wanted to know when the doctor would be returning to the finca. They wanted to continue family planning and felt frustrated by the lack of opportunity to do so.

The doctor did not speak to María at all about the program. She expressed positive attitudes toward family planning and was supportive of the finca program. She told people who complained about the program to go to the public health clinic if they didn't want to take the pills or injections on the finca:

> It is better to take them than to have a child every year, which is too much work. The times now are very trying. There is no money to maintain children. Some three or four is a sufficient family. The woman can't do it all. That's why I advise them to take the pills. Now it is better because there is a *remedio* (remedy or recourse). (1976)

However, María began expressing more negative opinions about modern contraceptive methods when one of her daughters became ill after using an IUD. She was diagnosed as having a tumor and underwent a hysterectomy. María attributed the tumor to the IUD. After that she advised women not to have intercourse during their period or for five days before or five days after if they do not want children. She claimed that the nurse at the health center taught her this. This belief has been reported as common in other areas, as well as in Hippocratic medicine (Browner and Ortiz de Montellano 1986; Newman 1985a:188). María understood the idea of timing, but unfortunately it was not the correct timing, according to scientific reproductive physiology.

What options did people on the finca have for family planning before the doctor's program and after the program was over? People mentioned using a variety of traditional methods, such as abstention, sleeping separately, breast-feeding, herbal and home remedies, and abortion. Herbs and home remedies include aspirin, purgatives, lemon juice, celery, emmenagogues and abortifacients. Siriaca said that when women ask her for advice, she recommends natural methods such as the use of avocado pits:

> What I recommend is to mash the avocado pit, boil it, and drink the water for three days during her period. On the third day, drink a cup of water. I told one woman to keep her avocado pits when it is the season for avocados. She had two bagfuls. She washed and boiled them every three days of her period, and she did not get pregnant. But she finished them and didn't have any more, so then she got pregnant. (July 1996, cited in Cosminsky 2001c:269)

Most women said they practiced postpartum abstention from sexual intercourse for one to three months, although there was a wide range; older women with more children tended to abstain for longer periods of time, not only postpartum but in general. In eight out of twenty-three families surveyed, the husband and wife slept separately, the husband with the male children and the wife with the female children (Taylor 1970).

The main sources for people from the finca to obtain biomedical forms of contraception are the Asociación Pro-Bienestar de la Familia (Aprofam), a nongovernmental family planning program that has a clinic in Retalhuleu and is affiliated with International Planned Parenthood, and the public health centers (*sanidades*) run by the Ministry of Health. Aprofam established clinics in Guatemala in 1965. The Ministry of Health opened family planning services in various parts of the country in 1967 (Monteith et al., 1985). Aprofam has a mobile unit that visits rural areas, but can go only when a doctor is available. Women have to have an initial gynecological exam, during which a pap smear is taken, and then an exam once a year. Women on the finca said they thought they had to have an exam each time they got the pills renewed, and this is one of their major reasons for not going. This miscommunication and misperception may be linked to the intense anxiety they feel about the gynecological exam, anxiety that is related to their values of modesty and *vergüenza* (shame).

The nurse at the health center said the reasons people give for not participating in the family planning program are some of the same reasons they offer for not using the clinic in general, whereas other reasons are specifically related to attitudes toward birth control. The reasons they don't participate include the cost of transport; not knowing what to do with their other children when they go to the health center; the cost of the pills; the belief that pills, injections, and IUDs are hot and will cause cancer, specifically tumors; a feeling of shame and the violation of their modesty when a male doctor administers the gynecological exam; and a belief that the husband is afraid that his wife will go with another man if she is protected from pregnancy.

Another biomedical option is *la operación*, or sterilization, which is done in the National Hospital in Retalhuleu. People had been told or believed that *la operación* had to be done after delivery. One woman, Veronica, had planned to deliver in the hospital because she wanted her tubes tied. However, she did not have time to get to the hospital and gave birth in the house. She sent for the local midwife, but the baby was born already when she arrived. She believed that she couldn't have her tubes tied unless she had another child.

Another woman who wanted to have the operation, Marta, had tuberculosis and was pregnant, and she was told it was dangerous for her to have more children so she should have the procedure. This was supported by her husband, and she went to deliver in the hospital instead of with María so she could have the operation. However, the child was born dead in the hospital, and consequently she did not have the tubal ligation.[3] These misconceptions again illustrate the need for better communication and understanding between family planning staff and the population they are supposed to be serving.

The reasons finca women gave for not participating in the finca family planning program were different from those discussed above because participants did not have to have an exam or secure transportation. Their reasons for not participating included the following: the woman wanted more children, the husband was not present because he worked off the finca, the husband didn't want to use family planning, the mother-in-law was against it, the woman had no husband, the woman held the common fear that contraception could be poisonous, the woman felt shame, and the woman was nursing and was concerned about the effects of contraception on her breast milk. Eleven people who initially rejected the program later accepted it and participated in it. Six of these were pregnant when the program started but expressed interest and then participated in it after the birth. Forty-five, or 30 percent of the finca women of childbearing age, used contraception at some time. Thirty-nine of them were in the finca program at some point during its brief duration.

As a woman moves through the family cycle, determinants affecting fertility decisions change. Younger women more frequently gave spacing between children as their reason for participating, whereas

TABLE 7.1. REASONS FOR JOINING FINCA FAMILY PLANNING
PROGRAM

Age	Spacing	No more children	Children shorten one's life	Total
15–24	11	2	1	14
25–44	5	23	1	29
Total	16	25	2	43

older women who had completed their families or reached their desired family size more frequently said that they didn't want any more children. Reasons women gave for not wanting more children included the fact that children get sick a lot, that it costs a lot to raise them, and that the mother gets sick a lot or has had difficult births. A couple of women said children "shorten one's life" (table 7.1) In 1976 no one worded their answer in terms of wanting fewer children. However, in 2013 several women who were using contraceptives did mention wanting fewer children than their parents.

Elena was taking birth control pills because she wanted to space her children. The doctor changed the type of pill she was to take from a pink one to a brown one that made her nauseous. She had suffered no side effects from the first kind. She asked Lucia, the person giving out the pills, for the other kind and was told that the brown pills were the only kind the doctor had brought. She said she would ask him to change them next month. The next month came, and she gave Elena the same type, with no explanation or additional information, either about the pills or about the nausea, so Elena stopped taking them. I don't know whether Lucia mentioned anything to the doctor about Elena's problem. This lack of explanation and communication about the problem caused Elena to drop out of the program.

What was the general sociocultural context within which the doctor's program occurred? A common belief among finca residents is that a woman is destined to have a certain number of children. One woman thought it was better to have them quickly when she was young than later when she would be old. The woman's role on the finca is to have children, and there are strong pressures to conform to this role. However, there are also strong pressures for an unmarried girl not to have

TABLE 7.2. REASONS FOR DROPPING OUT OF FINCA
FAMILY PLANNING PROGRAM

Reasons	Number
Side effects, such as anemia, hemorrhage, stomachache, inflammation, or pain	8
Pregnancy	2
Doesn't have a husband now	1
No longer getting period/too old	2
No answer	10

a child, even though several unmarried women have children on the finca. One such woman did not participate in the program because she wasn't married, although she had three children.

The reasons for women's decisions about participation in the family planning program reflect a double standard. In three cases women rejected birth control because the husband was away, three women rejected it because they were not married, and three women decided not to participate because the husband was against birth control and the women would not go against the husband's wishes. One informant said birth control was good if one has a husband. She participated for a while and then dropped out when her husband left her, saying she now had no husband. Another woman was a widow and therefore was not supposed to need birth control (table 7.2).

María and Siriaca expressed the same ideal. They used herbs to bring on a woman's period if it was delayed, but according to María, "a married woman doesn't get *detención*. If one is married and doesn't get her period then it is because of pregnancy, and it is a sin to cause an abortion."

Another belief commonly held is linked to the hot-cold principle of the humoral system. Pills and injections are considered hot and thus *hacen mal* (do harm); they can cause certain illnesses, especially vaginal inflammation, headache, and fainting. The IUD is believed to cause hemorrhage, nausea, and diarrhea, and to rot the stomach and make a woman thinner. Some women also believe that IUDs can cause permanent infertility. All the herbs used as emmenagogues and prescribed by the midwives to treat *detención* and infertility are of a hot quality. The most frequent negative comment (made by seventeen women) was that the modern contraceptives can cause tumors or cancer. This belief became even more prevalent on the finca after 1975 because of one of María's daughter's IUD incident. Concerns about tumors or cancer were not mentioned as a specific reason for rejecting or not participating in the finca family planning program. One woman had been taking birth control pills for two years and then got pregnant. She had a retained placenta, which she said had never happened with the births of her other children, and she thought it was a consequence of taking the pills.

Some women believed that oral contraceptives were good because they thought the pills contained vitamins and made a woman fatter. Other positive comments included the beliefs that they permit children to grow better and that the woman could earn more money. Some others said that contraception gives a woman control: if she wants to have more children she can stop taking them, and if she does not want more children she can keep taking them. This viewpoint sharply contrasts with that of the women who would not take birth control pills because their husbands would not let them. It is important to recognize the intracommunity variation in responses to family planning, as well as the differences between an expressed ideal of chastity and the reality of sexual activity.

Several women expressed ambivalent attitudes about contraception. Some women said that they were afraid of side effects but were thinking that it's good not to have more children, or that birth control is sinful but they don't want any more children, or that children are good because they can help you but they also cost a lot. Families were dependent on children's future contributions in wage labor and household help, but several people expressed concern about the costs of rearing children. Ambivalence was also revealed by comments about desired family size. These concerns sometimes reflected pressure to have children exerted by mothers, fathers, husbands, and mothers-in-law.

Despite the negative attitudes and rumors that many women expressed, they participated in family planning when the opportunity was offered. When contraception was made accessible, many women took advantage of it. Those who dropped out of the finca program because they experienced side effects were still interested in some form of family planning. Of those who participated in the program, 62 percent stayed in it and did not have any children between 1972 to June 1975, which is an important indicator of its success. When the program was no longer available, negative rumors and attitudes about birth control seemed to increase, especially the belief that contraceptives caused cancer. This increased negativity possibly reflected people's feelings of frustration and powerlessness. For several years after the finca program ended, nothing changed with respect to improving the accessibility of family planning for this population. In fact, access decreased. Although it is important to understand attitudes and beliefs relating to pregnancy and family planning in order to implement programs to promote effective use of family planning, the methods also have to be made accessible to people.

Other factors have influenced the availability of family planning to finca residents. The violence in Guatemala, especially in the early 1980s, resulted in the deaths of many community health workers and health promoters, and the cessation of many health programs. A large number of Mayans were killed during the period of violence, and this has led to some of the resistance to contraception in various Indian communities. In addition, the Reagan administration in the United States was complicit in the reduction or elimination of funding for international family planning programs, many of which depended on foreign aid.

Since the Peace Accords of 1996,[4] the government health system was reorganized as the Sistema Integral de Atención en Salud (SIAS) to expand and improve health services, especially to the rural and indigenous populations. The extent to which family planning has been included has varied, depending on who is president of Guatemala and the influence of the Catholic Church. For example, in 2006 the Guatemalan congress passed a family planning law requiring the government to promote the use of contraceptives and to provide sex education classes. Óscar Berger, the president at the time, vetoed the law, and the congress overrode his veto. The president and representatives of the Roman Catholic Church vowed to present legal challenges to the veto (BBC News 2006). Many Protestant evangelicals are also against contraceptive use, and some areas of Guatemala are now 20–30 percent evangelical.

On my returns to the finca in 2010 and 2013, people had a much greater knowledge about contraception. More young families were using various forms of birth control than did their parents had. Fathers as well as mothers now express a desire for smaller families, giving mainly economic reasons for this change. This may reflect a worsening economic situation and more job instability on the finca, but it also marks a change in male attitudes toward contraception.

TABLE 7.3. NUMBER OF LIVING AND DEAD CHILDREN OF A
SAMPLE OF MOTHERS ON FINCA SAN LUIS, 1996

Mother	No. of living children	No. of dead children
Felipa	11	1
Victoria	9	?
Margarita	9	2
Lucila	8	2
Valeria	4	6
Caterina	7	3
Santos	10	4 (including twins born dead)
Eugenia	12	2
Ampara	7	2
Juana	12	?
María	11	?

The younger generation's parents may have had nine to thirteen children, but some women of this younger generation want only three to five children and are using contraceptives. Of Juana's twelve children (ten of whom are living), her thirty-four-year-old daughter has seven children, from seventeen to two years of age, and more childbearing years ahead, and another is using Depo-Provera injections because she doesn't want any more children (she has three living children and one dead). A daughter-in-law of Victoriana, who had eight children, was pregnant with her fourth child and said she was going to have the *la operación* (tubal ligation). Her husband, Victoriana's son, said it is better to have fewer children. Another woman is taking Depo-Provera injections from the health center in San Felipe, where they are free. She does not want more children even though her husband does. One of the reasons women favor the injections is that it is easier to take them without the husband knowing. This reflects one strategy women use to cope with the prevailing patriarchal gender relations. Thus accessibility, availability, and affordability of contraceptives are necessary, though not sufficient conditions for their use.

When I returned to the finca in 1996, the women who had been in our sample in 1978 had now completed their families, and a number of their children already had several children. Table 7.3 lists a sample of mothers and the number of their living and dead children in 1996. Several of their children are now using various methods of contraception or having their tubes tied.

Family planning is being promoted not only to reduce maternal mortality and morbidity but also because of the very high rates of child malnutrition. Twenty-three percent of children under five years of age are underweight, and 54 percent are stunted; this is the highest level in the region and one of the highest in the world (Nybo 2009; Tran 2013).

Family planning is also promoted not only to encourage women to have fewer children but also to urge them to have longer birth intervals between children. Studies have shown that having children closer together, as well as having many children under the poverty conditions that exist in many areas in Guatemala, result in higher percentages of low-birth-weight babies, child malnutrition, and child morbidity—as well as maternal malnutrition and morbidity (World Bank 2004:118). Susceptibility to child malnutrition may result from fetal malnutrition, which results from maternal malnutrition. Causative factors of child malnutrition include depletion of maternal stores due to a rapid succession of pregnancies and lactation. In addition, a large number of children may limit the amount of food for each child, as well as the time available to care for each one. Large families and short intervals between births may unfavorably influence the children's nutritional status and thus increase mortality and morbidity from infectious disease (Taylor 1970; Haag 1995).

Family planning programs in Guatemala do not seem to involve midwives; nor do midwifery training programs seem to include much about family planning. Nevertheless, María was supportive of family planning until one of her daughters who was using an IUD developed a tumor and had to have a hysterectomy. Whether or not the IUD was a causative factor, she and other people on the finca attributed the tumor to the IUD. After that María supported natural methods of contraception, such as herbs and the rhythm method. Unfortunately, she was incorrect about which days of the monthly cycle women should abstain from sex if they don't want to become pregnant. This is a topic that could easily be incorporated into the training programs.

Siriaca is also supportive of family planning and having fewer children, and she also prefers natural methods of birth control, such as a remedy using avocado pits. However, when one of her daughters wanted to have her tubes tied, especially because her previous pregnancy had been a difficult one, Siriaca was very supportive. The private hospital Hilario Galindo in San Felipe had a special program in which visiting doctors from the United States were offering the procedure inexpensively. Siriaca went to register her daughter, but her daughter was required to come herself. She did so and signed up for the operation. When she went for the examination, however, she discovered that she was pregnant and thus could not have the surgery at that time. She had the baby, and after that she had the procedure done. Both María and Siriaca supported the concept of family planning but were concerned about the side effects of some of the biomedical methods of contraception.

CHILDREN'S ILLNESSES

In addition to treating women's conditions, such as *detención* and *descompostura*, María and Siriaca treated children's illnesses. These include folk illnesses that are not recognized by biomedicine, such as the evil eye, as well as common ailments such as diarrhea and respiratory illnesses. Several of the illnesses that midwives treat are thought not to be curable by doctors or biomedicine, although the doctor might be consulted and pharmaceutical remedies might be used for some of symptoms, like diarrhea. Some of the illnesses present symptoms similar to those accompanying malnutrition, which is rampant on the finca, as well as in many other areas of Guatemala.

The Evil Eye

One of the most common illnesses affecting infants and young children on the finca is the *mal de ojo* or *ojo* (evil eye). The concept of the evil eye is thought to have been transmitted to the New World by the Spanish (Hernandez Saenz and Foster 2001). Within the hot-cold principle, evil eye is characterized as hot and drying. The evil eye is believed to be caused by someone who is in a hot condition or has hot blood, such as a drunken man or a menstruating or pregnant woman, or by someone who likes the child and looks at the child. The heat is passed through that person's gaze because his or her blood is stronger, and thus hotter, than the child's. *Ojo* from a drunkard is considered the worst because it results in high fever and sudden diarrhea. Some deaths of children were attributed to *ojo*.

In Guatemala, evil eye is usually considered a child's illness. The symptoms are whining, crying a lot, diarrhea, vomiting, anorexia, and fever. María explained that the nape of the neck turns hot. The palms of the hands and the stomach are also very hot. Other symptoms reported for evil eye are yellowing of the eyes, the presence of a foul odor (a symptom of dehydration), the child stretching suddenly, and the child *brincando* (jumping). María also claimed that in the first few days after birth before the umbilical cord drops off, if the cord is jumping it is a sign of the evil eye and of fever. When *ojo* is strong, it is said, the gall bladder ruptures and leaks bile or *hiel*. After the age of two, a child will not become sick from *ojo*.

Usually, the person who gives the eye does so unintentionally and unknowingly.[5] María explained that there is a lot of evil eye on the finca because many people get drunk and give the eye to the little ones because they have too much heat from drinking and getting hangovers.

María treated and Siriaca continues to treat *ojo* with *pimienta de chapa*. They wrap nine or eighteen grains of *pimienta de chapa* in a cloth, with a leaf of *flor de muerto* and a little rue. María explained that you make it like a *tamalita*. You roll the cloth over the child's body, front and back, in the form of a cross, then over its head and face, then throw the *pimienta de chapa* into the fire. If the grains burst or crackle and let out a strong smell, it means that the child has *mal de ojo*; *el mal* (the bad or the heat) from the child has passed into the pepper. Thus the use of the *pimienta de chapa* is a form of both diagnosis and treatment.

María said that with two treatments, the child gets better. If the child has *ojo* very bad, three treatments a day are needed to cure him. Some curers on the finca use an egg instead of the pepper. It should be an egg from a black chicken, and it is passed over the child in a similar way. It is then broken into a bowl of water. If the heat from the child curdles or cooks the egg, it means the child has the evil eye. Although the midwives are known for their ability to treat the evil eye, at least three other people on the finca, including one male, also treat the evil eye. Some people believe that a doctor cannot cure the evil eye. According to María, the doctor would say that it is another illness such as worms "or perhaps much heat," but wouldn't know how to cure it.

To prevent evil eye, one should avoid taking a baby out in a street or any public place where he will be exposed to the gaze of others. I have suggested elsewhere that this placing the blame on the mother for her child's illness reinforces the restrictions on young women that are part of the system of gender relations on the finca and elsewhere in Guatemala and Latin America (Cosminsky 1976). Since pregnant women can give *ojo* to a child, their movements are also restricted. Nicole Sault (1990) argues that age is also a factor in the Zapotec village in Mexico where she did her study. Older women, more so than men, are believed to cause the evil eye, and older women use evil eye beliefs to control others and warn younger women to keep their child at home to protect them. On the finca, however, the giver of the evil eye was rarely identified, and in conversations between mothers more emphasis was put on the danger posed by drunken men than on older women as the cause of evil eye.

I agree with Sault that it is important to look at the context of social relations in which evil eye occurs—who is the victim, the agent, and the healer. Sault stresses that older women exercise power and social control over younger women. However, older women also cure the evil eye and give advice on its prevention, and thus older women are also a source of support and protection for younger women. On the finca the difference in emphasis may reflect the high prevalence of male drinking and the dangers that it presents to the family through both domestic violence and the spending of scarce resources on drink.

Mollera caída *(Fallen Fontanelle)*

Both María and Siriaca diagnosed and treated fallen fontanelle among sick infants of mothers they had visited, as well as babies who were brought to them because they were sick. The ailment is diagnosed when a baby has trouble nursing and chokes and throws up when it tries to nurse. The baby has trouble swallowing, and its throat is inflamed.

When María diagnosed a child with *mollera caída*, she explained, she first washed her hand, then put her finger in water boiled with salt and put the finger in the baby's mouth, taking out any mucus and pressing the palate upward to raise the fontanelle (figure 7.1). She said one had to be careful of one's fingernails, so they wouldn't cut the baby.

This is the same method Siriaca uses. When Siriaca diagnoses a child with *mollera caída*, she raises the fontanelle by putting her finger in warm water, then putting it in the baby's mouth, turning the finger upward to push on the palate and remove any mucus that might be in the mouth (figure 7.2). Siriaca related an incident of a woman who

FIGURE 7.1.
*María curing fallen
fontanelle (1979).*

FIGURE 7.2.
*Siriaca curing fallen
fontanelle (2000).*

treated *mollera* and had very long fingernails. She tore the palate, and when she took her finger out it was bathed in blood. The woman said that the throat had been very closed. The baby died three days later. She said, "You have to be very careful and not have long fingernails and raise it with much care and wash the throat" (personal communication, 1996).[6]

According to biomedicine, the fallen fontanelle is a sign of dehydration caused by diarrhea and insufficient liquid intake. However, people attribute difficulty nursing to the fontanelle falling because it pushes the palate down and thus causes the baby to have problems nursing. Difficulty nursing is thus perceived as a result, not a cause of fallen fontanelle.

George Foster reports that in Tzintzuntzán a jolt, such as from falling down, can cause the fontanelle to fall. He says it is "one of the most common Mexican culture-bound illnesses of children and in Tzintzuntzán can also afflict adults" (1994:31). According to Juan José Hurtado (1979) fallen fontanelle is one of the illnesses produced by a disturbance of the mechanical balance of the body. He says that it is mechanically caused by a fall, by inadequate handling of the baby, or by suddenly withdrawing the nipple from the infant's mouth during breastfeeding. The sunken fontanelle is believed to cause diarrhea, inability to suck the breast, loss of appetite, vomiting, fever, crying, restlessness, and weakness.

Susto *(Fright)*

Another illness that midwives may treat is *susto*, or fright. Fright may be caused when a child falls in the river, sees a snake, or suddenly hears or sees something for the first time. The child becomes pale and distracted, jumps when sleeping, and may swell. (Swelling may also be a sign of malnutrition.)

There are several treatments for *susto* involving herbs and rituals. One is to take the child to the river with some flowers, say the prayer Our Father, and leave nine flowers of different colors, calling the name of the child for each flower. Then with a branch or bulrush, one gives the child three knocks and three drinks from the river, then takes a little jar of river water and passes it in front of the child while calling its name, and finally drops the water on the road. This is done either by the parent or more often by one of the local curers. The child is then given a tea of rue and *cordial de susto* (bought in the pharmacy), some of which is sprayed on the child's head. Then they take the child to the priest, who says mass and sprinkles holy water on the child. María said, "The heart is frightened; it jumps a lot because his spirit went when he was frightened. You have to collect the Spirit again that way." This is an example of soul loss as a characteristic of *susto*, although soul loss doesn't always accompany *susto*.

One woman said regarding *susto*, "The doctor can't cure it. They say it is parasites." María similarly said:

> One doesn't go to the doctor. Better take only these remedies. There are some who take gospels to the church that the priest prays for. Others drink a tea of rue with *hoja de aire, hojita de naranja, barba de ajo*, and *tallita de cebolla*. Cook all of them and throw in a little anise. Give this tea for the *susto*. (1979)

Siriaca says that she learned how to cure *susto* from her mother, but her children never had it, and she has never treated it.

Chipil

Chipil, or *chipez*, is a childhood illness believed to be caused by the jealousy of a child who is displaced from the breast by a newborn (sibling jealousy syndrome). Barbara Rogoff (2011) reports that in San Pedro la Laguna, Guatemala, the youngest child, who was about one and a half or two years old and still nursing, would detect when its mother became pregnant. The baby would become fussy and whiny. In reference to Mexico, Foster (1994:53) says that the "knee child senses that its mother is again pregnant, and resenting competition for her affection from the forthcoming sibling, responds with *chipil*, the symptoms of which (whining, inconsolable crying, grasping the mother's apron, etc.) suggest protein calorie deficiency as well as sibling rivalry." Mellado, Zolla, and Castañeda (1989) report this illness for other parts of Mexico, with symptoms that include constant crying, loss of appetite, diarrhea, and sometimes aggressiveness, with the child appearing to sense that he or she will be displaced. Rosenthal reports that in Santa María de Jesus, *chipez* is believed to be caused by breast milk that "is no longer good" because the mother has become pregnant. The "bad" milk will cause diarrhea, and therefore the child should be weaned as soon as possible (1987:66).

The term *chipil* is derived from the Nahuatl word *tzipitl*, used to refer to "an anemic, feverish condition of recently weaned children, popularly attributed to envy of a yet unborn sibling" (Foster 1994:78). Siriaca referred to the baby as *chipero*. The symptoms of *chipil* may indicate the child has protein deficiency malnutrition, or kwashiorkor. The child usually also has diarrhea, a condition that Gordon (1964; Gordon, Chitkara, and Wyon 1963) terms "weanling diarrhea" because it occurs during the second year, when children are commonly weaned. Foster argues that the illness illustrates the "flexibility and adaptability of the humoral system" because it is considered a hot illness (jealousy is a hot condition) requiring cold medicines and foods (1994:53).

María also said:

> Some infants dirty their buttocks a lot from the diarrhea. They stiffen their knees, their skin becomes red, . . . they are *chipez*. When the mother bathes, she should put the baby on her knees like this [across her knees]. Then she bathes and throws the water for her hair on the baby. Nine nights she leaves the baby wrapped in her undergarments to sleep. Next day, goes to wash again, puts on another. It goes away. (1996)

This association of the maternal undergarments and water from her hair may symbolize that the displaced child is still closely tied to the mother.

In another case, the baby almost died of *chipez*. He was eleven months old when his brother was born, and the mother stopped breast-feeding him. He became very thin, all bones, and very sick. The mother gave the baby *mosh de avena* (oatmeal) with milk (this is usually made very thin or watery), and atole in a glass. In this case, the mother continued to breast-feed her older son while pregnant and stopped when the baby was born.

Pujido

Pujido is a condition in which the baby cries, stretches, and arches the back, and for males, the testicles swell because the baby is straining. It may be the same as *pujo*, or tenesmus. According to Siriaca, a baby feels like spines from sugar cane are on its back.

In 2000 Siriaca was examining a one-month-old baby boy, whom she said had *pujido*. She folded a cloth diaper in eight parts. She had the mother express some milk from the breast and rubbed it upward and across in the form of a cross on the back of the baby, and then cleaned it with the cloth. Then she turned the cloth to the other side and put more milk on the baby, rubbed it, and changed the side of the cloth again. She did this eight times, using a different part of the cloth each time. The baby was crying but after she treated him, then he slept. Siriaca also treated this baby for *mollera* because the baby was choking a little when nursing. With her finger she cleaned out mucus from his throat and pushed up on his palate with her finger, just like her mother had done.

Another remedy for *pujido* uses the leaves of the *platanillo*. These are broad large leaves from the banana tree, which are put on the mattress. The baby sleeps on top of them. The leaves should be changed every three days. Little by little the *pujido* goes away, not all at once. One mother said it can take up to three months to leave.

Another woman on the *finca* referred to a different remedy that she called *secretos* (secrets). You look for three children of the same age. If the sick child is a boy, then you look for three girls of the same age and size, and vice versa if the sick child is a girl. Then at 12:00 noon on Friday or Monday, you have the child lie down in the middle of the house, and you pray an Our Father. You place a cloth over him. Then you have the children jump in a cross, nine times this way and nine times that way over the child. Pray three Credos for nine Fridays and nine Mondays. You look for the *escobita* (whiskers) of a turkey, cut nine hairs from it, and throw it in a few coals. Then you put it in the cloth diaper that you are going to place on the child. You put the diaper on the child and wrap it around. Then you cut three shoots of *kishtan blanca* (*Solanum* sp.). You put them in a little boiling water and give the mixture to the child to drink three times a day for nine days.

When I asked how one knows whether the infant has the *ojo* or *pujido*, María said that with the eye, the child has fever in the head and hands and green phlegm, but with *pujido* he does not. With *pujido*, the baby gets red when stretching but doesn't have fever.

Lombrices *(Worms)*

A common belief both in the highlands and on the finca is that everyone is born with worms, which are believed to exist in a sac in the stomach. Supposedly they are natural and necessary, and they signal hunger: "Without them, we would not feel hunger, would not eat, and thus would perish" (Rosenthal 1987:iii). However, if the worms grow too much, if they leave the stomach, or if the bag breaks, they can cause sickness or death. When a child gets cold the worms rise, causing the child to vomit and have diarrhea, swelling of the stomach, and stomach pains. This is referred to as *alboroto de las lombrices,* or the agitation or arousal of the worms. The worms are also more likely to be aroused when one eats cold foods and in the rainy season because of the cold. Worms may also come from eating dirt or adobe.

Caroline Rosenthal writes that the condition is characterized by hyperperistalsis, excessive contractions of the stomach and bowels. "Children suffering from worms show signs of dehydration, with yellow or sunken eyes, wrinkled and pale skin, and dry mouth, because the 'liquid' of the body is finished" (1987:67). According to Rosenthal, "Most informants agree that the diarrhea caused by 'worms not being in their place' is the most serious of all because a child will not eat (not be able to feel hunger), will become malnourished, and possibly die" (1987:67).

Some remedies for *lombrices* are teas based on herbs that are bitter, which is thought to repel the worms so they go back into the sac, or a plaster on the abdomen with white honey or something that is thought to draw the worms back down into the sac. María gave a tea of *yerba buena* (*Mentha piperita*) mixed with the patent remedy Santamisina. A variation of this was a tea of *yerba buena, epasote* (*Chenopodium ambrosioides*), and lemon. Another mother added a spoon of bicarbonate to that tea.

Siriaca recommends a tea of verbena with Alka-Seltzer, or a tea of *yerba buena, flor de muerto* (*Tagetes erecta*), and garlic. These remedies are to *embolsar* the worms. Herbs are also used in enemas, which are administered for worms. One such enema given by the local school teacher to a sixteen-month-old infant for worms was made of *yerba buena, flor de muerto,* and *ruda* (*Ruta graveolens*) finely cut up and mixed with a little sulfate and some grains of salt, and mixed with water. The child was given two enemas with a three-inch bulb. The teacher then gave the baby about six tablespoons of the mixture and told the mother that it was important to keep giving this drink little by little throughout the day. She then got some *manteca* (lard) and rubbed it on the baby's stomach and on the back, and then placed a pair of leaves of *guineo morado* (purple banana) over the abdomen. She said that the baby's abdomen had a lot of heat. The *manteca* is *fresca* (cool) and thus helps lower the worms. Although this occurred in 1979, herbal enemas are still given today.

Colic

Cólico refers to an infant's stomach pains, possibly caused by too much cold or *aire*. It may also accompany other illnesses, such as *pujido* or evil eye. Treatment commonly involves herbal teas. María told the mother of a colicky child to prepare it a tea from onion stalk, garlic stalk, anise, and ten drops of *esencia maravillosa*. Another remedy she used for colic for a three-month-old child was the plant *cola de alacrán* (*Heliotropium angiospermum*).[7] She added rue, *hoja de naranja* (orange leaf), and a piece of charcoal. She then cooked the mixture and gave the child a half glass of the water to drink for nine mornings. These ingredients are all considered hot, and colic is considered a cold illness.

SUMMARY

This chapter has examined the healing roles that the midwives María and Siriaca play in diagnosing and treating a variety of women's and children's illnesses. Although they treat common children's ailments, such as diarrhea and respiratory illnesses, they also treat folk illnesses—that is, conditions that are understood as illnesses in the local ethnomedical classification, but not recognized as diseases by the biomedical system. María and Siriaca are recognized for their authoritative knowledge in diagnosing and treating these illnesses and for maintaining that knowledge.

Medicalization has taken place in the use of pharmaceuticals for family planning, in the performance of surgery for tubal ligation, and in the treatment of conditions like diarrhea that often are a symptom of children's illnesses such as the evil eye, *chipez*, and *susto*. These illnesses also seem to be manifestations of malnutrition, intestinal infection, or both. Often midwives combine patent medicines and pharmaceuticals with herbs, thus preserving some of their midwifery knowledge, as well as incorporating aspects of biomedicine. Furthermore, the midwives' diagnosis and treatment supports the existence of these illnesses in the face of the contrary position of biomedicine—that these are illnesses that the doctor cannot cure. This traditional expertise reinforces the midwives' position in the community. The midwives do not reject bio-medicine, and they will recommend its use, often in combination with herbal treatments, when they believe it is likely to be effective.

Despite midwives' extensive knowledge of plants, or what Siriaca calls *la naturaleza*, and the role midwives play as *naturalistas* (herbalists) in healing, the use of herbal remedies is one of the practices that are constantly condemned in the training programs. The doctors and nurses running these programs tell the midwives that they should not use herbs, whether in the form of teas or baths. This proscription is ironic because in the 1970s and 1980s WHO had several research projects about plants used for fertility regulation and about herbal medicine in general (Newman 1985b; Bannerman, Burton, and Wen-Chieh 1983).

Although the midwives know about plants that can be used for fertility regulation, family planning is an area that today is almost completely medicalized—that is, it comes under the biomedical system. The use of contraceptives marks a cognitive shift from the belief that the number of children a woman has is up to God to the belief that a woman has agency and can take an active role in determining how many children she wants and when she will have them.

People who use contraceptives refer to being in *tratamiento* (treatment). Thus, conceptually, family planning is seen as a medical treatment with the use of medical technology in the forms of pills, injections, IUDs, or surgery. Moreover, in order to be treated, one must go through the medical system and have a gynecological exam. If the doctor or nurse giving the exam happens to be male, issues of gender values, relationships, and hierarchy are all part of the medicalization process and affect people's attitudes toward contraceptives.

Women are often reluctant to see a male doctor for an exam, especially a gynecological exam, because they hold traditional values regarding modesty and shame. The bodily position required during a gynecological exam emphasizes even more than usual the hierarchical relationship between medical personnel and the patient.

Gender relations are also reflected in negative attitudes toward birth control. Sometimes the husband or partner suspects that a woman using birth control may be having sexual relations with someone else. This male attitude is one of the reasons some women prefer the injections over birth control pills: the use of injections is easier to conceal than oral contraception. Today young males tend to hold a more positive attitude toward family planning than men previously did on the finca.

The processes involved in medicalization are even more pronounced in the midwifery training programs. In the next chapter I review national and international policies and midwifery training programs, and I examine the local impact of these programs.

*Today the language that is used about childbirth is medi-
calized and imposes a medical view of birth.*

KITZINGER 1997:240

One of the primary mechanisms for medicalization of midwives has
been midwifery training programs. Guatemala has had a licensing program since 1935 that requires midwives to attend training (Hurtado
and Saenz de Tejada 2001). Additional regulations for obtaining a license, which requires examinations and training, were introduced
in 1953. In 1969 the creation of the Division of Maternal and Child
Health increased the number of training programs. Some of these have
been sponsored by the Guatemalan Ministerio de Salud Pública y Asistencia Social, while others have been funded or carried out by various
international agencies, such as USAID, the World Health Organization (WHO), and nongovernmental organizations such as John Snow,
Inc., the Johns Hopkins Program for International Education in Gynecology and Obstetrics, and religious missions.

These training programs reflect the impact of shifts in WHO's political and economic policies. In the 1970s and 1980s WHO promoted
the incorporation of traditional health care providers, including midwives, into government health services (Bannerman, Burton, and Wen-
Chieh 1983; Hurtado and Saenz de Tejada 2001:217; Leedam 1985).
Integrating midwives into government health services was part of the
strategy promoted in the Declaration of the Alma-Ata, adopted by the
International Conference on Primary Health Care in 1978 to achieve
"Health for All by the Year 2000." Training courses emphasized the
upgrading of midwives' practices. Midwives were urged to wash their
hands, to use the supine or horizontal position for delivery, to cut the
cord with a sterile instrument, and to treat the umbilical cord with
alcohol, merthiolate, and talcum powder rather than substances like
cow dung or cobwebs.

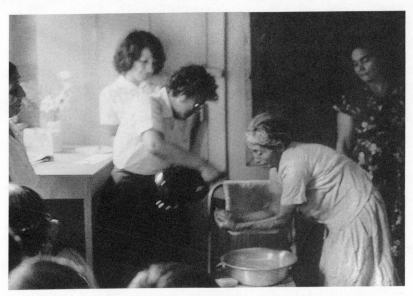

FIGURE 8.1.   *Teaching how to wash hands with a small amount of water during a midwifery review session in Retalhuleu (1978).*

Figures 8.1 and 8.2 are from a review session in 1978 for all the *comadronas* in the Department of Retalhuleu. This was the first regional session to be held in several months, so many midwives attended. The room that the session was supposed to be in was locked, and the person with the key had left. They found another room to have the session in, but it was overcrowded and hot. Midwives were standing outside and looking in, trying to hear, while others were standing in the back of the room because there was not enough space. These conditions were not conducive to learning. Consequently, they changed the session to a half-day instead of a whole day.

The session attended by Siriaca was attended by fewer midwives because it covered a smaller geographical area and the original date had been changed, which some midwives were not aware of (figure 8.3). In contrast to the session attended by María, the arrangements were much better: roomier and fresher, with a raised stage so all could see what the instructor was presenting. Symbolically, however, the stage also meant that the people on the stage, who were biomedical personnel, were in a superior position to the midwives, who were sitting below.

The pedagogical strategies used in the 1978 and 2013 sessions sometimes undermined the main purpose of the sessions: to train the

FIGURE 8.2. *María attending a midwifery training review session in Retalhuleu (1978).*

FIGURE 8.3. *Siriaca attending a midwifery training review session in the health center in San Sebastián (2013).*

midwives in medical practices. Pictures of both sessions illustrate the same modes of teaching and learning that Brigitte Jordan has referred to as "waiting out" a lecture (1993:173). Nicole Berry has called for educators to pay more attention to the types of pedagogy used in the training programs rather than abandoning midwife education entirely, as is now being promoted by WHO (2009:439). When experiential or participatory methods are used, midwives are more engaged, livelier, and more animated (Jordan 1993:173), as shown in the hand-washing lesson depicted in figure 8.1.

In that session, however, one of the nurses asked the midwives to comment about or criticize the person doing the hand washing. The midwives were very reluctant to do this, as it contradicted their basic social values to shame someone in public. In addition, such criticism could have set up antagonisms between midwives, some of whom may have already been competitors if they were from the same area. Thus the midwives did not discuss each other's performance due to the cultural inappropriateness of this particular strategy. Although the nurse trainers tried to get the midwives to more actively participate, instead they silenced the women. In thirty-five years some things have not changed. Anita Chary writes that at some Ministry of Health–sponsored midwife training sessions that she and colleagues from the Maya Health Alliance have observed, they were surprised at "how unsophisticated some of the lessons are"—such as instruction on the basics of hand washing (2014).

Midwives were also muted during a discussion about the use of the sweat bath in the 1978 review session. The nurse said in a condescending tone that some midwives still use the sweat bath, or *temascal*. "I am sure none of you still do that," she remarked. Needless to say, no one would say that she did still use it. Because this was a regional meeting, many of the midwives attending were from Mayan villages where the sweat bath was still used, especially as part of the postpartum treatment of the mother. I asked the nurse what the problem was in using the sweat bath. She turned the question back to the midwives. María answered that the sweat bath is like a den of an animal and that she had heard of an incident in which the midwife attending the pregnant woman fainted in the sweat bath from the heat and then couldn't assist the birth. The nurse agreed and went on to say that if the heat was too high or the time in the bath was too long, the woman could become dehydrated, which could cause problems, including fainting.

The nurse's words implied that neither the midwife nor the mother would know how hot was too hot or how long was too long to be in the sweat bath. To my knowledge, no scientific studies of the effects of sweat baths have been carried out. It is unknown how often someone faints in the sweat bath, but medical personnel used a single such incident to back up their negative view of the sweat bath. Ironically, in the United States, we not only believe that the sweat bath, a type of sauna, is healthy, but we pay to have one. Yet Guatemalan biomedical personnel constantly condemn its use. This condemnation is at least in part because it is a Mayan custom; it reflects biomedical personnel's negative and prejudicial attitudes toward Mayan health practices. Another argument that has been made against sweat baths is that they are a breeding ground for bacteria because of the dark and damp conditions. However, the argument can also be made that the heat promotes healing and that hot steam and water help cleanse the woman.

In an attempt to modernize the teaching methods, trainers are now using PowerPoint. The nutritionist who was a guest speaker in the review session I observed in July 2013 used a PowerPoint presentation to illustrate her talk about the importance of breast-feeding. Although some of the pictures in the PowerPoint were useful, much of the content was text. This was problematic for midwives who were illiterate or were slow readers. The presentation was also still basically didactic in form; the speaker followed a lecture format along with the Power-Point, and there was little interaction with or participation by the midwives. During the session the instructor used a model of a woman's torso to illustrate how the fetus is positioned in the uterus, and a model of the breast to show how to position the breast and the baby to maximize nursing (figure 8.4). These were very useful and interested the midwives. Because there were only about a dozen midwives in attendance, it would have been helpful to let them examine and touch the models.

Linda Greenberg (1982) has analyzed the various problems of these training programs and their relations with midwives, mothers, and communities. Unfortunately, most of these problems continue today, even though the emphasis in training has shifted. The Guatemalan health system (Sistema Integral de Atención en Salud; SIAS) was reorganized in response to the 1996 Peace Accords and began to focus more on training midwives to recognize risk and urging them to refer patients with risk factors to the hospital. Since then, another shift has occurred, and WHO is emphasizing emergency obstetrics. The preg-

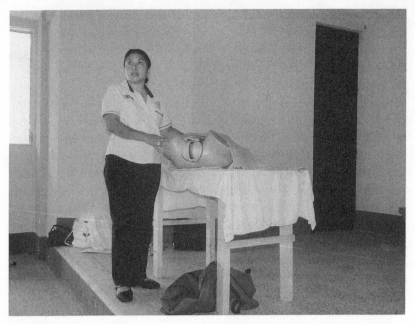

FIGURE 8.4. *Model of woman's torso used in midwifery review session (2013).*

nant woman is supposed to develop an emergency obstetric plan with her family and the midwife, including saving money and arranging a means of transport to the hospital if necessary (Hallowell 2012) for delivery by "skilled attendants."

Guatemala has continued training programs for midwives, although, as Berry has noted, conflicting aims have produced difficulties in relationships between medical personnel and midwives (2010). Below I discuss some of the more well-known programs. Information on these programs comes from published literature, unpublished dissertations and theses, personal communications, and websites, not from my own observations.

MOTHERCARE MIDWIFERY PROJECT

The MotherCare/John Snow Quetzaltenango Maternal and Neonatal Health project has been included in a number of different evaluations of training programs (Sibley, Sipe, and Koblinsky 2004; Hurtado 1998; Hurtado and Saenz de Tejada 2001; Koblinsky 1996; O'Rourke

1994, 1995a, 1995b; Bailey, Szaszdi, and Glover 2002). Carried out from 1988 to 1993, it was a collaborative project between the Quetzaltenango Health Area, the Institute of Nutrition of Central America and Panama (INCAP), and MotherCare/John Snow, and was funded by USAID. According to Barbara Schieber and her colleagues, "the primary goal was to reduce the high rates of maternal cases and neonatal mortality through more efficient use of existing resources and through intervention at all levels, from the community to the hospital" (Schieber, Goldman, and Bartlett 1993:i). As part of the training program, meetings were held with health service personnel to increase their sensitivity to and respectful treatment of traditional birth attendants (TBAs) and acceptance of TBAs and their patients into the health care service. Also:

> Preliminary data from the evaluation phase show a significant increase in TBA referrals of complicated obstetric cases to the hospital. Neonatal mortality in the hospital has decreased from 38/1000 live births in 1989 to 32/1000 live births in 1992. The TBAs report better acceptance by the hospital personnel, who are beginning to welcome their participation during the hospital births of their referred patients. (Schieber, Goldman, and Bartlett 1993:ii)

According to the training manual for the project, the Quetzaltenango MotherCare program differed from other training programs in its basic approach:

> The traditional risk-based approach that has been promoted in our country is not used in this manual. In the traditional risk-based approach, a series of variables or risk factors, such as age, primiparity, grand multiparity, malnutrition, illiteracy, and bad obstetrical history are used to identify "high risk" women. If one applies this focus with these risk factors to the study's population, more than 80 percent will be high risk and will need to deliver in the hospital. If one refers only the "primigravida" (who represent 30 percent of all deliveries) the capacity of the nation's hospitals would be exceeded as they can attend only 20 percent of the births nationwide. (Schieber, Goldman, and Bartlett 1993:2)

Nevertheless, Kathleen O'Rourke writes that the principle objective of the Quetzaltenango program was to train the midwives in the identification of obstetric situations of high risk ("En Quetzaltenango, el principal objetivo del programa fue capacitar parteras en la identifica-

ción de situaciones obstetricas de alto riesgo"; 1995b:504). The midwives were told that in the case of emergencies, such as postpartum
hemorrhage, they should refer the woman to the hospital. However, it
is not clear that the midwives received any specific "information about
how to detect postpartum hemorrhage, how quickly women can die,
and what immediate measures should be taken to improve the possibility that the woman will survive the trip to the hospital (e.g., massage the uterus, have the woman urinate, stimulate the nipple—give
the baby the breast, give fluids)" (Schieber, Goldman, and Bartlett
1993:2), even though these are mentioned in the training manual for
the trainers. In Retalhuleu, this is still the case. Midwives are told to
refer any case of hemorrhaging to the hospital, but are not given information about what to do in the meantime, even though it may take
over an hour to get to the hospital if transportation is available. One
of the recent training programs offered in Guatemala by an NGO was
a one-to-two-day course specializing in postpartum hemorrhage, but
it was not offered in the Department of Retalhuleu (Garcia, Morrison,
and Savrin 2012).

The training manual for trainers of TBAs in the Quetzaltenango
MotherCare program stresses the need for "participatory adult education" methods and techniques, or "active learning": "using concrete
activities that permit the learner to actively experience" (Schieber,
Goldman, and Bartlett 1993:7). The authors continue: "Education is a
two-way process. All of us have something to teach and something to
learn, 'teachers' as well as 'students'" (8). Strategies that were used included case studies followed by discussion, simulation exercises, ani-
mation techniques, skits, role playing, and supporting students with
praise and positive reviews rather than criticizing them. Chairs were
placed in a circle to encourage communication, and classes were conducted in Spanish and Mam. "Within the Quetzaltenango training
program TBAs were treated respectfully and encouraged to share their
experiences and feelings about topics under discussion. Traditional
practices were supported unless they were determined as harmful. In
that case culturally acceptable alternatives were provided" (O'Rourke
1994:50).

An example of a practice considered harmful is the use of oxytocin injections by the *comadronas* to give "force" to labor, a practice
associated with perinatal mortality (Bartlett and Paz de Bocaletti,
1991). Ironically, this is a modern practice associated with biomedicine
that midwives have learned and sometimes use. In class, instructors

discussed other means of strengthening labor, such as encouraging women to maintain a more upright position, which is in accordance with the local culture.

O'Rourke evaluated the Quetzaltenango training program by comparing the pattern of hospital referrals by midwives before and after the training and by comparing midwives from communities where the training was offered with midwives from communities where it was not available. After the training there was a 200 percent increase in the number of mothers referred to the hospital by the TBAs. However, there was no difference between the midwives who participated in the intervention program and those who did not. O'Rourke attributed the referral increase not to the training of midwives, but to the training of hospital personnel (1994, 1995b:512). When midwives were treated with more respect, they referred more pregnant women. Although, according to Patricia Bailey and her colleagues, "the large percentage increase in the number of referrals to the hospital was based on small numbers" (Bailey, Szaszdi, and Glover 2002:21), there was improvement in the ability of the midwives in the training group to refer women with obstetric complications to the hospital, and there was a small reduction of perinatal mortality; this occurred in both the intervention and control groups, though magnitude of the change was not statistically significant. O'Rourke recommends that in the future researchers concentrate on evaluating the interaction between programs that train hospital personnel and those that train midwives, to estimate their proportional effect.

Both the Quetzaltenango training program and the evaluation of it raise several problems. The training of the midwives was a three-day course. The training emphasized "detection, management and timely referral of the complicated obstetrical and neonatal cases that present the greatest risk of mortality. Indications for referral included bleeding, swelling of hands and face during pregnancy, malpresentation, prolonged labor, retained placenta, asphyxia, postpartum bleeding, and maternal and neonatal infections" (Bailey, Szaszdi, and Glover 2002:16). The question can be asked whether three days was sufficient time to cover the necessary information effectively with the midwives.

Another problem is that the evaluation was based on interviews administered to mothers who had given birth during the study period (1990–1993). The physician interviewers determined whether the pregnancy and birth had been normal or complicated, whether the midwife referred the woman to the hospital, and whether the referral was complied with on the basis of information from the mother. To my knowledge, there were no interviews with the midwives concerning these specific births. The main reasons given by mothers for not following referrals were "their lack of confidence in or distrust of the hospital, transportation difficulties, and inadequate financial resources" (Bailey, Szaszdi, and Glover 2002:20).[1]

Bailey and her colleagues also raise the question of whether a reduction in morbidity or complications is a realistic indicator for the evaluation of TBA training "because there is little that TBAs can do to prevent an antenatal or intrapartum complication. The TBAs' greatest potential for effective intervention is during the postpartum period, especially in cases of hemorrhage or infection, which is where this study did detect a positive change" (Bailey, Szaszdi, and Glover 2002:20). O'Rourke stresses that the "sensitization of the hospital staff to the culture of birthing in the community it served, including opening its doors to welcome in the family and TBA of the woman" was an extremely important, if not the most important, intervention because it affected the willingness of TBAs to refer patients to the hospital, and patients more willing to accept such referrals (O'Rourke 1995a). Despite this finding, such sensitization and openness have not been instituted at the hospital in Retalhuleu and at most other hospitals in Guatemala. The doors of the hospital in Retalhuleu remain shut to the midwife and to family members who accompany a mother.

MotherCare subsequently received funding for another five-year period starting in 1994, and it began sponsoring additional activities, including the broadcast of radio spots. "Other high priorities included intense training of facility staff in the treatment of obstetric emergencies and a continuation of efforts to improve relationships between hospital staff and TBAs to make hospitals more family- and TBA-friendly in Quetzaltenango as well as neighboring departments" (Bailey, Szaszdi, and Glover 2002:22). The program was also extended to other areas, including Sololá (Berry 2010:96). However, the results were used to argue against further training of the midwives because the training did not appear to decrease maternal mortality rates, which was WHO's policy and one of the Millennium Development Goals. Although the training of hospital personnel had a positive outcome, I think it was ultimately discontinued. Hospital personnel should be trained to have a greater understanding of and respect for the midwives and their beliefs and practices, and such training should be extended to other hospitals and to training programs in other departments.

Berry (2010:96) points out that MotherCare's strategies were closely aligned with the early Safe Motherhood Initiative, which centered on midwife training and prenatal care as strategies for decreasing maternal mortality. However, WHO and Safe Motherhood changed their orientations in the project's second decade because the training of midwives and emphasis on prenatal care were considered mistakes. MotherCare lost its contract, and the Safe Motherhood project in Sololá was taken over by the Johns Hopkins Program for International Education in Gynecology and Obstetrics (JHPIEGO). The project shifted emphasis toward improving emergency obstetric care through referrals to the hospital by the midwives. With this shift, monetary support for midwifery training ceased; instead funding was made available for efforts to increase emergency obstetric care (Berry 2009, 2010:98). However, the use of emergency obstetric procedures depended on referrals from the midwives.

This shift put people like the director of JHPIEGO in Sololá in a difficult position. After years of building up relationships with the local midwives, the program was now neglecting them. For example, no one resupplied the kits that they had been given in the past. This was symbolic of the new policy: it didn't matter what the traditional midwives thought. Because of the confusion resulting from the changed policy, the director of JHPIEGO decided to work more directly with midwives in developing a program, regardless of what the official JHPIEGO plan stated. The midwives would help on the maternity ward, with staffing twenty-four hours a day, seven days a week, despite the disdain and resistance of some of the hospital personnel (Berry 2009:438, 2010, 2012:99).

Hospital policy does not allow family members to stay with the patient, and thus the midwife plays an important supportive role for the patient. Although the midwives were rarely allowed to deliver babies at the hospital and instead spent time helping the patients in other ways, they felt that their work in the hospital was important (Berry 2010:101). The costs for this program were comparatively minimal, but it was difficult to piece together sources of funding. As Berry emphasizes, "pretending that one can stop funding work with midwives and still work on safe motherhood is not at all realistic." Emphasizing emergency obstetric care instead of reduction in maternal mortality "may have done more harm than good by both alienating midwives and tying up all of the resources available for programs under one, ineffective agenda" (2010:102).

Berry (2005) describes a program to integrate midwives into the state health system that involved training one group of midwives about obstetrical complications, so they could then train other midwives. Although this was an innovative program, Berry shows how the training was still didactic in form. Moreover, it was completely one-sided in that it did not acknowledge any of the midwives' own system of knowledge about whether, when, and how one can change the position of the fetus. The training focused on the referral of cases involving complications and on further educating midwives in biomedical procedures; it did not consider the realities of the midwives' worlds. Berry also suggests bringing midwives into the emergency room to get experience with obstetric complications and learn how they could be resolved. They would also be a comfort to patients, and "knowing what happens to a client in the hospital might make them more willing to refer" (Berry 2009:439).

SISTEMA INTEGRAL DE ATENCIÓN EN SALUD (SIAS) PROGRAM

Health reforms in Guatemala mandated by the 1996 Peace Accords have resulted in a reorganization of health care through the Sistema Integral de Atención en Salud (SIAS) (the comprehensive health care system). An important part of this neoliberal health reform is contracting with NGOs for the financing and delivery of health services. This was part of a model of decentralization and increased civil participation defined in the peace accords, but was also influenced by the World Bank and International Monetary Fund policy of structural adjustment, which involved restrictions on government providing and paying for health services (Maupin 2009; Chary and Rohloff 2015).

One aspect of this reorganization was to integrate the *comadronas* into the health care system through midwifery training programs in order to decrease maternal and infant mortality rates. Jonathan Maupin has analyzed these programs in his excellent study of the SIAS health care reforms (2008, 2009). He analyzed the effect of the reforms on midwifery practice and identity in San Martín Jilotepeque in the Department of Chimaltenango. He did not evaluate or critique the training program, but showed how it is redefining the role, practice, and authority of the midwife through a different model of recruitment and relationship to the biomedical system.

Young midwives are elected by the community to attend the midwifery training program instead of being recruited through the traditional means of divine calling, apprenticeship, inheritance, or assisting successfully in a birthing emergency. These new young recruits in turn accept biomedical practices and denigrate those of the traditional midwives. In addition, a different relationship between the midwife and the mother is promoted—one that is more hierarchical and authoritarian and is based on the doctor-patient relationship characteristic of the biomedical model. These new midwives accept their attenuated role, which stresses referral to the health center or hospital for prenatal care, for deliveries that are high-risk or have complications, and for postpartum checkups of the baby. However, as of the time of Maupin's study, hardly any of those recruited in this manner who had gone through the training program had delivered any babies, suggesting that women prefer to use experienced midwives whom they know and trust. The new midwives are under intense pressure to limit their practice, to increase their hospital referrals, and to behave in an authoritarian manner toward the women under their care.

MIDWIVES FOR MIDWIVES

A different type of training program was run by Midwives for Midwives, which, together with the Ixmucane Birth Center, operated in Antigua from 1997 to 2005. Perhaps the most distinguishing characteristic of this program, in contrast to the government and Safe Motherhood programs, was its respect for the midwives and for the roles they play in their communities (Houston 2000). "We weave together Guatemalan traditional values, professional midwifery modeling in knowledge acquisition and skills competency, biomedical intervention when appropriate, and respect for women's rights" (Foster et al. 2014:26).

The project started as a women's health and birth center. Local midwives brought women there, and the staff—non-Guatemalan certified nurse-midwives and certified professional midwives—worked with local midwives and encouraged them to remain and to participate in their clients' care, to share information, and work as a team: "Ixmucane provided an environment not only for a respectful interface and exchange of ideas but also for hands-on skills practice for the traditional midwives" (31). The result was a place where accommodation and coexistence of science and nonharmful traditional practices was possible (32).

However, due in part to the difficulty of staffing the clinic, the emphasis of the program gradually shifted toward training the *co-madronas*. In-depth interviews were conducted with more than two hundred traditional midwives concerning their knowledge, how they became midwives, and how they acquired their skills. The staff found that "there were many areas where traditional midwives did not have the knowledge and skills important for promotion and care of normal pregnancy and birth" (Foster et al. 2014:35). As a result of listening to and observing the midwives, Midwives for Midwives developed "a training curriculum weaving together scientific evidence, practical skills, and nonharmful traditional methods with nonharmful technological methods" (36). A unique aspect of the training was the midwives' respect for each other's work.

According to Jennifer Foster and colleagues (2004:222), adult learning principles and the traditional midwives' knowledge formed the basis of the training program. The twenty-seven-week, one-day-per-week, program eventually was carried out in six different departments. The Sololá group also participated in ten clinical sessions in the Sololá hospital, collaborating with hospital staff and supervised by Midwives for Midwives' training team. Although they had the support of the Guatemalan Ministry of Health and the administrator of the hospital, the program's professional midwives and the traditional midwives met with daily opposition and resistance from both doctors and nurses (Foster et al. 2014:44). Nevertheless, the *comadronas* did experience supervised clinical practice within the hospital. Unfortunately, with the shift in WHO policy away from training traditional midwives, the program was unable to get continued funding and closed in 2005. However, Midwives for Midwives is currently planning on restarting their program in a new clinic in Chimaltenango (Jennifer Houston, personal communication, September 2015).

ASOCIACIÓN DE COMADRONAS DE AREA MAM (ACAM)

Several of the *comadronas* from Concepción Chiquirichapa, a town near Quetzaltenango, organized themselves at the end of the civil war for mutual support, to improve their education, and to preserve their Mayan medicine and childbirth practices (ACAM 2014; Christiani 2011; Proechel 2005).[2] In 2000, the Asociación de Comadronas de Area Mam (ACAM) was officially recognized as an organization within Guatemala. With the assistance of a married couple who returned in 1999 after fleeing to the United States due to the violence, together with a midwife from the United States, Judy Luce, who was working with them in Concepción Chiquirichapa, they were able to raise enough money to buy some land and build a health center. In June 2004, they opened the Casa Maternal de Nacimiento y la Comienza de Esperanza in Concepción Chiquirichapa. These midwives have attended the government's midwifery training courses, have received their licenses, and attend the monthly review sessions. One of the novel aspects of their program is that they are training younger people to become midwives through an apprenticeship with older, experienced midwives. To varying degrees, Guatemalan midwives have incorporated elements and techniques of biomedicine, such as fetoscopes, latex gloves, vaginal exams, commercial pregnancy tests, and oxytocin injections, into their existing indigenous methods of delivering care, which include massage, external versions, use of medicinal herbs, and the sweat bath.

The birth center is staffed and run by the midwives of ACAM, who rotate their working hours so at least two midwives are always there, including at night. They give prenatal exams, attend births, provide postpartum care, thus providing continuity of care. Families of the mothers accompany them on prenatal visits and are allowed to be present and stay overnight if necessary at the time of a birth. As Christiani (2011) states, "At ACAM, the midwives care for the entire family. When a mother labors over the course of the night at ACAM, the midwives drag out mattresses to the waiting room and make atole and warm tamales for the family." This is a stark difference from most hospital deliveries, where relatives and midwives are not allowed to come in and must wait outside the hospital.

When women can receive care and deliver with *comadronas* at a maternity center, objections about unsanitary conditions in poor rural homes can no longer be an excuse for hospital delivery. *Comadronas* will refer cases with complications, such as hemorrhaging or a retained placenta, to the hospital. The ACAM center is unique and represents both a compromise and a solution. Birth does not occur in either the home or the hospital, but in a place in which the midwives are in control and are operating within certain constraints set by the state, integrating elements from biomedicine and the Mayan birthing system on their own terms.

CURRENT SITUATION

WHO currently emphasizes the use of skilled attendants, claiming that training TBAs has failed to lower the maternal mortality rate, and thus no longer deserves support. WHO does not consider *comadronas* or traditional midwives, who are not formally or biomedically trained, to meet the definition of skilled birth attendants (WHO 2004:1). With this shift, traditional midwives are considered not only unfit or unable to handle birth complications and emergencies, but insufficiently skilled to "manage normal deliveries and diagnose, manage, and refer obstetric complications" (Kruske 2004:308). This statement ignores factors such as poverty and insufficient access to health services, which also play a role in maternal and infant mortality (Cosminsky 2012).

The current emphasis in WHO is to replace TBAs rather than train them or incorporate them into the biomedical system. The implication is that traditional midwives have no skills, rather than that they have valuable skills that are different from biomedical ones.

In 2008, President Álvaro Colom announced an initiative to train fifteen thousand lay midwives. He explained that this five-month program would "provide midwives with training in the basics of gynecology and obstetrics, including how to identify complicated pregnancies and avoid preventable deaths" (MSNBC 2008). Thus, in spite of WHO's policy of not training midwives anymore, the Guatemalan government recognizes their importance and the necessity of continuing to train them. As Jennifer Lang and Elizabeth Elkin write, "No other person has a more direct and profound impact on the well-being of the childbearing woman, her infant, and the rest of her family" (Lang and Elkin 1997:31). The type of midwife training advocated by the government, however, seems to stress referral to the hospital for an increasing list of what are considered high-risk pregnancies and obstetrical emergencies.

Today, a plethora of midwifery programs exist in Guatemala. These are run and financed by a variety of NGOs, international development agencies, religious missions, and universities. They range from one-day programs specializing in specific topics, such as postpartum hemorrhage, the number one cause of maternal deaths in Guatemala (Garcia 2013; Garcia, Morrison, and Savrin 2012) to a complete sixteen-week curriculum covering the whole birth process from prenatal to post-natal (Oliveira 2015).

A one-day program was carried out by nurses and nurse-midwives from the United States working with the NGO Refuge International, which runs a health clinic in Sarstun, a remote village in the eastern central part of Izabal, Guatemala. The curriculum was based on the Home Based Life Saving Skills program developed by the American College of Nurse-Midwives, combined with teaching methods from Paulo Freire's theory of popular education. The teaching emphasized cultural sensitivity in an oral format, and the course was delivered in Kekchi, the local Mayan language. The project included pretest and posttest evaluations.

Another one-day program, carried out by Timmy's Medical Program in the Department of Sololá, worked with the organization Pop Wuj and focused on infant asphyxiation and on training *comadronas* on neonatal resuscitation techniques using the Helping Babies Breathe model. The goal of the project was "to cultivate collaboration between traditional rural Maya healing and modern, urban medicine" (Aue 2014). The local doctor trained the nurses and assigned staff to the health centers in the region, and they would train the midwives in the area. The sessions began with an open dialogue in which the midwives told about their experiences with complications. The midwives participated in group discussions with facilitators fluent in the local Mayan languages, and they practiced the techniques on models. A review and evaluation of the training were to be held a month later, and midwives who were successful would receive the resuscitation equipment (Aue 2014).

The Safe Motherhood Project, which started in 2003, is a member project of Rose Charities Canada. This is not the same project as WHO's Safe Motherhood Initiative. A group of Canadian health care workers, including a registered maternity nurse, an obstetrician, and a registered nurse with the International Red Cross, volunteer to go to Guatemala and train *comadronas* in emergency birthing skills in a four-day course. They have returned to teach a more advanced course to some of the graduates so they can become teachers themselves. They have since gone back to Guatemala and taught the course in San Andrés, Nahualá, and other towns.

Saving Mothers, another NGO, has established the School of

POWHER (Providing Outreach in Women's Health and Educational Resources), which carried out a sixteen-week training program for local midwives in Santiago Atitlán (Saving Mothers 2015). They use a curriculum developed by two nurse-midwives based in New York and adapted to be culturally appropriate to the Mayan culture. The course also included clinical hours in the Sololá hospital, where the midwives got hands-on experience. At the end of the course, the midwives received a birthing kit that included a blood pressure cuff, stethoscope, headlamps, measuring tape, and scissors, among other items. Jessica Oliveira, the Guatemalan Project Director for Saving Mothers, said some *comadronas* were also trained to use fetal dopplers and received them at the end of the course (personal communication, 2015). Siriaca and the other midwives in the Department of Retalhuleu whom I met were never given any of the above items, except scissors; nor were they trained in their usage. The course will be carried out in 2016 in another part of the country (Saving Mothers 2015).

The NGO Médicos Descalzos Chinique (Chinique Barefoot Doctors), with support from the Canada Fund for Local Initiatives, has carried out participatory research on gynecological and obstetric problems from the viewpoint and traditional nosology of the midwives, and manages a program aimed at strengthening coordination between the public health system and midwives in the Quiché area. They have also had support from the NGO Solidarität mit Lateinamerika of Austria. The research has resulted in the 2013 publication of a manual titled *Con comadronas: Conocimiento tradicional de las comadronas sobre salud reproductiva* (With Midwives: Traditional Knowledge of Midwives about Reproductive Health). The manual has been distributed to midwives and health services as a complementary educational tool for use in the training activities of midwives. The midwives of Chinique had been meeting monthly since 1994, but have extended their organization to include a group of midwives from several municipalities of the Department of El Quiché, forming the Departmental Council of Traditional Midwives of Quiché, which includes twelve different municipalities. One of their aims is to improve dialogue, coordination, and negotiation with the health services and authorities (Médicos Descalzos Chinique 2013, 2015).

Midwives have also organized in other parts of the country. ACOTCHI is the Asociación Civil de Comadronas Traditionales de Chimaltenango (Association of Traditional Midwives of Chimaltenango) and was founded in 2004. In addition to promoting training and defending the rights of the midwives, it also held Spanish reading and writing classes weekly for affiliated midwives. However, this group seems to have been inactive in recent years.

Another organization formed by midwives is Cooperativa K'exeloma, a cooperative in the western highlands with a hundred members who gather monthly for educational sessions and now have a new clinic. The impetus for organizing was in large part the midwives' reaction to the negative and discriminatory manner in which they had long been treated by the clinic biomedical staff. They have been able to gain support and garner resources from various NGOs and private biomedical practitioners (King, Chary, and Rohloff 2015).

These are just a few of the programs that are being carried out in Guatemala. Many NGOs, both Guatemalan and foreign, have midwifery training programs, some delivered via short-term medical missions, usually from the United States, others longer term or permanent. Even those organizations that are centered or based in Guatemala have some relationship with an organization or university in the United States, Canada, or a European country on which they depend for funding or personnel or both. This raises the question of the sustainability of these programs. In addition, there seems to be little or no communication or sharing of information among these programs and organizations—or even awareness of one another. Parts of programs that have been shown to be effective in increasing the midwives' referrals—such as training biomedical hospital personnel to have more understanding and respect for the midwife, her patients, and their culture, or allowing the midwife play some role within the hospital or at least accompany the woman she is referring—are not carried out in programs in other parts of the country. Thus programs must keep reinventing the wheel, and they are less able to achieve the outcomes of reduced maternal and infant morbidity and mortality.

Nicole Berry (2014) has recently critiqued short-term medical missions in the area of Sololá. Many of these missions depend on volunteers. She found that conflicts may exist between the volunteers and the NGO hosts, who maintain long-term residence, concerning obligations, what they consider helpful, and the aims of the mission. These volunteers may be students or they may be medical personnel, such as doctors, nurses, or certified midwives from outside Guatemala, especially from the United States or Europe.

The information in the training programs is presented as authoritative and scientific. However, sometimes it reflects outdated medicine that has been replaced by more recent information and evidence. There is a time lag in the provision of training, so outdated medicine is taught as modern medicine (Greenberg 1982). An example of this is the insistence that midwives use the horizontal or supine position in delivery instead of a vertical, squatting, kneeling, or semireclining position, which uses gravity to help the baby descend and emerge. In the United States a semireclining position is often used now. María let women use whichever position they felt best able to push in, whereas Siriaca tells women they have to lie down because she was instructed to do so in the training course and review sessions.

María had been taught to use alcohol, merthiolate, talcum powder, and *licopodio* on the umbilicus to disinfect and dry it after she cut the cord. Because she believed that cauterizing the cord with a candle was also beneficial on the basis of evidence that this left a smaller umbilicus that did not become infected, she adapted her practice by being flexible and combining the two approaches. Cauterizing the cord leaves it sterile and thus prevents neonatal tetanus. Siriaca continues to cauterize the cord for the same reasons. WHO said that putting anything on the cord is harmful, and the midwives are now told not to cauterize the cord or put anything on it. In their evaluation of midwifery care Noreen Goldman and Dana Glei (2003) categorize as harmful the application of any substance to the cord, even though the specific items they use were those they were taught to use in earlier courses. WHO now reports that dusting powders formulated with talc, starch, or zinc oxide have been shown to promote healing of the stump (World Health Organization 1998); this is a practice they had condemned after previously promoting it. Thus María's and Siriaca's synthesis of Mayan-derived and biomedical practices is beneficial, even though biomedicine had previously condemned their approach as harmful.

Various studies, including Cosminsky (1977b) and Goldman and Glei (2003), have attempted to classify practices as beneficial, harmful, neutral, or unknown. Goldman and Glei state:

> The assessments were based on scientific evidence of the potential effects of these practices as well as their appropriateness given midwives' training and the circumstances under which they practice in rural Guatemala. . . . Our measure does not reflect the potential social and psychological benefits associated with some of the pro-

cedures used by midwives. More generally, our measure gives considerably less weight to traditional as compared with biomedical practices. (2003:690)

Such classifications are problematic. Goldman and Glei were unable to classify some procedures because of the lack of scientific data regarding the practices. For example, there is inconclusive or insufficient information in the scientific literature regarding the potential benefits or harm associated with specific herbal remedies, massage, the sweat bath, and binding the woman's stomach after delivery. Yet each one of these practices has been or is presently condemned by biomedical personnel in the training courses in spite of the lack of scientific data— and these are all practices associated with Mayan or traditional births.

Some practices, such as prayer, rituals, and massage, may allay the woman's anxiety and thus be beneficial. However, these practices are usually classified as neutral or are ignored because the effects may be considered psychological and thus difficult to measure. Another problem with such classifications is that as new scientific evidence emerges the classification changes, as in the case of delivery position and using dusting powders on the umbilicus. There is often a time lag with regard to what is taught as scientific or modern, and in the process of medicalization, sometimes biomedical practices that are outdated and have been superseded by more recent evidence are encouraged or even imposed (see Jordan 1993:185).

The United Nations' Millennium Development Goals of reducing maternal and infant mortality are supposedly based on a human rights approach, especially from the perspective that women's rights are human rights and that humans have a universal right to health. However, implementation of projects to meet those goals assumes that the enactment of laws and regulations, along with training programs that can make childbirth safer, are culture-free and can be applied universally. In the process, projects may actually violate some women's human rights, and the practices may not be safer (Berry 2010). For example, a mother and midwife may be penalized for not having an emergency plan if there is a birth complication and they do not go to the hospital, or they might have a plan but be unable to find transportation at the specific time, especially if it is in the middle of the night. The midwife may be legally liable and lose her license in such a case. How is such a policy protecting women's rights, whether those of the mother or those of the *comadrona*? Lynn Morgan and Elizabeth Roberts raise the question of diverse rights claims and conflicts between different actors and the state; these should be considered as issues of reproductive governance (2012).

CONCLUSION

These few examples show that, contrary to the attitude of some medical personnel that it is too difficult to get midwives to change, these training courses do have an impact, and some midwives do change their practices when they perceive that the changes are beneficial to the patients or themselves. These changes reflect increasing voluntary medicalization on the part of the midwives. They are exerting agency, and while they may continue certain practices, such as cauterizing the cord, they deliberately and voluntarily decide to change by either adding or substituting other practices. In other cases they are becoming medicalized through force or threats. That is, if they do something deemed wrong or risky, such as delivering a firstborn baby, they might lose their license.

Innovative programs or aspects of programs that seem to be successful are often discontinued, usually because of lack of funding or shifts in WHO policy, instead of being more widely supported and incorporated into the national programs. Midwives who have attended an innovative training program that uses participatory methods and have received their licenses, may then go to the government's monthly review meetings, which are usually taught didactically and condescendingly. Even though the midwives have been allowed to accompany their referrals into the hospitals in Quetzaltenango and Sololá, to this date a midwife bringing or referring a woman to the hospital in Retalhuleu is not allowed in. In fact, she and the patient both might be scolded for attempting a home delivery. In one case, a patient was scolded for consulting with and using Siriaca at all, and the doctor told Siriaca, "The time of the midwife has passed."

Chapter 9

MEDICALIZATION THROUGH THE LENS OF CHILDBIRTH

The time of the midwife has passed.

DOCTOR IN HOSPITAL IN RETALHULEU
(SIRIACA, PERSONAL COMMUNICATION, 2013)

Birth on the finca and in Guatemala in general is becoming increasingly biomedicalized. Using the medicalization model proposed by George Lowis and Peter McCaffery (2000), we can see how very intensive and extensive this process has been and continues to be at all levels with regard to the role of the midwife in birth events. The different levels of their model include technology, conceptual, interactional, control, and gender/status aspects of the birthing system and the role of the midwife. I now examine these aspects in more detail, focusing on their impact on María and Siriaca. The various interrelated aspects of biomedicine are integrated, accommodated to, articulated, and resisted or rejected differently by each midwife and at different rates. By comparing the impact on and responses of María and Siriaca, we can gain a greater understanding of the dynamics involved in the process of medicalization and the relationships between the local, the state, and the global levels.

TECHNOLOGY

The use of new technology, especially surgery, is perhaps the primary way in which biomedicine has gained its dominant position worldwide in defining childbirth. Various types of technology used in the birth process include oxytocin injections, sonograms, electronic fetal monitors, antibiotics, anesthesia, analgesics, cord clamps, forceps, and stirrups. Most midwives in Guatemala are denied access to this technology, including even the most basic tools, such as stethoscopes, fetoscopes, and blood pressure meters. Such exclusion may be based on an assumption that these instruments are too complicated for the midwives to use, or they may be a way of symbolizing control of the birth process. Although these tools are not provided in the training programs by the Ministry of Health, a few programs, such as Midwives for Midwives (when it was running) and Saving Mothers' School of POWHER, do instruct the *comadronas* on the use of these tools and provide them in the midwifery kits they give to the midwives who finish the course. Providing the midwives with instruction and the instruments may contribute to safer births, as well as reinforce the authoritative knowledge and status of the midwife.

Recently the prenatal clinics have strongly encouraged the use of ultrasounds, especially in cases where they suspect that the fetus is malpositioned. However, there are no machines in the clinics or health centers; the result is that the mother has to go to a private lab to have an ultrasound that in 2012 in Retalhuleu cost around Q250 ($32), plus transportation costs. Referral for an ultrasound may be an additional source of stress for a pregnant woman, not only because of the cost, but also because failure to undergo the procedure can be anxiety producing. If she does have the ultrasound, her anxiety may be allayed if it comes out well or increased if the results are problematic. A problematic ultrasound usually results in a cesarean delivery.

The use of cesarean surgery is the primary technological way in which obstetrical complications and risks are dealt with in the biomedical system. This means that in many of the cases the midwives refer to the hospital, the babies are delivered by a cesarean section. Although this is one way in which the doctor resolves a number of biomedically labeled risks, for the mothers and midwives the surgery entails its own set of risks, not only physical risks of infection and future medical problems, but also social and psychological risks.

Although Siriaca refers first-time mothers to the hospital for delivery, she does it mainly because of the threat that she will lose her license if she doesn't, not necessarily because she believes the specific birth is risky. In other cases, she has ignored the prenatal clinic's recommendation for a hospital delivery or C-section because her manual examination of the mother when she determined the position of the fetus and the possible due date indicated that the baby's position and condition were fine and that nothing was problematic. She also asked the mother how she felt, and if she felt movement from the baby, she continued to attend the woman and delivered a healthy baby without any problem.

Medicalization also occurs with respect to low-tech or simple technology, as illustrated in the cutting of the umbilical cord and treatment of the umbilicus. Both María and Siriaca cut the cord after the placenta has been expelled. They explain that otherwise the placenta will rise up in the body and choke and kill the woman. The doctor, on the other hand, cuts the cord right away. By 2010 Siriaca had been given clamps and was now cutting the cord even if the placenta had not yet been expelled. However, waiting until the cord stops pulsing before cutting allows the baby to receive more oxygen and iron than clamping and cutting immediately. Kitzinger states that there is no reason the cord has to be cut before the placenta is delivered: "it is separated only for convenience" (1997:351).

The treatment of the cord illustrates both the pluralistic and the syncretic nature of the midwives' practice. María and Siriaca both cauterized the cord with a candle after it was cut so it was left sterile and dry. They then applied alcohol and merthiolate as disinfectants, followed by talcum powder or *licopodio*, as they had been taught in one of the earlier courses. Next they dressed the umbilicus with gauze and tied it with a piece of cloth or a binder. The advantages of cauterization are recognized by the midwives and thus they continue the practice. Yet biomedical personnel constantly condemn it and blame the midwives for refusing to change. Both María and Siriaca said they had been repeatedly told by the doctors and nurses not to cauterize the cord and not to put anything on it, after they had incorporated the practice of applying disinfectant and powder for years as they had been taught earlier by the nurses. Now WHO says that "dusting powders" like talc and zinc oxide are beneficial and promote healing (WHO 1998). The midwives are blamed if they change and blamed if they don't! The nurses don't ask the midwives their reasons for a particular practice, possibly because of their biased assumptions that the *comadronas* are ignorant.

One type of medical technology, injections, is particularly controversial. Midwives' use of injections, especially an oxytocin like Pitocin to speed up labor, illustrates that midwives do incorporate changes from biomedicine, but this is a change that biomedical personnel do not want them to make. The midwives can get Pitocin from the pharmacy, and they know the doctors use it. On some occasions the midwives are responding to pressure from mothers to use Pitocin. According to the health workers, the midwives may give too much of the medication to the woman, and this may cause problems that result from overly strong contractions. On the other hand, injecting oxytocin can be helpful to stop bleeding in cases of severe postpartum hemorrhaging (Klein, Miller, and Thomson (2009:345).

Neither María nor Siriaca said that they gave injections during labor, although they knew of other midwives who did. Siriaca has been trained in a health promoter course to give injections and sometimes gives injections of vitamins or antibiotics when people request them. Usually people obtain the medicines from the pharmacy and ask her to administer them.

Medicalization thus also involves withholding technology from the midwives on the assumption that they do not have the basic knowledge to use the technology properly. Withholding is also a way of maintaining power and control through the possession of authoritative knowledge. For example, both María and Siriaca listened to a baby's heart by placing their ear on the mother's abdomen. In the review session in July 2013, the nurse told the midwives that they should listen to the baby's heart with a stethoscope, seemingly unaware that the midwives didn't have any. When one of the midwives informed her of that, the nurse said she would look into seeing if they could get some and how much it would cost to provide them. However, it is relatively easy to make a simple fetoscope from wood, clay, or a hollow tube of bamboo to listen to the baby's heart (Klein, Miller, and Thomson 2009:139, 445), and they could have done that in one of the review sessions. Lack of access to even basic technology challenges the authority of the midwives, whose practice is characterized by low-tech tools and one-to-one supportive care. In contrast, one of the new training programs, Saving Mothers, has taught the midwives to use blood pressure cuffs and ultrasound fetal dopplers.

One type of recently available technology that has been a big help to midwives with respect to supporting their position—facilitating their work and saving time and energy—is the cell phone. The use of cell phones recently has become widespread on the finca and in surrounding areas. Someone can call Siriaca at any time of the day or night to request her services without having to walk or take transport to her home, and they can give her vital information concerning labor or symptoms. Similarly she can call for a taxi from the *aldea*, where there are now several taxi services, if time is problematic. Cell phones also makes it easier for the midwife to arrange for prenatal and postnatal visits and massages. The cell phone also may make it easier to obtain transportation to the hospital in case of any emergency.

The cell phone can also be used to increase communication between the hospital staff and the midwife so they can give her advice concerning life-saving measures until the mother gets to the hospital. They can tell about interventions that can help stop or reduce postpartum hemorrhage on the way to the hospital. If the woman has signs of going into shock, hospital personnel can recommend to the midwife measures such as having the woman lie with her feet higher than her head, and with her head turned to one side (Klein, Miller, and Thomson 2009:239). To my knowledge, Siriaca and other midwives have not used cell phones for such communication with the hospital, but they could thus be used for both saving lives and for reinforcing the midwife's status and authority.

CONCEPTUAL LEVEL

On the conceptual level, medicalization affects conceptions of time and risk, as well as ideas about the causation and classification of illnesses.

The Concept of Time

One of the major impacts of medicalization is the imposition of a time framework on almost every aspect of the birthing process. It is commonly said that the Maya are obsessed with time (but see Tedlock 1992 for a critique and reinterpretation of the meaning of time among the Maya). However, the modern "Western" culture is much more governed by and concerned with time.[1] Biomedicine uses time frames that it considers normal and, by extension, universal; presumably these are based on statistical and epidemiological studies. Thus medicalization entails imposing a time dimension on many processes that in some cases is affected by cultural values such as efficiency rather than letting nature take its course. In other cases, a length of time may be indicative of potential risk, such as the amount of time after birth required for the placenta to be expelled.

The ways in which time is conceptualized and managed may reveal how power and resistance play out (McCourt 2010:3). Biomedicine assumes that the various time frames that it incorporates and imposes are universal—the same for every woman everywhere—whereas many midwives assume that there is individual variation, often around a general, flexible time frame. Midwives examine each case by considering its particular characteristics separately and within the woman's individual, family, and social context. Nicole Berry also explains that midwives tailor their practices to the characteristics of each individual woman and disagree with health workers who insist "that one can set a time after which you know a baby will not change position in utero" (2010: 216). Aspects of time include the length of pregnancy or the baby's due date, the timing of the process of fetal development, the length of time spent in labor, the time it takes for the cervix to dilate, how long after the birth the placenta is expelled, when breastfeeding is begun, the ideal length of time for exclusive and supplemented breastfeeding, and desirable birth intervals.

One of the major functions of the prenatal exam is to estimate how far along the pregnancy is and to predict the due date of the baby. Both María and Siriaca did this through external examination of the position of the baby—for example, to see whether it had dropped and whether the head had engaged. Sometimes the midwife's estimation will differ from the doctor's. Although the due date may be calculated on the basis of the time since a woman's last menstrual period, many women do not keep track of their periods, and some women have amenorrhea, going from pregnancy to lactation to pregnancy without getting their period.

One young, unmarried mother consulted both Siriaca and the prenatal clinic. The doctor in the clinic said she was only five months pregnant. However, when Siriaca examined her, she said the birth was going to be soon, and eight days later the baby was born. The mother was fortunate to be able to go to the hospital in the finca car at 3:00 a.m. She gave birth in the hospital because it was her first baby, and Siriaca said she was not allowed to attend her. The mother said she should have gotten an ultrasound, which would have supported Siriaca's estimated due date rather than the doctor's, but she couldn't because she didn't have the money.

Delivery is influenced by concepts of time not only with respect to due date, length of labor, and dilation, but also in relation to values of efficiency and convenience that are part of the way biomedicine is often practiced. Thus when Siriaca and a patient arrived at the hospital at 11:00 p.m., they were scolded for coming so late at night because it was an inconvenience for the staff. If the patient had come earlier and was not fully dilated and it was not yet time for the delivery, she would have been scolded for that as well (Smith-Oka 2013a, 2013b). Siriaca gave the time frame of around twelve to fifteen hours of normal labor as a guide for considering that there might be a problem and referring the woman to the hospital. This advice coincides with the recommendation of Klein and her colleagues: "Labor is too long when strong contractions last more than 12 hours for women who have given birth before, or 24 hours for women giving birth for the first time" (Klein, Miller, and Thomson 2009:186). WHO guidelines defined prolonged labor as labor lasting more than twelve hours (Verderese and Turnbull 1975). Medicalization shortens the time before a delivery is considered risky and increases the number of cesareans.

Many labor definitions were set in the 1960s, and what doctors were taught then was incorporated into guidelines regarding normal time in labor that are still in use. One obstetrician who co-wrote the guidelines was asked recently how long labor should take. He said, "There's no clear-cut deadline, and every woman is different. . . . It can run the gamut from six hours long, start to finish, to three and four days" at the other extreme (Neergaard 2014:A6). He also mentioned the difficulty of changing long-term practices among physicians. Ironically, physicians and other biomedical personnel complain that midwives don't want to change.

New recommendations have been published by the American College of Obstetricians and Gynecologists and the Society for Maternal-Fetal Medicine indicating that "contemporary labor progresses at a rate substantially slower than what was historically taught" (Caughey, Cahill, Guise, and Rouse 2014:179) and that current guidelines that may rush labor have been a factor in the overuse of C-sections (Caughey 2011; Barclay 2014). In some places performing a C-section is a way of controlling time—that is, controlling when the baby is born.

Siriaca has been affected more than María was by the concept that the norm for the time of labor is shorter than it may be in an individual case. Both midwives gave herbal teas to help with labor, but neither gave injections like Pitocin to speed it up. However, many midwives do give Pitocin injections, having learned to do so from the nurses and doctors, regardless of the fact that medical personnel constantly tell them not to give the injections. Midwives can get Pitocin from the pharmacy, and in some cases the mothers request it. This is a case in which some midwives have changed their practice and have become more medicalized than medical personnel want them to be.

Time is considered critical with respect to expulsion of the placenta. María said that if the placenta doesn't come within fifteen minutes, the mother should go to the hospital. To help push the placenta out, María had a mother put her braid in her mouth to cause her to gag. The gagging reflex caused the muscle to contract, helping expel the placenta. Siriaca said that the placenta should be expelled within twenty to thirty minutes. If it takes longer, the mother needs to go to the hospital. This is what she learned from the training course and what she practices. In the training session that I observed in 2013 with Siriaca, the nurse said the midwives should massage the mother fifteen minutes after the birth and then five minutes each half hour to facilitate the delivery of the placenta. Meanwhile, she should have the mother go to the hospital.

Breast-feeding is another area where time is contested. Ideas about when to start breast-feeding, how often to feed, for how long to continue breast-feeding, and when to supplement with other foods have changed and are continuing to change. Both María and Siriaca urged their clients to start breast-feeding immediately after the birth and helped them to do so, as they had been taught in the training courses. They explained that the colostrum is good *alimento* (nutritious) for the baby. They accept that the colostrum is healthy, contains vitamins and antibodies, and is good for the baby. Still, some finca women still believe that the colostrum is dirty, so they wait until the new milk comes in, usually within three days. In the meantime they give the baby boiled sugar water, a cloth soaked in anise to suck on, or water with anise in a spoon.

In the 1970s, midwives and mothers were told by doctors and nurses that infants should be fed every three hours instead of on demand, as was the customary practice. Fortunately, María did not accept this impractical, unrealistic, and unscientific medical advice but continued telling her clients to breast-feed their babies on demand. However, in the 2013 training session I observed, the nurse told the midwives that infants should be fed on demand because that is now the accepted scientific advice and is considered healthier for the baby. Ironically, there was no acknowledgement that breast-feeding on demand was and is the customary practice of most rural Guatemalan women.

Today, six months of exclusive breast-feeding is the policy promoted by WHO and the medical profession, and this guidance is passed on to the midwives, who are to pass it on to the mothers they attend. After six months mothers can start complementary feeding with cereals and other foods while continuing to breast-feed until the child is two years old. In actuality, complementary feeding of babies usually occurs much earlier on the finca, as it does in most countries. This policy of six months of exclusive breast-feeding is an aspect of the medicalization of breast-feeding; it is based on epidemiological and clinical research that has shown exclusive breast-feeding to have nutritional and health benefits (Van Esterik 2002). The policy is assumed to have universal applicability without consideration of the possible constraints of the nutritional and health status of the mother (especially in areas such as the *finca*, where many mothers are malnourished), work demands, available help and economic resources which may make exclusive breastfeeding for that long a period difficult.

The Concept of Risk

The discourse of risk is another way that medicalization has permeated birthing. Much of the emphasis on the correct timing at the different stages of labor revolves around the concept of risk. If the medically determined timing differs from that of the mother's or fetus's body then the assumption is that either the mother or the fetus is in danger. In a sense, every pregnancy is at risk and that the health of both the mother and the fetus is at risk. This is a change from the more commonly held medical belief that "some subset of pregnancies had complications that had to be managed, such as obstetric emergencies that required physical intervention" (Dudgeon 2012:19).

Underlying this medical concept of risk is the treatment of pregnancy as a "disease"—a physiological disturbance, abnormality, or pathology that departs from the normal state and thus should come under the purview of the medical system. Furthermore, as Peter Conrad points out, risk itself has become medicalized. "Risk is treated not as some statistical potential for the future, but as a near-disease state. Risk means the potential for disease, but is increasingly treated as if it were an illness in and of itself" (2007:163).

WHO has defined a number of general risk factors in pregnancy. They include personal factors such as the age of the mother (under sixteen or over thirty-five), parity (first birth or having given birth to several children), previous cesarean section, high blood pressure, anemia, and preeclampsia. They also include external factors like traditional practices, such as the midwives' practices of massage and use of the sweat bath, and unpredictable factors, such as prolonged labor, malpresentation, and hemorrhaging.

Pregnancy as understood by María and Siriaca and the finca mothers is a state in which the body is out of balance—it is a hot state until the woman gives birth. Birth is conceived of as social and sacred, not just a physical event. Midwives see birth as dangerous or risky if certain practices are not followed, and these risks may be different from those defined by the biomedical system. In Santa Lucía, one woman told me that "every pregnancy (birth) is an illness which weakens the woman." The concept of risk has shifted from a statistical or epidemiological concept based on probability with either a positive or negative correlation, to a negative understanding of risk as a predictor of danger or harm (Douglas 1990, 1992) that attributes blame or calls for accountability (Dudgeon 2008).

Siriaca has adopted the discourse of risk that she learned during the review sessions, especially in reference to the prohibition against midwives attending *primíparas* because there is a greater chance of some type of birth complication in first births. Similarly, she has given examples of mothers who have had previous cesareans, or whose babies were malpositioned, whom she could not attend because they were considered *alto riesgo* (high-risk). She says "the doctor forbids it." If she did attend such a delivery and there was a complication, she could lose her license, her kit, and the right to practice. There is some confusion as to whether these restrictions are legal ones from the state because they are issued by the Ministry of Health, but some midwives believe that they are the law, rather than just expressions of the doctor's authority. Siriaca's repeated use of the phrases "the doctor forbids it" and "high-risk" to discuss aspects of pregnancy reflects medicalization not only at the conceptual level, but also at the control level. Blame and accountability fall on the midwife, not on the patient, the family, or the doctor, all of whom are contesting for power and control of the mother's and baby's bodies.

In the biomedical system, for the most part, risks are handled technologically. The reason most often given by biomedical personnel for referral to the hospital is that the hospital staff have the technology to discover potential risks, to resolve such risks, and to deal with obstetrical problems and emergencies. Medicalization involves midwives and mothers acknowledging the hospital staff's authoritative knowledge and skills, and being willing to submit to the doctor's, nurses', and other skilled attendants' use of technology and procedures that are considered superior to their own.

Concepts of Illness Causation and Classification

Concepts about the body and illnesses illustrate the sharp differences between biomedicine and the local ethnomedicine. María, Siriaca, and the finca population continue to believe in the basic principles of the ethnomedical system, which includes the birth beliefs and practices. These revolve around the hot-cold principle, or the humoral balance of the body, in which pregnancy is considered a hot state, and after the birth both the mother's body and the newborn are in a cold and vulnerable state. Therefore, during pregnancy, the woman should avoid hot substances, and postnatally she should avoid cold ones. Illnesses are caused by an imbalance of too much heat or too much cold, and treatment is based on restoring the balance. Pharmaceuticals and patent remedies are also classified within this system—for example, Alka-Seltzer is considered cool and is used for a stomachache, which is caused by too much heat in the stomach.

Biomedicine does not subscribe to humoral medicine. The conflict with the basic hot-cold principle that interviewed mothers most frequently mentioned had to do with hospital practices. Woman who had just delivered in the hospital, and were thus in a cold state, had to wash or shower with cold water and eat foods they classified as cold. Occasionally individual medical personnel would refer to a treatment or practice in terms of hot or cold, as when the doctor told Siriaca not to heat her hands before massaging a pregnant woman because it might cause her to have arthritis; this belief was possibly derived from the Ladino folk system. On the other hand, Siriaca was more concerned about the effect of her cold hands on the woman, who was in a hot condition.

The finca population still believe that strong emotions, especially anger, fright, and sadness can cause birth-related problems, including miscarriages, premature labor, and cessation of breast milk production, as well as other conditions, such as *nervios*. These conditions are usually treated by local healers, including the midwives. Because these are related to disrupted social relations, including violence, the biomedical staff treat the symptoms, such as high blood pressure or stomach pains, but do not consider the social and psychological parameters, which are considered to be outside the biomedical system.

María and Siriaca had some notion of the germ theory of biomedicine. They washed their hands with soap before a massage or a birth, and they cut the cord with either a new razor blade or a pair of scissors that, according to Siriaca, had been boiled. However, Siriaca, as María did before her, also cauterizes the cord with a candle after it is cut, which leaves it sterile. Thus when medical staff tell the midwives not to cauterize the cord, they may actually be discouraging a beneficial practice that prevents neonatal tetanus and other infections (Mata 1995:36). Germs are usually conceived of as *animalitos* (little animals) that are killed by boiling. However, due to the poverty of many of the *finca* families, conditions within some of the households are crowded and unsanitary in ways beyond the control of the midwives.

Siriaca still identifies and treats folk diseases, such as the evil eye, fallen fontanelle, fright, anger, *chipez*, and *pujido*. However, someone may go to the clinic or pharmacy for treatment of specific symptoms of these illnesses, such as diarrhea or fever, but also go to the *comadrona* or other healer for treatment of the illness itself and its cause. The ultimate cause or source of the disease may be witchcraft, God, or an imbalance of hot and cold. These are not in the realm of the biomedical system but call for diagnosis and treatment by a traditional healer (Cosminsky 1977c). Medicalization occurs primarily at the immediate causation level, which answers the question of how one got sick, but not at the ultimate causation level, which answers the question of why.

María and Siriaca learned from the medical staff how to recognize conditions such as preeclampsia, eclampsia, anemia, and hemorrhaging, and to refer women with these conditions to the hospital. However, they might differ from the biomedical personnel concerning the causation of the mother's specific case.

INTERACTIONAL LEVEL

The one-to-one relationship between the mother and the midwife, and social relationship with the mother's family, present one of the sharpest differences between the biomedical and the midwifery practice at the interactional level. Doctors and nurses treat women as medical problems, and treat birth with medication and technological intervention. Patient management is devoid of any social or emotional relationship between the doctor or nurse and the family, community, and midwife.

The biomedical model imposes a hierarchical relationship, with the doctor at the top overseeing the nurses, who oversee the patient and the midwife, each having authority over and commanding the ones who are considered below them. The phrase that Siriaca uses, "the doctor forbids it," reflects this hierarchical and authoritarian attitude and relationship. Many of Siriaca's statements that are not as forceful, as when she explains that "the doctor says" she shouldn't use herbs in the postnatal bath, or the water should be "warm not hot," similarly reveal this assumption of the doctor's authoritative knowledge, as well as doctor's and nurses' negative and condescending attitudes toward the midwives.

The medical personnel assume that the midwife has the same type of hierarchical and authoritarian relationship over her client. For example, the nurse giving the training session tells the midwife that she should tell the mother that if the mother does not go to the prenatal clinic, the midwife will not attend her. Many midwives believe they have a divine calling and will be punished by God if they refuse to help someone. Threatening someone is not part of the midwife's repertoire, although she herself may be threatened by the nurses and doctors.

On the other hand both María and Siriaca would employ the phrase "the doctor says" as a way of using the doctor's authority to bolster their own authority in relation to their clients. The relationship between midwife and mother is a horizontal one based on respect for the midwife's position and for her knowledge and ability; the midwife is not granted the total decision-making power over her clients and their families that the doctors and nurses assume she possesses.

The medical hierarchy is embedded in a bureaucracy that reinforces an emphasis on efficiency and technology at all stages of the birth process. Paperwork certification is characteristic of the bureaucracy. This paperwork includes the midwife's license, a medical certificate of a tuberculosis exam, forms that need to be signed by a midwife in order for parents to get a birth certificate, and reporting the births she has attended to the health center. These papers provide numbers or statistics that are used by the Guatemalan National Institute of Statistics in various reports.

According to Vania Smith-Oka (2013a) the role of bureaucracy is a critical factor in the routinization and increasing frequency of cervical examinations in hospitals in Mexico. A new government program, Oportunidades, pays women to deliver in the hospital. However, Smith-Oka says, the hospitals are overwhelmed and can not handle the load, so they hasten births with techniques to speed up dilation and labor, often causing birth to be more painful for the mothers, in order to meet the new requirements for hospital births. She shows how bureaucracy and routine are almost unconscious practices in which clinicians engage to expedite labor and move patients rapidly through the system (2013a:604, 2013b). This conflicts with an idealized norm of patient care. If the same type of program is instituted in Guatemala, the likelihood that similar problems would occur are very strong because for the past several years it has been estimated that hospitals in Guatemala can handle only 20 percent of the births, and no new national hospitals have been built.

The training programs and review sessions in Guatemala are vertically organized, from the top down, with virtually no input or feedback from mothers, midwives, or the communities the midwives serve. They mirror the relationships between biomedical personnel and the midwives and mothers. Medicalization is not only a process in which new concepts of disease and their causation and treatment are communicated, and in which new or different forms of technology are used. Medicalization is also characterized by the bureaucratic organization of the health system, the authoritarian manner in which information is communicated, and the hierarchical and impersonal relationships among biomedical personnel, and between biomedical personnel and the midwives, the patients, and their families. The Midwives for Midwives program in Antigua was an exception. Mutual interaction was built into the design and content of its program, which is now defunct, although there are plans for restarting in 2016 in Chimaltenango (Jennifer Foster, personal communication).

The mother, the family, the midwife also interact with the spirit world. This interaction is enacted through prayer and ritual. María had a divine calling and was guided by the spirits of dead midwives; she lit candles and prayed before going to see a client, and when she returned home, she prayed for a safe birth and for the lives of the mother and child. Siriaca believes that her hands are guided by God. She prays to an image of *el Niño de Atocha* or *el Niño Jesús* before she goes to visit a woman, and she gives thanks to them after a successful delivery.

The hierarchical interaction between biomedical staff and the *comadrona* and her client reflects ethnic and class prejudices and discrimination. The staff of the clinics, health centers, doctor's offices, and hospitals where finca residents are treated are all staffed by Ladinos from higher socioeconomic classes than the patients. Although there are a few Mayan staff in some biomedical facilities, there are none in the facilities serving the finca population. Although not all staff treat the midwives and patients rudely and brusquely, many of them do. They assume that the patients are Mayan or poor or both, and they discriminate accordingly.

CONTROL LEVEL

The issue of control is pervasive throughout the medicalization process, as seen in the hierarchical and bureaucratic organization of medicine. The doctors and nurses control access to knowledge and to instruments and procedures that are used in the birthing process, such as anesthesia, stethoscopes, blood pressure meters, IVs, surgery, and administration of oxytocin. This is not the case everywhere in Guatemala. The midwives of the Asociación de Comadronas de Area Mam, in Concepción Chiquirichapa, have access to and use stethoscopes, blood pressure meters, and oxytocin injections in their maternity center. The Saving Mothers program in Santiago Atitlán trained midwives to use fetal dopplers, as well as blood pressure meters.

Control is manifested in the shift of power from midwives to doctors not only because of the redefinition of birth as risky and dangerous, and the characterization of midwives as unskilled, but also with obstetric control of midwifery by the state and the Ministry of Health. The Ministry of Health increasingly defines what the midwife can and cannot do. The policies being promoted by WHO through USAID and the Guatemalan government aim at eventually displacing or replacing the midwife. This leads to her loss of control of the birthing process, which is being transferred increasingly to the obstetrician and hospital (Lewis and McCaffery 2000:28). We have seen how this process has accelerated: much more authority has been taken from Siriaca than was taken earlier from María.

GENDER/STATUS LEVEL

Gender is starkly highlighted in the medicalization process by the male doctor's increasing dominance over the female midwife and the transferring of authority from the midwife to the doctor and the hospital (Lewis and McCaffery 2000:28). Doctors in Guatemala, especially in the rural areas, are primarily male. Gender is also an issue in the relationship between the doctor and the mother, whose body is being contested and is reduced to a birthing machine in the biomedical system. Emphasis is placed solely on the mother's physicality, without consideration of her social, emotional, spiritual, or cultural dimensions, unless they are considered to be problems or impediments. Interaction between the male doctor and the female patient sharply contrasts with the female-to-female supportive relationship of the midwife to the mother and her female relatives.

Another aspect of the influence of gender is the pervasiveness of patriarchal roles in the relationship between the mother and the father of the child. If the mother and father are living together, he or his parents may decide whether the mother will use a midwife or the hospital. If the midwife suggests that it is necessary to refer the mother to the hospital for some complication, it is often up to the husband or partner to make the decision, a reflection of the *machismo* that pervades Guatemalan culture. Another problem is that the number of young, single *primípara* mothers on the finca is increasing; in some cases the father of the baby has abandoned the mother and refuses to acknowledge patrimony. In these cases, decisions about how the birth is to be managed may be made by her parents. Biomedicine, on the other hand, focuses on the individual patient and assumes that she can make her own decisions. It ignores her social context and her family, whose members may be her support system as well as decision makers about her care.

The low rate of literacy among midwives also reflects the impact of gender relations: in Guatemala literacy rates are lower for women than for men. When a family has limited resources, they usually go toward the health and education of sons first, while the daughters stay at home to help with household chores. Illiteracy has been problematic for the midwifery training programs. Jennifer Foster and her colleagues argue that *machismo* and the devaluation of women contribute to high maternal and infant mortality and morbidity. On the basis of their evaluation of the Midwives for Midwives project, they conclude that "traditional midwives must be able to read and write and that governmental and charitable programs need to include traditional midwives" (Foster et al. 2014:46).

Class and ethnicity also affect medicalization. Doctors and nurses are usually Ladinos from a higher socio-economic class, and they are more educated and usually from a more urban background than María, Siriaca, and other midwives and their clients, who are from rural, poor backgrounds, whether they are Maya or Ladino. Biomedical personnel often speak to midwives and their clients condescendingly, both in the training programs and at health facilities. Midwives and their clients may accept the biomedical information and practices as more modern and beneficial, but the superior and patronizing attitude of biomedical staff can lead midwives and local people to reject the health facilities, their personnel, and the information they present.

Age is another status dimension that is an important factor in medicalization. The midwife training programs and the attitudes and behavior of many medical personnel reflect an underlying ageism. Respect for elders is a strong value in Mayan culture (Carey 2001) and among the finca population. This respect underlies in-laws' and parents' authority to decide where a young pregnant woman will give birth and which midwife she will use. The doctors and nurses, most of whom are Ladino, tend to be more Westernized and to value the individual, youth, and economic achievement. Many of the arguments against training midwives who are already practicing, and in favor of training younger people are based on condescending attitudes toward and negative stereotypes of more senior people. These stereotypes include beliefs that because many of the older *comadronas* are illiterate, they are more difficult to teach, and that they are more entrenched in their ways or tied to their beliefs and practices, and thus are less willing to change. Younger people, on the other hand, have more education, are less tied to the past, and are more willing to follow the authority of biomedical personnel, who have greater status and power and who symbolize modernity. Examples from the work of practicing midwives such as María and Siriaca challenge such assumptions about older midwives' limitations.

RECOMMENDATIONS

In the discussion of training programs and review sessions in chapter 8, I indicated some of the many problems that have reduced the programs' effectiveness. Many of the same problems exist with respect to health facilities and the relations between the biomedical staff and the patients. Unfortunately, many of the same criticisms have been made since the 1970s, with little change (Cosminsky 1977b; Greenberg 1982; Putney and Smith 1989; Berry 2010; Jordan 1993; Hinojosa 2004; Chary 2014; Edvalson et al. 2013; Chomat et al. 2014). Given the present poor state of the Guatemalan health system, midwives will still attend the majority of births, especially in rural and indigenous areas. To stop midwifery training programs is short-sighted. Rather than blame midwives for high infant and maternal mortality rates, as WHO, nurses, and physicians have been prone to do (Cosminsky 2012; Garces et al. 2015), it would be better to improve relations between midwives and biomedical health care providers. In a recent meeting of CARE, the Guatemalan vice minister of health and social assistance, Pablo Ramirez, explained that "the Ministry recognizes the important role that midwives play in rural areas and that any successful government plan to reduce maternal mortality needs to recognize the role of midwives" (CARE 2015). My recommendations toward this end are derived from and influenced by a number of sources, including Chary (2014), Medicos Descalzos Chinique (2013, 2015), Hurtado and Saenz de Tejada (2001), and Hoban (2002).

First and foremost is the matter of respect. Nurses, doctors, and auxiliaries should treat midwives with respect, not scorn or disregard. They should be friendly to them, not scold them or treat them like children. This is especially important when a midwife brings a client to the health center or hospital.

Second, biomedical staff should learn about the midwives' culture, their values, their beliefs and practices concerning birth, and the meaning that pregnancy and birth have for them. When a particular topic is discussed in a training session, the midwives should be asked what they would do in that particular situation so sharing of knowledge and practices is promoted.

Third, hospitals and other health facilities should be more patient-, family-, and midwife-friendly. In her evaluation of the Quetzaltenango training program, Kathleen O'Rourke (1995a) showed that one of the aspects of the program that was most effective in increasing referrals by the midwives was the training of health facility staff about the patients' and midwives' culture. For example, one of the main concerns of new mothers in the hospital is disturbance of the hot-cold balance of their body and its effect on breast milk. For better hygiene as well as restoration of balance to their bodies, women should have warm water to wash and shower, and they should have tortillas, their basic food, rather than bread to eat.

Fourth, midwives should have input into their training. Trainers should ask them which themes and problems they need to learn more about and what they are interested in understanding better. The trainers should ask why midwives maintain certain of their own practices and reject or accept certain biomedical ones. There should be a mutual exchange of information, whether or not the trainers agree with specific beliefs and practices. Trainers should listen to the reasons behind midwives' practices, rather than simply ordering them to discontinue them. The constant barrage of proscriptions results in a negative response and tends to turn the midwives off, rather than helping them to find a way to modify a current practice, if it has been proved harmful, or incorporate new ones.

Fifth, midwives should be given information that adds to, rather than conflicts with what they already know. People are more likely to learn and incorporate new information and practices when they are additive. It is helpful for midwives to learn how to tell if a woman is anemic by examining her eyes, how to take blood pressure with a sphygmomanometer, and how to listen to the baby's heart with a fetoscope or fetal doppler—especially if they are provided with instruments to do so. Rather than just telling a midwife to refer a hemorrhaging patient to the hospital—which may be a death sentence if the hospital is far away—it would be better to teach her measures she can take to stop or lessen the flow while she and her client are on the way to the hospital (Garcia, Morrison, and Savrin 2012; Garcia 2013).

Sixth, if possible, training sessions and consultations should be in the local Mayan language if the midwives do not speak Spanish. If that is not possible, someone who is bilingual should act as a translator and interpreter. Participation, retention of new information, and development of new skills are increased when presentations are in the midwives' primary language.

Seventh, teaching needs to be participatory rather than didactic (Foster et al. 2004; Jordan 1993; Garcia, Morrison, and Savrin 2012; Oliveira, personal communication, 2015). In her classic study of Yucatecan Maya midwives, Brigitte Jordan (1993) stressed the need for trainers to use apprenticeship-type methods that are experiential, rather than more formal ones based on lectures. Although the latter still tend to dominate training sessions, some trainers are using models and mannequins; more frequent use of them would be beneficial. Most of the programs discussed in chapter 8 incorporate a variety of teaching methods and strategies that are more appropriate for adults and for illiterate participants. Rather than sitting on benches in rows, participants sit on chairs or at desks in a circle so everyone is looking at each other. This manner of communication is more conducive to sharing and absorbing information. Other appropriate methods include participatory interaction, short lectures, discussions, development of skits, role playing, live-model demonstrations, clinical practice with pregnant clients, hands-on skill labs, and small-group work involving case studies. If parts of the course require writing or reading, midwives who are literate should assist those who aren't.

Eighth, midwives should have guided visits to the prenatal clinic and the hospital, especially the maternity ward. Hospitals should allow the midwife to accompany her client when she refers her, and they should grant her access to her client during labor and delivery.

CONCLUSION

María and Siriaca are pragmatic and eclectic in their perceptions of their roles as midwives. Like other midwives (King, Chary, and Rohloff 2015), they are eager to learn and improve their practice. However, they weigh the concepts and practices they learn about against their own experiences and knowledge. They choose from the alternatives available in the pluralistic world in which they practice according to what they believe is in the best interests of the mother and baby.

In certain cases, options in birth practice are becoming more and more limited; midwives' roles are becoming attenuated as the process of medicalization is backed by the state and becomes increasingly political. Some of the proscriptions that are presented as scientific or evidence-based in midwifery training and review sessions are not necessarily so. Instead, they exist to maintain the authoritative position of the doctor and nurse. The government enforces that authority by threatening midwives with loss of their license or even imprisonment. Biomedical personnel enforce it by scolding and humiliating midwives in front of their clients or in front of other midwives during review sessions.

Although on an individual level, both midwives and mothers articulate, synthesize, and integrate practices and beliefs from the different systems, no official attempt is made to integrate the midwives into the biomedical system. Attenuation of the midwives' role can be viewed as a process of demedicalization—that is, removing or limiting those areas of the midwives' role that are considered physical, including attending the birth, while leaving in place its social, ritual, and sacred aspects.

Lock and Nguyen argue that "medicalization desocializes illness and further 'depoliticizes' what are fundamentally political questions revolving around the distribution of wealth and social justice" (2010:71). Although that is true, I argue that birth has also become politicized, and politics have become medicalized by international bodies such as WHO and USAID. Consequently the results of poverty and discrimination are ignored as possible determinants of maternal and infant mortality and morbidity. Instead, reproductive problems are believed to be amenable to resolution by the replacement of midwives and the local birthing system with medicine and medical personnel. Related to the "desocialization" of illness that is a consequence of medicalization is what Conrad calls the "individualization of social problems." He explains: "The general mode is to solve the problem in the individual, not the society," and to treat "complex societal problems with technological fixes. . . . Medicalization reinforces the individualized approaches to social problems" (2007:152–153).

One of the aims of this monograph is to show that midwives are eager to learn to improve their practice and are capable of change. It also seeks to show that when midwives maintain their practices, there are often valid, logical health reasons that are backed by recent scientific evidence. This is the case with cauterizing the cord, giving prenatal and postnatal massages, employing a vertical birth position, and delaying the cutting of the cord. On the other hand, some of the biomedical practices used in Guatemala are outdated and, according to the most current findings, need to change. Although it can be claimed that María and Siriaca are unusual practitioners, I would argue that they are representative of many of the Guatemalan midwives I have met and about whom others have written (see Rogoff 2011; Berry 2010; and Carey 2006). Nora King and her colleagues present a more positive argument about the role that NGOs and privatization play. They show that some midwives are able to leverage resources from NGOs to enhance both their own biomedical knowledge and medical facilities within their community, while maintaining their authoritative role and traditional local practices (King, Chary, and Rohloff 2015).

In 2001 I wrote that the training program run by Midwives for Midwives, which was based on a working philosophy of mutual respect and cooperation between professional, mostly North American midwives and lay Guatemalan midwives, gave rise to some optimism concerning the future of midwifery in Guatemala. On the other hand, the increasing governmental restrictions on midwives fostered a more pessimistic view. Because the Midwives for Midwives program was ended in 2005 due to lack of funding, and the current WHO strategy is to gradually eliminate lay or traditional midwives, I am more pessimistic about the future of midwifery and women's reproductive health in Guatemala. However, the Guatemalan government is still supporting training courses for both old and new midwives, primarily through a proliferation of NGOs and development agencies, and it seems to realize they are necessary because of the lack of medically trained personnel and medical resources, including hospitals, and because of the important role they play in maternal and child health. Unfortunately, the underlying problems of poverty, resource maldistribution, and discrimination are not being adequately addressed. Under these conditions, midwives continue to provide a critical resource for the people of Guatemala. Consequently, I have a small amount of optimism that the time of midwives has not passed. Hopefully their knowledge and practices will not be completely lost, and they will be increasingly incorporated as respected practitioners into a more pluralistic and holistic reproductive health system.

MEDICINAL PLANTS AND REMEDIES
MENTIONED BY MIDWIVES

Herbal remedies are one of the midwives' main areas of authoritative knowledge and expertise. Their usage is also constantly condemned by biomedical
personnel and in the various training programs for the midwives. Much of
this knowledge is not being passed on partly because of the negative pressure.
Negative attitudes are also communicated to younger people in the prenatal
clinics and to those who are being trained as health promoters and new midwives in various NGO and WHO programs.

Several of these plants have been analyzed and found to produce the effects that they are used for (Browner and Ortiz de Montellano 1986; Ortiz
de Montellano and Browner 1985; Lozoya and Lozoya 1982; Caceres 1996).
Ironically, the use of some of these herbs is condemned precisely because they
are so effective. The assumption is that the midwife may overprescribe and
cause injury to the fetus or the mother. However, when used in the proper
amounts as specified by the midwives, these herbs can be very helpful.

The plants are presented according to the manner of preparation specified
by the informants, as well as the part of the plant used, if specified. In many
cases, plants are used according to the humoral theory with the goal of restoring a hot-cold balance. In other cases, they may be used according to a tan-
gible attribute or according to the "doctrine of signatures" of like produces
like—for example, a plant containing a white, milk-like liquid is used as a ga-
lactagogue to increase the production of breast milk. The number of leaves,
the amount of medicine administered, or the number of times a medicine is
taken is often linked to numbers considered significant in Mayan culture and
Catholic religion, such as three and nine.[1]

In contrast to how they are combined in many herbal remedies, in pharmacological investigations plants are analyzed separately. However, combi-
nations of plants may have synergistic, additive, potentiating, and antagonis-
tic effects that may accrue when different constituents interact (Etkin 1986:4);
they may diminish the toxicity of individual constituents or neutralize activities. These effects may not occur when a plant is analyzed separately.

Lorin Nevling of the Field Museum of Chicago identified specimens I collected. Specimens that remained unidentified are left as such, as are plants for
which no specimen was collected. In such cases, the common name in Spanish

or English is used without the scientific nomenclature. In a few cases, I have noted identifications made by others.

This is not meant to be a complete list of medicinal plants or herbal remedies used by the midwives. Rather, the list includes those that were mentioned in the course of interviews or visits to midwives' clients. Also, it does not include the various remedies that were mentioned by other people on the finca. Some of these remedies were published in Cosminsky (1982b).

The remedies are presented below according to their usage. Initials indicate the source. MC refers to María de la Cruz, S to Siriaca, and SLU to a midwife from Santa Lucía Utatlán. In some cases the instructions are addressed to the midwife. In other cases they are addressed to the woman using the remedy.

EMMENAGOGUES

For *detención* (delayed menstruation). Some of these may also be abortifacients.

Massage the abdominal area and then have the woman drink a tea of boiled *salvia santa* (*Lippia dulcis*) leaves with oregano,[2] white honey, rum, and *esencia maravillosa* for nine days, after which the woman should get her period. (MC)

A variation was massaging the woman, then having her drink a tea from boiling three sprigs of *salvia santa*, oregano, and white honey; this should be drunk three times when the moon is full. (MC)

Tea made from boiling three sprigs of *artemisa* (*Artemisia mexicana*). (SLU)

Tea made from mustard leaves (*Brassica nigra*), pink honey from the pharmacy, and the root of *escorcionera* (*Eryngium carlinae*). (SLU)

Tea made from nine flowers of *sanguinaria* or *botoncillo* (bloodwort; *Gomphrena dispersa*) for nine days. (MC)

PREGNANCY PREVENTION; BIRTH CONTROL

Mash an avocado pit, boil it, and drink the water for three days during a woman's period. On the third day, drink a cup of water. Do this during every menstrual period. (S)

INFERTILITY OR BARRENNESS

Cook a piece of dried umbilical cord with clove, cinnamon, cumin, oregano, *pimienta de castillo*, *balsamito de aire*, two *octavos* of rum, and white honey. Put in a bottle and drink a cup each morning until you finish the bottle. (MC)

Boil *balsamito de aire* with oregano. Put in a bottle and add white honey. Drink before each meal. (MC, S)

Cook three tips of *eneldo* (unidentified) and drink water with a glass of rum (aguardiente), in two parts.[3] (SLU)

PRENATAL CARE

For prenatal pains, bathe in hot water with avocado pit, avocado leaves, and salt to soften the body before birth.[4] (MC)

Variation: if a woman has a lot of pain, but it's not yet time, she should eat avocado. Then cut out three or four avocado pits, boil them, add a little salt, and bathe from the heart downward. (MC)

Bathe in hot water with avocado leaves and salt. Drink boiled water with ten drops of *esencia maravillosa* for prenatal pains. (SLU, MC)

Bathe with avocado leaves and boiled *hierba del cáncer*[5] for swollen feet and legs. (S)

To prevent a miscarriage, first raise the uterus by massage from the tip of the toes upward, then apply a plaster made of egg white, mashed rue leaves (*Ruta chalepensis*), *pimienta gorda*, and rum in a cloth on both sides and the back of the abdomen. (MC)

Siriaca used the same remedy but also gave a drink of coconut water, wasp's nest, *cogollo* (heart or shoot) of a *huisquil* (chayote squash; *Sechium edule*), and a shoot of *cordoncillo* (*Piper auritum*) for pains, for hemorrhage, and to prevent miscarriage. (S)

To prevent miscarriage, drink a tea made from leaves of *membrillo* (*Cydonia oblonga*) boiled with shavings from kaolin tablets called *pan del Señor*, which are from the shrine of the black Christ at Esquipulas). Cut upward in the form of a cross, saying three "Our Fathers." (SLU)

For a hemorrhage from a miscarriage, give medicine of *cordoncillo* (*Piper auritum*). Rub it from the tip of the toes up the arms and abdomen to stop the pain. (S)

For anemia, drink a cup of tea of *hierba mora* (*Solanum americanum*) every day. Siriaca says it refreshes the stomach and has vitamin B and iron. (S)

LABOR AND DELIVERY

Tea of boiled *pimpinela* (*Poterium sanguisorba*) with rum (aguardiente) for pain or delayed birth. (SLU)

Tea of clove, cinnamon, and *pimpinela* (*Poterium sanguisorba*) to quicken labor. (MC)

Variation of above: tea of clove, cinnamon, *pimpinela*, oregano, nine leaves of *flor de pascua* (poinsettia; *Euphorbia pulcherrima*), and nine leaves of avocado to soothe birth pains, give strength, and speed up birth. (MC)

If pains are very bad, add twenty drops of *esencia maravillosa* to the above mixture. It will either stop the pains or make them come stronger, and will give the woman strength. (MC)

Tea of the root of *azucena* (*Lilium longiflorum*) for pains or delayed birth. (SLU)

Decoction of *kispar* (*Petiveria alliacea*) to calm pain and for delayed birth. (SLU)

POSTPARTUM CARE

Tea of five boiled sprigs of *artemisa* (*Artemisia mexicana*) for afterbirth pains. (SLU)

Tea of *pimpinela*, (*Poterium sanguisorba*), oregano, and white honey for afterbirth pains. (SLU)

Tea of *artemisa* (*Artemisia mexicana*) with *pimpinela* to stop hemorrhaging. (SLU)

Tea of *ajenjo* (*Artemisia* sp.—probably absinthe) to stop hemorrhages. (S)

For inflammation of the uterus and kidney, bathe with *sanguinaria* (*Gomphrena dispersa*) and *ala de murciélago* (unidentified) before going to bed. (MC)

For hemorrhaging take four leaves of *Santa María*, put a small amount of hot ashes and two or three burning coals in the ashes so they don't get cold, and make like a tamale. Put it in a cloth and put it on the legs, the stomach, the knees, and the heels, and then put on a large sash. (MC)

For *aire* or wind (a cold illness), drink a tea of oregano, cumin, clove, cinnamon, lavender, *pimiento de castillo*, white honey, and *balsamito de aire*. (MC)

Sitz bath (*vaho*) of hot water containing leaves of peach tree (*Prunus persica*), cherry tree (*Prunus capuli*), *espina valudo* (unidentified), *wachulin* (*Lepechinia caulescens*), *lanten* (*Plantago australis*), and half a bottle of milk. Sit over bucket, cover body, and let steam enter from below. (SLU)

To lower and heat the milk in the breasts and calm pains, give bath of hot water with *ciguapate* (*Pluchea odorata*), *siquinai* (*Vernonia* sp.), *guaruma* (*Cecropia peltata*), and *Santa María* (*Piper* sp.) on third and eighth days after the birth. (MC, S)

To increase production of breast milk, heat *alhucema* (lavender), put a cloth in the smoke, and place the cloth on front and back of chest. (MC)

Tea of quequexte (*Xanthosoma robustum*), the veins of which contain a white liquid to increase production of breast milk. (MC and S)

Toast and grind a *zapote* pit. Mix with other spices to form a black substance called *suchela*. Drink in atole to increase breast milk (MC). Some women said it also contained sesame.

Breast abscess from nursing: Boil *manzanilla* (*Matricaria courrantiana*), wet a cloth, and put it on abscess. (MC)

ANGER

In a pot, cook a stalk of onion, a stalk of garlic, some rue, *cogollo* (shoot) of orange, one lime, anise, and three burning coals, and drink it. (MC)

BILIS

Squeeze juice from one sweet orange, one sour orange, and one lemon into half an octavo of *guaro* (rum), add a spoonful of carbonate (from the pharmacy), strain it into a glass, and drink it. Next day, repeat before having coffee. (S)

INFANT CARE

Give a tea made from anise, sugar, onion stalk, and garlic to newborn the first few days until breast milk comes in. Some mothers give a cloth soaked in anise tea to baby to suck on. (MC)

Bathe baby with leaves of mango, avocado, and eucalyptus to prevent rash on head. (MC)

Colic

Give child a tea made of onion stalk, garlic stalk, anise, and ten drops of *esencia maravillosa*. (M)

Mal de ojo *(Evil Eye)*

Wrap nine or eighteen grains of *pimiento chapa*, a leaf of *flor de muerto (Tagetes erecta)*, and a little *ruda* (rue; *Ruta chalepensis*) in a cloth, like a little tamale. Pass the rolled cloth over the child's body in the form of a cross, and throw the *pimiento de chapa* into the fire. If the grains burst and let out a strong odor, the child has evil eye, and the heat from the child has passed into the pepper. Repeat two or three times. (MC, S)

Pujido

Put leaves of the *platanillo* (banana) tree on the mattress and have baby sleep on top of them. Change the leaves every three days. The *pujido* goes away little by little. (MC, S)

Susto *(Fright)*

Tea of *ruda* (rue; *Ruta graveolens*) with *hoja de aire (Bryophyllum pinnatum)*, leaf from an orange tree, onion stalk, and beard of garlic. (MC)

Take the child to the river with some flowers, say the Catholic prayer "Our Father," leave nine flowers of different colors, and call the name of the child for each flower. Tap him three times with a branch, give him three drinks from the river, pass a little jar of river water in front of the child calling his name, and drop the water on the road. Then give the child a tea of rue and *cordial de susto* (from the pharmacy), and spray some on the child. (MC)

OTHER ILLNESSES

Cough

Boil flowers of *bombilia* (*Bougainvillea glabra* Choisy) and *canela* (cinnamon), sweeten with white honey, and drink. (SLU, S)

Cook three pieces of the *cogollo* of flower of *izote* (*Yucca elephantipes*) with egg, *granadillo*, and *panela*. Strain it so it becomes like a cough syrup. (S)

Variation: Tea from cinnamon, *violeta* (*Ageratum conyzoides*), *flores de bombilia* (*Bougainvillea glabra*), three pieces of the heart of *izote* (*Yucca elephantipes*), leaf of *orasus* (*Salvia microphylla*), and white honey. For asthma and bronchitis. (S)

Make a tea from *tomillo* (thyme), cinnamon, and a small eucalyptus leaf, and add white honey. (MC, S)

Make a tea from *tomillo*, three *violeta* flowers (*Ageratum conyzoides*), cinnamon, and bombilia. (S)

Cook nine tendrils of *guisquil* (*Sechium edule*) or chayote with *orasus* (*Salvia microphylla*), and cinnamon. Sweeten, add ten drops of *esencia maravillosa*, and drink. (MC)

Tea of leaves of eucalyptus, *orasus* (*Salvia microphylla*), and three pieces of armadillo shell. (S)

Diarrhea, Stomachache, Worms

Drink a tea of *hierba buena* (*Mentha piperita*) for diarrhea in baby. (MC, S)

Tea of *flor de muerto* (*Tagetes erecta*), *hierba buena*, and garlic for worms to go back into their sack (bitterness makes the worms go back into their sack). (S)

Verbena (*Verbena litoralis*) with Alka-Seltzer for worms and stomach pains. (MC)

Pericón (*Tagetes lucida*): make a tea for stomachache and diarrhea. (S)

Tea from orange leaves, *ruda* (rue; *Ruta graveolens*), beard of garlic, beard of onion, *cola de alacrán* (scorpion's tail), and *esencia maravillosa*.[6] For vomiting, diarrhea, and colic. (MC)

For worms give two *lavados* (enemas) of *hierba buena*, *flor de muerto* (*Tagetes erecta*) and rue (*Ruta graveolens*). Cut up finely, mix with a little *sulfato* (from the pharmacy) and some grains of salt, and mix with water for worms. Then give the baby about six tablespoons. Keep giving the baby this mixture throughout the day. (Schoolteacher)

Fever

Dissolve a piece of tobacco in *guaro* (rum) in a dish, wet a cloth with the mixture, and tie around the head to take out the fever. (MC).

Take some shavings of the bark of the pinyon tree, scorch them, add some pieces of toasted salt, and tie them to the person's feet in place of shoes. It pulls the heat downward. (MC)

Toast a handful of salt, *pimienta de chapa*, and a little olive oil. Rub downward to the feet and to the toes, wrap the ankles, and have the sick person lie down. It will cut the fever. (MC)

Measles, Chicken Pox

Cebada (barley; *Hordeum vulgare*), water, toasted yellow corn, and *mejoral* (acetaminophen) to soothe child with chicken pox and measles. (MC, S, SLU)

Diabetes

Wash the fruit *noni* (*Morinda citrifolia*), soak it in a pitcher of purified water, and mash it into juice. Drink one glass daily for diabetes. (S)

One informant puts the *noni* fruit in a *licuadora* (blender) that her daughter who works in Guatemala City sent her. She strains it, adds purified water, and drinks a glass daily after eating, for gastritis.

Urinary Tract Infection

Give a tea made from a mixture of fourteen herbs that includes fenugreek, seven *negritos*, bark from *palo jiote* (*Bursera simaruba*),[7] bark from *cuajilote*, bark of *pancojuch*, *hoja de pescado*, *palo de la vida*, *flor de azúcar*, *salvia santa*, *ismut*, *violeta*, *hoja de arnica*, and avocado pit or four *coquitos tiernos* (tender or soft), and *flor de volvo*. Drink before each meal and before going to bed for three days. (S)

Drink a tea of *hoja de aire* (*Bryophyllum pinnatum*) with some bark from *cancerina*. (MC)

Make a tea of *chaya*.[8] But you must ask permission first or it will itch or sting: "Buenos días, por favor, Doña Chaya. Dame permiso para cortar para usar por _____ (el nombre de persona)." ("Good day, please, Doña Chaya, give me permission to cut to use for _____," followed by the person's name.) (S)

Descompostura *or* caida de matriz *(Fallen Uterus)*

Drink a tea of oregano, lavender (*alhucema*; *Lavandula vera*), cumin, *salvia santa* (*Lippia dulcis*), cinnamon, *pimienta de castillo*, and *balsamito de aire* with a half bottle of white honey and a quarter of an *octavo* of rum. Drink every morning until the bottle is finished. (MC)

Mix a half ounce of each: *espíritu de anís, agua colonia, espíritu de asares, balsamito de aire, balsamito de pepito, pimienta de castillo*, clove, cinnamon, lavender, cumin, and oregano. Cook and mix with white honey. Drink a cup each morning until the bottle is finished, for eight days. (MC)

COMMON AND SCIENTIFIC NAMES
OF MEDICINAL PLANTS

Appendix II

Common Name			Scientific Name		Use
Spanish	K'iche'	English	Genus/Species	Order	
aguacate	oj	avocado	*Persea americana*	Lauraceae	birth control; prenatal pains
alhucema		lavender	*Lavandula officinalis*	Labiatae	increase production of breast milk
azucena		lily	*Lilium longiflorum*	Liliaceae	calm birth pains; delayed birth
artemisa, ajenjo			*Artemisia mexicana*	Asteraceae	regulate menstruation; afterbirth pains; hemorrhage
bombilia			*Bougainvillea glabra*	Nyctaginaceae	cough
cebada		barley	*Hordeum vulgare*	Gramineae	chicken pox, measles
chaya			*Cnidoscolus chayamansa*	Euphorbiaceae	urinary tract infection
ciguapate			*Pluchea odorata*	Compositae	postnatal herbal bath
cordoncillo			*Piper auritum*	Piperaceae	hemorrhage; prevent miscarriage
eneldo		fennel	*Foeniculum vulgare*	Umbelliferae	infertility
escorcionera			*Eryngium carlinae*	Umbelliferae	delayed menses
flor de muerto		Aztec marigold	*Tagetes erecta*	Compositae	evil eye, worms, diarrhea
flor de pascua		poinsettia	*Euphorbia pulcherrima*	Labiatae	calm birth pains, delayed birth
guaruma			*Cecropia peltata*	Moraceae	postpartum bath

Common name	Indigenous name	English name	Scientific name	Family	Medicinal use
hierba mora	imut		Solanum nigrescens; Solanum americanum	Solanaceae	anemia
hoja de aire			Bryophyllum pinnatum	Crassulaceae	fright
izote			Yucca elephantipes		calm pain; delayed birth
kispar			Petiveria alliacea	Phytolaccaceae	breast abscess
manzanilla		chamomile	Matricaria courrantiana	Compositae	
membrillo			Cydonia oblonga	Rosaceae	prevent miscarriage
mostaza	mostansash	mustard	Brassica nigra	Cruciferae	delayed menses
orasusia	orasus		Salvia microphylla	Labiatae	cough; asthma
oregano		oregano	Oregano vulgare	Labiatae	delayed menses
pericón	iya	sweet marigold	Tagetes lucida	Compositae	diarrhea; stomachache
pimpinela			Poterium sanguisorba	Rosaceae	quicken labor; afterbirth pains; hemorrhage
quequexte			Xanthosoma robustum	Araceae	increase production of breast milk
ruda	rora	rue	Ruta chalapensis	Rutaceae	evil eye; fright; anger
salvia santa		sage	Lippia dulcis	Verbenaceae	delayed menses
sanguinaria		bloodwort	Gomphrena dispersa	Acanthaceae	delayed menses; inflammation of uterus

(continued)

Common Name			Scientific Name		
Spanish	K'iche'	English	Genus/Species	Order	Use
Santa María			Piper sp.	Piperaceae	hemorrhage; postpartum bath
siquinai			Vernonia sp.	Compositae	postpartum bath
tomillo		thyme	Thymus vulgaris	Labiatae	cough
verbena			Verbena litoralis	Verbenaceae	worms; stomachache
violeta			Ageratum conyzoides	Compositae	cough; asthma

NOTES

CHAPTER I

1. *Doña* is a term of respect used to address or refer to a woman. I use the term to introduce Doña María and Doña Siriaca, but for convenience, I use their first names throughout most of the monograph.

2. In previous publications, I used the name Finca San Felipe, a pseudonym. However, the *finquero* has kindly granted permission to use the plantation's real name, Finca San Luis. I continue to use pseudonyms for people to protect their privacy, except in the case of Doña María and Doña Siriaca, who are publicly recognized figures due to their status as *comadronas*.

3. According to the World Health Organization, a skilled attendant is "an accredited health professional—such as a midwife, doctor, or nurse—who has been educated and trained to proficiency in the skills need to manage normal (i.e., uncomplicated) pregnancies, childbirth, and the immediate postnatal period, and in the identification, management, and referral of complications in women and newborns. Traditional birth attendants, who are not formally trained, do not meet the definition of skilled birth attendants" (2004:1).

4. A different model of medicalization is proposed by Kathryn Pauly Morgan (1998), who distinguishes "five dialectically related components" (86): conceptualization through theories and paradigms; macro-institutionalization through social, economic, political, and symbolic structures; micro-institutionalization through direct and mediated doctor-patient relations; micro-institutionalization through the lived subjective experience of personal medicalized self-management, and ordinary lifeworlds.

5. "Hegemony refers to the process by which one class exerts control of the cognitive and intellectual life of society by structural means as opposed to coercive ones. . . . Doctor-patient interactions frequently reinforce hierarchical structures in the larger society by stressing the need for the patient to comply with a social superior's or expert's judgment" (Baer, Singer, and Susser 2003:15). In time, the patient comes to agree with the expert.

6. Elsewhere I have defined *midwife* as a "position that has been socially differentiated as a specialized status by the society. Such a person is regarded as a specialist and a professional in her own eyes and by her own community"

(Cosminsky 1977b). The K'iche' term *iyom* is used for the midwife or *comadrona* in Santa Lucía Utatlán in the highlands.

7. We selected a sample of thirty-five households with at least two children in each, one of whom was under two years of age, for intensive interviewing and observation. The households were selected to represent a range of nutritional and health statuses as measured in previous studies of the finca.

8. We began on market day, analyzing the "market basket" (food brought home). Households were revisited at least three times a week for two-week periods, which is the pay period of a *quincena*, to check on all expenditures during that period. Detailed information was obtained on who buys or procures what, from where, and how (credit, cash, or exchange). All illness episodes and health-seeking behavior were recorded for the same two-week period. Three or four two-week periods were studied: in May and June, the height of the lean season, when cash and corn were scarce; in July and August, when the harvest begins but cash is low; and in October, the peak season, when both corn and cash are relatively plentiful. The October sample consisted of a subsample of twelve households selected from the previous samples. Interviews were held with the administrative personnel of the finca, who kindly allowed us access to the finca records to obtain information about wages (Scrimshaw and Cosminsky 1991:66).

CHAPTER 2

1. The term *finca* encompasses both the plantation and the hacienda polar types proposed by Wolf and Mintz (1957), who classify as haciendas only those plantations that raise crops for local consumption, not for export. In Guatemala the distinction is confusing because many small plantations raise such crops as coffee exclusively for export, while some larger ones raise large amounts of their crops of corn and sugar for internal markets.

2. Regina Wagner has written two detailed and beautifully illustrated books: one on the history of coffee in Guatemala (2001) and one on the history of sugar (2007). Other sources that discuss the history of agriculture and labor, including the place of coffee in Guatemala and its relationship to the Liberal Revolution of 1871, the presidency of General Barrios, increased control by the state, and changes in land ownership and labor include McCreery (1994, 1990); Cambranes (1985); Handy (1984); Whetten (1961); Adams (1970); Bossen (1984); Melville and Melville (1971); Plant (1978, 1995); Carey (2001); and Grandin (2000). However, there have hardly been any studies of life on a coffee population (COVERCO 2003) or sugar plantation (Bossen 1984; Pansini 1977).

3. According to Bossen, "Farms or plantations with more than 45 hectares comprise about 2.1 percent of all farms, but control about 62 percent of the farm land. . . . These plantations are capitalist enterprises, concentrated

in the fertile coastal plains, where 4 percent of the farms control 80 percent of the land" (1984:26). Johnston and Low (1995:8) state that less than 1 percent of all farms take up more than half the agriculturally productive land on which primarily export crops, such as coffee, cotton, bananas, and sugarcane, are grown.

4. The measurements used for land vary depending on the region and local custom. For *caballería*, I am using 1 *caballería* equals 110.7 acres, which is the definition Ascoli uses in his report (1970). Other equivalents of a *caballería* are 111.5 acres, 64 *manzanas*, or 45 hectares (Wagner 2001), 112 acres (McCreery 1994), and 109.8 acres (Melville and Melville 1971). One *manzana* equals 1.73 acres.

5. Guatemala is now the fifth largest sugar producer in the world and is second in terms of exports.

6. For more details on these seasonal differences, see Scrimshaw and Cosminsky 1991.

7. Although I do not have figures on crop production from these *surcos*, according to some informants they were less productive and harder to plant and harvest than the previous *cuerdas* given for *milpa* plots.

8. These greens include *chipilín* (*Crotalaria longirostrata*), *hierba mora* (*Solanum nigrum* and *Solanum americanum*), *kishtan* (*Solanum wendlandii*), *berro* (watercress), *bledo* (wild amaranth), and squash leaves.

9. For mechanized cutting the land needs to be flat and clean of stones, and the cane must be planted in straight lines. It is cut green and does not require burning. The cutting machine is directed by GPS (Wagner 2007:213). According to Wagner, "All these operations are aimed at increasing cutting productivity, streamlining the gathering and transporting of the cane to the mill, rapidly and constantly, so that the raw material does not lose sucrose, the sugar mill is supplied continuously, and milling is uninterrupted. The end result is quality sugar" (213).

Wagner continues: "In other words, renting farms out so as to increase the cultivation of cane requires excellent coordination and efficient supervision of all operations pertaining to the fields and to transportation as mentioned above, so as to reduce wasted time to the minimum as the cane goes from being cut to the mill so as to obtain optimum yield, i.e., pounds of sugar per ton of cut cane" (213).

10. In 1976 María's household was at the mature stage in the domestic cycle and consisted of herself, her husband, three daughters (twenty-six, twenty-three, and ten years old), four sons (twenty-five, seventeen, fifteen, and fourteen years old), one daughter-in-law, one son-in-law, and seven grandchildren. One of the daughters had just had a baby, which María had delivered. In 1978, however, ten people were living in the house. One of the daughters had moved to Finca Buena Vista with her husband and their four children. Another of her daughters had gotten married and moved out. One of her sons, his wife, and

their child had moved to another house on the finca, but one of her other sons had gotten married, and his wife and their child were living with María.

11. María's husband and one son were working at a nearby finca, and each gave her Q6. Her grandson and another son were working at a different finca. The older gave her Q8 and the younger Q6, and another son working at Finca San Luis gave her Q8. (In 1978, Q1 = $1.)

12. Bruce Barrett (1995) offers an excellent discussion of the historical and social context of pesticide use and exposure in Guatemala, including nutritional and health consequences. A later report by Peter Hurst (1999) specifically examines the Safe Use Project in Guatemala, which is supposed to address the criticisms of pesticide use. More recent research is needed to look at the effects of pesticide use.

13. Barbara Rogoff (2011) shows this type of interethnic mixture in the family background of Chona, a midwife in San Pedro la Laguna, who identifies as Mayan but whose ancestry contains some Ladino members.

14. A spiritist is a religious specialist to whom finca residents often turn for diagnosis and treatment of illnesses (Cosminsky and Scrimshaw 1980). Spiritism is derived from a European tradition that spread throughout Latin America. Spiritists follow the teachings of Allan Kardec and consider spiritism to be the "science of the interrelationship between the material world and the espiritus . . . of the invisible world" (Greenfield 2008). A spiritist becomes possessed by a spirit while in trance.

15. At the time these surveys were done, the most widely used system for measuring malnutrition was the Gómez classification system, which was based on weight for age. Third-degree malnutrition is defined as less than 60 percent of standard weight for age, second-degree from 60 to 74 percent, and first-degree from 75 to 90 percent. The most commonly used standard values are those of the fiftieth percentile of the Harvard Standards. UNICEF now uses moderate or severe wasting as a measure of malnutrition, which is now defined as more than two standard deviations below median weight for height of the reference population.

16. Pyelitis is an inflammation of the kidney or urinary tract resulting from chronic or recurrent infections, which may be caused by the presence of a stone or stagnation of urine. Symptoms are smelly urine discharge, diarrhea, vomiting, fever, and bladder irritability. However, on the finca, the term *pielitis* was used to refer to an infection or inflammation in the skin around the penis area in a male child.

CHAPTER 3

1. Brigitte Jordan (1993) reports a similar custom in the Yucatan.

2. Coparenthood, or *compadrazgo*, is the ritual kinship relationship established between a child's parents and godparents at baptism. It entails a re-

lationship of respect with certain rights and obligations both for the other coparents and for the child. Compadrazgo extends networks of support to include people who are not relatives but who become quasi-kin (Mintz and Wolf 1950). Should something happen to the parents, the godparents are supposed to raise the child in the Catholic faith. Although this relationship is a ritual one, financial and emotional obligations are also important to the parents. For example, when Elena needed money for medicine for her sick son, she sold some corn to her *comadre*, who felt obligated to buy it from her to help her, even though she did not need the corn at the time.

María was asked to be godmother not only because of her midwife role, but also because her neighbors perceived her as being economically better off. She used a variety of strategies to extend her resources, including baking and selling bread, and raising and selling pigs.

3. Since 1935 the Guatemala Ministry of Health has had licensing requirements for midwives (Carey 2006:46).

4. The K'iche' term *ajq'ij* has been variously translated as Mayan priest or daykeeper (Carey 2006), diviner, shaman, and shaman priest or daykeeper (Tedlock 1992; using the spelling *ajk'ij*). It refers to a person who uses the 260-day Mayan ritual calendar and the red seeds of the *tz'ite*, has undergone apprenticeship and initiation by an established shaman-priest, has suffered a serious illness, and has had dreams and visions that signify the calling or gift (Tedlock 1992).

5. Burning refers to cauterizing the cord with a candle.

6. Arnfried Kielmann (1970) estimated a 17 percent underregistration of births and 28 percent underregistration of deaths by comparing vital registry records with reproductive histories of the finca women. He had calculated an average of 50.4 births for the years 1960–1970. If we assumed 17 percent underregistration, then the years 1971–1975 would have a 43.2 birth rate. This was approximately the same as the 1975 birth rate for Guatemala as a whole, which was 44 (Center for International Health Information 1996).

7. *Esencia maravillosa* is a liquid concoction sold in the pharmacies. It contains alcohol, aloe, pear, rhubarb, sassafras, chamomile, jaborandi, peach, and water. The accompanying information says it is an antipyretic, diaphoretic, expectorant, antispasmodic, and eupeptic.

CHAPTER 4

1. The doctor may have recommended orange juice because it contains folic acid, which is important in preventing birth defects such as spina bifida. Part of the message was understood (the importance of drinking orange juice), but part of the message was miscommunicated or misunderstood (that not drinking orange juice leads to a risk of birth defects rather than malpresentation).

2. The poor nutritional status of women was confirmed by a World Bank report that found that malnutrition among women in Guatemala had increased from 24 percent in 1995 to 26 percent in 2000. "Under-nutrition among women is of particular concern because of its potential consequences for their babies, including low birth weight and infant mortality" (Marini and Gragnolati 2003:31).

CHAPTER 5

1. For similar spiritual aid and instruction see Rogoff 2011:103–5, citing Paul and Paul 1975:710–11.

2. In their book written specifically for midwives and health promoters in villages around the world, Susan Klein, Suellen Miller, and Fiona Thomson state, "It is usually not good for the mother to lie flat on her back during a normal birth. It can squeeze the vessels that bring blood to the baby and the mother, and can make the birth slower. But if the baby is coming very fast, it is OK for the mother to lie on her back" (2009:200).

3. According to Jo Murphy-Lawless, the earliest description of an episiotomy occurs in Fielding Ould's treatise on midwifery from 1742.

4. According to Gelis, up until the nineteenth century in France, the placenta was seen as the child's "other self," its double (1991:165).

5. This is a sharp contrast with the situation in Costa Rica that Jenkins describes where the medical personnel giving the midwives training courses considered the syringe too difficult for the midwives to use and excluded it from the kit provided for the midwives.

6. This incident also illustrates that some women want family planning services—contrary to popular opinion and contrary to some findings in Mayan communities—but have difficulty obtaining them.

7. I don't have statistical data on the number of C-sections performed at the National Hospital in Retalhuleu.

CHAPTER 6

1. Twenty days is the *tzolkin*, the period of the Mayan ritual calendar that is still used for divinatory and ritual purposes. The ancient Mayan numerical system is based on multiples of twenty, whereas ours is a decimal system based on multiple of ten.

2. Food from CARE (Cooperative for Assistance and Relief Everywhere) was given out by the clinic in San Felipe to pregnant women and women with infants if the mothers had been to prenatal care and if they attended the nutrition and cooking classes held by the clinic.

3. Previously WHO had recommended four months of exclusive breast-feeding.

4. The bag stated that you boil two glasses of water for three or four minutes and mix in two tablespoons of Vitacereal. This differed from the instructions I found online, which say that after mixing the Vitacereal with water, you cook the mixture for fifteen minutes. There is a big difference in the amount of the cereal used in preparing something to be drunk in a glass, in the form of an *atole*, compared to preparing cereal in a bowl.

CHAPTER 7

1. I was fortunate to be invited in 1977 to participate in a consultative group from this task force investigating medicinal plants that might be used for regulating fertility and have potential as contraceptives. The interdisciplinary group included pharmacognosists, anthropologists, physicians, chemists, and botanists, and was chaired by Norman Farnsworth. Although the computer database that he started, NAPRALERT, continues today, there seems to be little interest in scientific research on plants or other natural substances in the field of fertility regulation and contraception; primarily biomedical forms of contraception are promoted.

2. This program was begun at least in part as a result of a recommendation made in a report by Yvonne Taylor that was part of an extensive study done on the finca in 1970 by a group of physicians led by Nevin Scrimshaw (Taylor 1970).

3. She said she was afraid to have the operation because she does not like to be cut. She said she heard that they make you double up your knees and give you a big injection in the buttocks. We explained to her about the minilaparoscopy and told her that she did not have to be pregnant to have the operation. Later that year she had this "button" type of operation done at the hospital in Champerico for ten dollars. She felt weak and dizzy in the morning for some time but then recuperated nicely and went back for tuberculosis treatments.

4. The Peace Accords of 1996 marked the end of the civil war in Guatemala and included several agreements concerning the rights of the indigenous population and regarding the poverty, discrimination, and social inequity that characterize much of Guatemalan society. The reorganization of the health system as the Sistema Integral de Atención en Salud involved extending medical services, including the training of midwives, to the rural and indigenous populations of the country (Berry 2010; Maupin 2008, 2009).

5. This belief that the evil eye is given unintentionally differs from Foster's contention that the heating threat of envy is the cause of the evil eye in Tzintzuntzán (Foster 1994:57–58).

6. Juan José Hurtado (1979) reports that doctors were concerned about cases they saw of palates damaged either from too much pressure exerted by the finger or with tears from the fingernails.

7. I did not have a specimen of *cola de alacrán*. This is the scientific name listed in UNAM (2014).

CHAPTER 8

1. For a critique of the use of referrals and reduction of mortality and morbidity rates as evaluative criteria, see Cosminsky (2012).

2. I had the great pleasure of meeting some of these midwives at an international conference on traditional midwifery in Oaxaca, Mexico, in 2003. At this conference they were not only making a presentation about their Mayan birth system, but also interacting and learning with midwives from many different countries. This was neither their first nor their last such conference. They were eager to learn but also were self-confident about the knowledge they possessed from their own birthing system, together with what they had added and integrated from the biomedical system and various midwifery systems represented at the conference.

CHAPTER 9

1. For an excellent and comprehensive historical analysis of time and birth, see McCourt (2010).

APPENDIX I

1. The numbers three and nine have special significance and appear in many remedies, referring to the number of leaves in the preparation or the number of times or days the remedy is to be taken. Three may symbolize the three hearthstones in the Mayan household. Nine may refer to the nine months of pregnancy. It also may signify the nine layers of the underworld and the corresponding nine lords of the dead, whom the ancient Maya believed to influence the effectiveness of the treatment. The numbers are sacred in the Catholic tradition as well, symbolizing the Trinity, the novena, and the nine-day wake. However, for the most part people are unaware of these possible origins and ancient significance.

2. I did not collect a specimen of oregano. According to Margarita Kay, oregano has been identified as a species of *Lippia*. However, the culinary herb that has the common name oregano in English is identified as *Oreganum vulgare* (1996:183).

3. *Eneldo* is identified as *Foeniculum vulgare* by Caceres (1996:230), and as *Anethum graveolens* by Morton (1981:642).

4. Mam midwives in Concepción Chiquirichapa use a tea from *pimpinela* to heat the body, especially the uterus, during every stage of birth. Often chamomile and *pericón* (*Tagetes lucida*) is added and drunk daily in the

last few weeks of pregnancy to prepare the woman's body for birth. The tea is also used in labor to give the woman strength for pushing and to soften and warm the mother's body to allow the baby to turn more easily and to facilitate delivery. After the birth it warms the uterus, which promotes healing (Proechel 2005:129, 144).

5. I had previously collected specimens of *hierba del cáncer coral* (*Hamelia patens*) and *hierba del cáncer capulla* (*Acalypha arvensis*), but unfortunately Siriaca did not specify which kind of *hierba del cáncer* she used in this remedy.

6. Rosita Arvigo and Michael Balick (1993) identify this plant as *Heliotropium indicum*.

7. Caceres (1996:296).

8. I did not get a specimen for identification. Kunow (2003:117), and Garcia et al. (1999) identify *chaya* as *Cnidoscolus chayamansa* and say it is used for bladder infection. Morton (1981:430) has the same identification and notes that it is a laxative and diuretic.

BIBLIOGRAPHY

ACAM (Asociación de Comadronas de Area Mam). 2014. "History of the Project." www.mayamidwifery.org.

Adams, Richard N. 1970. *Crucifixion by Power: Essays on Guatemalan National Social Structure, 1944–1966.* Austin: University of Texas Press.

Adams, Walter, and John Hawkins, eds. 2007. *Health Care in Maya Guatemala: Confronting Medical Pluralism in a Developing Country.* Norman: University of Oklahoma Press.

Aguilar Girón, José Ignacio. 1966. *Relación de unos aspectos de la flora útil de Guatemala,* 2nd ed. Guatemala: Tipografia Nacional.

Ahearn, Laura. 1999. "Agency." *Journal of Anthropological Linguistics* 9: 12–15.

Ardener, Shirley. 1975. *Perceiving Women.* London: Malaby.

Arms, Suzanne. 1975. *Immaculate Deception.* Boston: Houghton Mifflin.

Arvigo, Rosita and Michael Balick. 1993. *Rainforest Remedies: One Hundred Healing Herbs of Belize.* Twin Lakes, WI: Lotus Press.

Ascoli, Werner. 1970. "The Guatemalan Finca and Finca 'San Luis.'" Paper No. 1 in *Ecological Assessment of the Nutritional Status of a Guatemalan Finca Population.* Unpublished INCAP-MIT study. Department of Nutrition and Food Science, Massachusetts Institute of Technology.

Aue, Ashley. 2014. "Building Futures with Midwives in Rural Guatemala." Timothy Global Health. https://timmyglobalhealth.org/building-futures -with-midwives-in-rural-guatemala/.

Baer, Hans, Merrill Singer, and Ida Susser. 2003. *Medical Anthropology and the World System,* 2nd ed. Westport, CT: Greenwood.

Bailey, Patricia, Jose Szaszdi, and Lucinda Glover. 2002. "Obstetric Complications: Does Training Traditional Birth Attendants Make a Difference?" *Revista Panamerica Salud Publica/Pan American Journal of Public Health* 11:15–23.

Bannerman, Robert, John Burton, and Ch'en Wen-Chieh, eds. 1983. *Traditional Medicine and Health Care Coverage.* Geneva: World Health Organization.

Barclay, L. 2014. "New Guidelines Advise Longer Labor Time to Avoid Cesareans." Medscape. www.medsape.org/viewarticle/821419.

Barrett, Bruce. 1995. "Commentary: Plants, Pesticides, and Production in Guatemala; Nutrition, Health and Nontraditional Agriculture." *Ecology of Food and Nutrition* 33:293–309.

Bartlett, Alfred, and Maria E. Paz de Bocaletti. 1991. "Intrapartum and Neonatal Mortality in a Traditional Indigenous Community in Rural Guatemala." *Acta Paediatrica Scandinavia* 80:288–96.

BBC News. 2006. "Family Planning Row in Guatemala." BBC News, February 2. http://news.bbc.co.uk/2/hi/americas/4673160.stm.

Berry, Nicole. 2005. "Incorporating Cultural Diversity into Health Systems: An Example of Midwives Teaching Midwives." *Women in International Development Forum* 27 (January): 1–9.

———. 2006. "Kaqchikel Midwives, Home Births, and Emergency Obstetric Referrals in Guatemala." *Social Science and Medicine* 62:1958–1969.

———. 2008. "Who's Judging the Quality of Care? Indigenous Maya and the Problem of 'Not Being Attended.'" *Medical Anthropology* 27:164–189.

———. 2009. "Making Pregnancy Safer for Women around the World: The Example of Safe Motherhood and Maternal Death in Guatemala." In *Anthropology and Public Health*, ed. Robert Hahn and Marcia Inhorn, 2nd ed., 422–446. New York: Oxford University Press.

———. 2010. *Unsafe Motherhood: Mayan Maternal Mortality and Subjectivity in Post-War Guatemala.* New York: Berghahn.

———. 2014. "Did We Do Good? NGOs, Conflicts of Interest and the Evaluation of Short-Term Medical Missions in Solola, Guatemala." *Social Science and Medicine* 120: 344–351.

Bossen, Laurel. 1979. "Plantations and Labor Force Discrimination in Guatemala." *Peasant Studies* 8 (3): 31–44.

———. 1984. *The Redivision of Labor: Women and Economic Choice in Four Guatemalan Communities.* Albany: State University of New York Press.

Browner, Carole. 1983. "Male Pregnancy Symptoms in Urban Colombia." *American Ethnologist* 10:494–510.

Browner, Carole, and Bernard Ortiz de Montellano. 1986. "Herbal Emmenagogues Used by Women in Colombia and Mexico." In *Plants in Indigenous Medicine and Diet: Biobehavioral Approaches*, ed. Nina Etkin, 32–47. Bedford Hills, NY: Redgrave.

Browner, Carole, and Carolyn Sargent, eds. 2011. *Reproduction, Globalization, and the State: New Theoretical and Ethnographic Perspectives.* Durham, NC: Duke University Press.

Bryant, Carol, Kathleen DeWalt, Anita Courtney, and Jeffrey Schwartz. 2003. *The Cultural Feast.* Belmont, CA: Wadsworth.

Caceres, Armando. 1996. *Plantas de uso medicinal en Guatemala.* Guatemala City: Editorial Universitaria.

Callister, Lynn Clark, and Rosemarie Vega. 1998. "Giving Birth, Guatemalan Women's Voices." *Journal of Obstetric, Gynecologic, and Neonatal Nursing* 27:289–295.

Cambranes, Julio Castellano. 1985. *Coffee and Peasants in Guatemala: The Origins of the Modern Plantation Economy in Guatemala, 1853–1897.* Stockholm: Institute for Latin American Studies.

CARE. 2015. "Healthy Moms, Healthy Sisters: Global Investments to End Maternal and Child Mortality in Guatemala." Washington, DC: CARE. www.care.org/sites/default/files/documents/Guatemala_Trip_Report_2015_print.pdf.

Carey, David, Jr. 2001. *Our Elders Teach Us: Maya-Kaqchikel Historical Perspectives.* Tuscaloosa: University of Alabama Press.

———. 2006. *Engendering Mayan History.* New York: Routledge.

Caughey, Aaron B. 2011. "Is There an Upper Time Limit for the Management of the Second Stage of Labor?" *Obstetric Anesthesia Digest* 13 (1): 27–39.

Caughey, Aaron, Allison G. Cahill, Jeanne-Marie Guise, Dwight J. Rouse. 2014. "ACOG/SMFM Consensus: Safe Prevention of the Primary Cesarean Delivery." *America Journal of Obstetrics and Gynecology* 210 (3): 179–193.

Center for International Health Statistics. 1996. *Guatemala: Health Statistics Report, 1996.* Arlington, VA: Center for International Health Statistics. http://pdf.usaid.gov/pdf_docs/PNACC635.pdf.

Chary, Anita. 2014. "Improving Midwife Training Programs: Indigenous Lay Midwives' Recommendations from Guatemala." Global Health Hub. www.globalhealthhub.org/2014/05/27/improving-midwife-training-programs-indigenous-lay-midwives-recommendations-guatemala/.

Chary, Anita, Shom Dasgupta, Sarah Messmer, and Peter Rohloff. 2011. "'But One Gets Tired': Breastfeeding, Subjugation, and Empowerment in Rural Guatemala." In *An Anthropology of Mothering*, ed. Michelle Walks and Naomi McPherson, 172–182. Bradford, Ontario, Canada: Demeter.

Chary, Anita, Anne Kraemer Diaz, Brent Henderson, and Peter Rohloff. 2013. "The Changing Role of Indigenous Lay Midwives in Guatemala: New Frameworks for Analysis." *Midwifery* 29:852–858.

Chary, Anita, Sarah Messmer, Erik Sorenson, Nicole Henretty, Shom Dasgupta, and Peter Rohloff. 2013. "The Normalization of Childhood Disease: An Ethnographic Study of Child Malnutrition in Rural Guatemala." *Human Organization* 72 (2): 87–97.

Chary, Anita, and Peter Rohloff. 2015. *Privatization and the New Medical Pluralism: Shifting Healthcare Landscapes in Maya Guatemala.* Lanham, MD: Lexington Books.

Chomat, Anne Marie, Noel Solomon, Gabriela Montenegro, Caitlin Crowley, and Odilia Bermudez. 2014. "Maternal Health and Health-Seeking Behaviors among Indigenous Mam Mothers in Quezaltenango, Guatemala." *Revista Panamericana de Salud Pública* 35 (2): 113–120.

Christiani, Nora Marie. 2011. "'I Have to Carry Them Both.' Negotiating the Global and Local in Mayan Midwifery." BA honors thesis, Wesleyan University, Middletown, CT.

Conrad, Peter. 1979. "Types of Medical Social Control." *Sociology of Health and Illness* 1:1–11.

———. 2007. *The Medicalization of Society*. Baltimore: Johns Hopkins University Press.

Conrad, Peter, and Joseph W. Schneider. 1980. "Looking at Levels of Medicalization: A Comment on Strong's Critique of the Thesis of Medical Imperialism." *Social Science and Medicine* 14A (1): 75–79.

Cosminsky, Sheila. 1972. "Decision Making and Medical Care in a Guatemalan Indian Community." PhD diss., Brandeis University (INCAP T-142).

———. 1975. "Changing Food and Medical Beliefs and Practices in a Guatemalan Community." *The Ecology of Food and Nutrition* 4:183–191.

———. 1976. "The Evil Eye in a Guatemalan Indian Village." In *The Evil Eye*, ed. Clarence Maloney, 163–174. New York: Columbia University Press.

———. 1977a. "Alimento and Fresco: Nutritional Implications for Health Care." *Human Organization* 36:203–207.

———. 1977b. "Childbirth and Midwifery on a Guatemalan Finca." *Medical Anthropology* 1 (3): 69–104.

———. 1977c. "The Impact of Methods on the Analysis of Illness Concepts in a Guatemalan Community." *Social Science and Medicine* 11:325–332.

———. 1982a. "Childbirth and Change: A Guatemalan Case Study." In *Ethnography of Fertility and Birth*, ed. Carol MacCormack, 205–230. New York: Academic Press.

———. 1982b. "Knowledge and Body Concepts of Guatemalan Midwives." In *Anthropology of Human Birth*, ed. Margarita Kay, 233–252. Philadelphia: F. A. Davis.

———. 1987. "Women and Health Care on a Guatemalan Plantation." *Social Science and Medicine* 25:1163–1173.

———. 1994. "All Roads Lead to the Pharmacy: Use of Pharmaceuticals on a Guatemalan Plantation." In *Medicines: Meaning and Contexts*, ed. Nina Etkin and Michael Tan, 103–122. Amsterdam: University of Amsterdam Press.

———. 2001a. "Midwifery across the Generations: A Modernizing Midwife in Guatemala." *Medical Anthropology* 20:345–378.

———. 2001b. "Maya Midwives of Southern Mexico and Guatemala." In *Mesoamerican Healers*, ed. Brad Huber and Alan Sandstrom, 179–210. Austin: University of Texas Press.

————. 2001c. "Midwives and Menstrual Regulation: A Guatemalan Case Study." In *Regulating Menstruation*, ed. Etienne van de Waale and Elisha Renne, 254–273. Chicago: University of Chicago Press.

————. 2012. "Birth and Blame: Guatemalan Midwives and Reproductive Risk." In *Risk, Reproduction, and Narratives of Experience*, ed. Lauren Fordyce and Aminata Maraesa, 81–101. Nashville, TN: Vanderbilt University Press.

Cosminsky, Sheila, and Mary Scrimshaw. 1980. "Medical Pluralism on a Guatemalan Plantation." *Social Science and Medicine* 14B:267–278.

————. 1981. "Sex Roles and Subsistence: A Comparative Analysis of Three Central American Communities." In *Sex Roles and Social Change on Native Lower Central American Societies*, ed. Christine Loveland and Franklin Loveland, 44–69. Urbana: University of Illinois Press.

COVERCO (Commission for the Verification of Codes of Conduct). 2000. *The Culture of Coffee in Guatemala*. Guatemala City: COVERCO.

————. 2003. *Women and Children: The Precarious Lives behind the Grains of Coffee*. Guatemala City: COVERCO.

Csordas, Thomas. 1990. "Embodiment as a Paradigm for Anthropology." *Ethos* 18:5–47.

Cunningham, Alan. 1995. "Breastfeeding: Adaptive Behavior for Child Health and Longevity." In *Breastfeeding: Biocultural Perspectives*, ed. Patricia Stuart-Macadam and Katherine Dettwyler, 243–264. New York: Aldine de Gruyter.

Davis, Dona Lee. 1989. "The Variable Character of Nerves in a Newfoundland Fishing Village." *Medical Anthropology* 11:63–78.

Davis-Floyd, Robbie. 1992. *Birth as an American Rite of Passage*. Berkeley: University of California Press.

Davis-Floyd, Robbie, and Elizabeth Davis. 1997. "Intuition as Authoritative Knowledge in Midwifery and Home Birth." In *Childbirth and Authoritative Knowledge: Cross-Cultural Perspectives*, Robbie Davis-Floyd and Carolyn Sargent, 315–349. Berkeley: University of California Press.

Davis-Floyd, Robbie, and Carolyn Sargent. 1997. "Introduction: The Anthropology of Birth." In *Childbirth and Authoritative Knowledge: Cross Cultural Perspectives*, ed. Robbie Davis-Floyd and Carolyn Sargent, 1–51. Berkeley: University of California Press.

Dissanayake, Wimal, ed. 1996. *Narratives of Agency: Self-Making in China, India, and Japan*. Minneapolis: University of Minnesota Press.

Douglas, Mary. 1970. *Natural Symbols*. New York: Pantheon.

————. 1990. "Risk as a Forensic Resource." *Daedalus* 119:1–16.

————. 1992. *Risk and Blame*. New York: Routledge.

Douglas, William 1969. "Illness and Curing in Santiago Atitlán." PhD diss., Stanford University.

Dudgeon, Matthew. 2008. "Risk and Reproductive Health in Guatemala." Presented at the American Anthropological Association conference, San Francisco, November 19–23.

―――. 2012. "Conceiving Risk in K'iche' Maya Reproduction." In *Risk, Reproduction, and Narratives of Experience*, ed. Lauren Fordyce and Aminata Maraesa, 17–36. Nashville, TN: Vanderbilt University Press.

Edvalson, Rebecca, John Edvalson, John Hawkins, James McDonald, and Walter Adams. "Barriers to the Political Empowerment of Nahualense Midwives." 2013. In *Crisis of Governance in Maya Guatemala: Indigenous Responses to a Failing State*, ed. John Hawkins, James McDonald, and Walter Adams, 175–194. Norman: University of Oklahoma Press.

Etkin, Nina. 1986. "Multidisciplinary Perspectives in the Interpretation of Plants Used in Indigenous Medicine and Diet." In *Plants in Indigenous Medicine and Diet: Bio-Behavioral Approaches*, ed. Nina Etkin, 2–29. Bedford Hills, NY: Redgrave.

Fabrega, Horatio, and Peter Manning. 1979. "Illness Episodes, Illness Severity, and Treatment Options in a Pluralistic Setting." *Social Science and Medicine* 13B (1): 41–51.

Finkler, Kaja. 1991. *Physicians at Work, Patients in Pain: Biomedical Practice and Patient Response in Mexico*. Boulder, CO: Westview.

―――. 1994. *Women in Pain: Gender and Morbidity in Mexico*. Philadelphia: University of Pennsylvania Press.

Fleischer, Soraya. 2006. "Pasando por comadrona, midwife y médico: El itinerario terapéutico de una embarazada en Guatemala." *Anthropologica* 24:51–75.

Foster, George. 1960. *Culture and Conquest*. Chicago: Quadrangle.

―――. 1982. "Responsibility for Illness in Tzintzuntzan: A Cognitive-Linguistic Anomaly." *Medical Anthropology* 6:81–90.

―――. 1994. *Hippocrates' Latin American Legacy: Humoral Medicine in the New World*. Langhorne, PA: Gordon and Breach.

Foster, Jennifer, Angela Anderson, Jennifer Houston, and Maya Doe-Simkins. 2004. "A Report of a Midwifery Model for Training Traditional Midwives in Guatemala." *Midwifery* 20:217–225.

Foster, Jennifer, Jennifer Houston, Ann Davenport, Angela Anderson, Virginia Lamprecht, and Gal Frenkel. 2014. "Weaving Traditional and Professional Midwifery: The Story of Midwife, Birth Center, and the Empowering of Midwives in Guatemala." In *Global Case Studies in Maternal and Child Health*, ed. Ruth White, 25–50. Burlington, MA: Jones and Bartlett.

Foucault, Michel. 1975. *The Birth of the Clinic: An Archaeology of Medical Perception*. New York: Vintage.

Frazao, Elizabeth. 1976. "Energy Expenditure of Pregnant Women in Rural Guatemala." MS thesis, Massachusetts Institute of Technology.

Garces, Ana, Elizabeth McClure, K. Michael Hambridge, Nancy F. Krebs,

Lester Figueroa, Marta Lidia Aguilar, Janet L. Moore, and Robert L. Goldenberg. 2015. "Trends in Perinatal Deaths from 2010 to 2013 in the Guatemalan Western Highlands." *Reproductive Health* 12 (Suppl 2): S14: 1–8.

García, Hernan, Antonio Sierra, and Gilberto Balám. 1999. *Wind in the Blood: Mayan Healing and Chinese Medicine*. Berkeley, CA: North Atlantic Books.

Garcia, Kimberly. 2013. "Mixed Methods Evaluation and Teaching with Guatemalan Traditional Midwives' Regarding Nursing Interventions to Manage Postpartum Hemorrhage." *Journal of Nursing Education and Practice* 3 (1): 120–128.

Garcia, Kimberly, Barbara Morrison, and Carol Savrin. 2012. "Teaching Guatemala Midwives about Postpartum Hemorrhage." *Maternal-Child Nursing Journal* 37 (1): 42–47.

Garrard-Burnett, Virginia. 2000. "Indians Are Drunks and Drunks are Indians: Alcohol and Indigenismo in Guatemala, 1890–1940." *Bulletin of Latin American Research* 19:341–356.

Gelis, Jacques. 1991. *History of Childbirth*. Boston: Northeastern University Press.

Georges, Eugenia 1996. "Fetal Ultrasound Imaging and the Production of Authoritative Knowledge in Greece." *Medical Anthropology Quarterly* 10 (2): 157–175.

———. 2008. *Bodies of Knowledge: The Medicalization of Reproduction in Greece*. Nashville, TN: Vanderbilt University Press.

Gilbert, D. 1976. *A Dietary Survey of Guatemalan Women on the Finca San Luis*. Unpublished manuscript, Department of Nutrition, Massachusetts Institute of Technology.

Ginsburg, Faye, and Rayna Rapp. 1991. "The Politics of Reproduction." *Annual Review of Anthropology* 20:311–343.

Glei, Dana, and Noreen Goldman. 2000. "Understanding Ethnic Variation in Pregnancy-Related Care in Rural Guatemala." *Ethnicity and Health* 5:5–22.

Goldin, Liliana, and Brent Metz. 1991. "An Expression of Cultural Change: Invisible Converts to Protestantism among Highland Guatemala Mayas." *Ethnology* 30:325–338.

Goldman, Noreen, and Dana Glei. 2003. "Evaluation of Midwifery Care: Results from a Survey in Rural Guatemala." *Social Science and Medicine* 56:685–700.

Gonzales, Nancie, and Moises Behar. 1966. "Child-rearing Practices, Nutrition, and Health Status." *Milbank Memorial Fund Quarterly* 44:77–96.

Gordon, John. 1964. "Weanling Diarrhea." *Nutrition Reviews* 22:161–63.

Gordon, John, I. D. Chitkara, and John Wyon. 1963. "Weanling Diarrhea." *American Journal of Medical Science* 245:345–377.

Grajeda, Ruben, Rafael Escamilla, and Kathryn Dewey. 1997. "Delayed Clamping of the Umbilical Cord Improved Hematologic Status of Guatemala Infants at Two Months of Age." *American Journal of Clinical Nutrition* 65 (2): 425–431.

Grandin, Greg. 2000. *The Blood of Guatemala: A History of Race and Nation.* Durham, NC: Duke University Press.

Greenberg, Linda. 1982. "Midwife Training Programs in Highland Guatemala." *Social Science and Medicine* 16:1599–609.

Greenfield, Sidney. 2008. *Spirits with Scalpels.* Walnut Creek, CA: Left Coast Press.

Guarnaccia, Peter, Victor De La Cancela, and Emilio Carrillo. 1989. "The Multiple Meanings of Ataques de Nervios in the Latino Community." *Medical Anthropology* 11:47–62.

Guarnaccia, Peter, and Pablo Farias. 1988. "The Social Meanings of Nervios: A Case Study of a Central American Woman." *Social Science and Medicine* 26:1223–1231.

Guarnaccia, P.J., M. Rivera, F. Franco, C. Neighbors, and C. Allende-Ramos. 1996. "The Experiences of *Ataques de Nervios*: Towards an Anthropology of Emotion in Puerto Rico." *Culture, Medicine, and Psychiatry* 20: 343–367.

Haag, John. 1995. "Family Planning as a Promoter of Child Survival and Growth." In *Child Growth and Nutrition in Developing Countries*, ed. Per Pinstrup-Anderson, David Pelletier, and Harold Alderman, 176–198. Ithaca, NY: Cornell University Press.

Haire, Doris. 1975. "The Cultural Warping of Childbirth." *International Childbirth Education Association News.* Minneapolis: International Childbirth Education Association.

Hallowell, Elizabeth. 2012. "Planning for Obstetrical Emergencies: Maternity Care, Sovereignty, and Governance in Guatemala." *Anthropology News* 53 (9): 9–10.

———. 2014. "'Between the Wall and the Sword': Reproductive Governance and the Technology of Emergency in Guatemalan Maternity Care." *Feminist Formations* 26 (3): 100–121.

Handy, Jim. 1984. *Gift of the Devil.* Boston: South End Press.

Harvey, T. S. 2013. *Wellness beyond Words: Maya Compositions of Speech and Silence in Medical Care.* Albuquerque: University of New Mexico Press.

Harwood, Alan. 1971. "The Hot-Cold Theory of Disease: Implications for Treatment of Puerto-Rican Patients." *The Journal of the American Medical Association* 216 (7): 1153–1158.

Hernandez Saenz, Luz Mara, and George Foster. 2001. "Curers and Their Cures in Colonial New Spain and Guatemala: The Spanish Component. In

Mesoamerican Healers, ed. Brad Huber and Alan Sandstrom, 19–46. Austin: University of Texas Press.

Hinojosa, Servando. 2004. "Authorizing Tradition: Vectors of Contention in Highland Maya Midwifery." *Social Science and Medicine* 59:637–651.

Hoban, Elizabeth. 2003. "We're Safe and Happy Already: Traditional Birth Attendants and Safe Motherhood in a Cambodian Rural Commune." PhD diss., University of Melbourne.

Hopkinson, Amanda. 1988. "Midwifery and Rural Health Care in Guatemala." In *The Midwife Challenge*, ed. Sheila Kitzinger. London: Pandora.

Houston, Jennifer. 2000. "Weaving Cultural Exchange: Midwives Working Together." *Midwifery Today* 53:34–35.

——- 2001. "Final Report: Midwives for Midwives." Behrhorst Partners for Development, Antigua, Guatemala. Unpublished manuscript.

Hoyt, Elizabeth. 1955. "The Indian Laborer on Guatemalan Coffee Fincas." *Inter-American Economic Affairs* 9 (1): 33–46.

Huber, Brad, and Alan Sandstrom, eds. 2001. *Mesoamerican Healers*. Austin: University of Texas Press.

Hurst, Peter. 1999. "Safe Use in Guatemala—Are Industry Projects Effective?" *Pesticides News* 43:8–9.

Hurtado, Elena 1984. "Estudio de las Características y Prácticas de las Comadronas en una Communidad Indígena de Guatemala." In *Ethnomedicina en Guatemala*, ed. E. M. Villatoro. Guatemala City: Centro de Estudios Folklóricos.

———. 1998. "Evaluación de la capacitación de comadronas tradicionales del Proyecto MotherCare/Guatemala. Final report, Guatemala, unpublished manuscript.

Hurtado, Elena, and Eugenia Saenz de Tejada. 2001. "Relations between Government Health Workers and Traditional Midwives in Guatemala." In *Mesoamerican Healers*, ed. Brad Huber and Alan Sandstrom, 211–242. Austin: University of Texas Press.

Hurtado, Juan José. 1979. "La mollera caída: Una subcategoria cognitivia de las enfermedades producidas por la ruptura del equilibrio mecanico del cuerpo. *Boletin Bibliografico de Antropologia Americana* 50:11–20.

Index Mundi. 2015. "Guatemala Demographics Profile 2014." www.index mundi.com/guatemala/demographics_profile.html.

Isakson, S. Ryan. 2009. "'No hay ganancia en la milpa': The Agrarian Question, Food Sovereignty, and the On-Farm Conservation of Agrobiodiversity in the Guatemalan Highlands." *Journal of Peasant Studies* 36 (4): 725–759.

Izurieta, Lilian, and Lora Beth Larson-Brown. 1994. "Child Feeding Practices in Guatemala." *Ecology of Food and Nutrition* 33:249–262.

Jenkins, Gwynne. 2000. "Bureaucratizing Midwives, Biomedicalizing Birth in Rural Costa Rica." Paper presented at the Department of Anthropology, Wayne State University.

———. 2001. "Changing Roles and Identities of Midwives in Rural Costa Rica." *Medical Anthropology* 20 (3): 409–444.

Johns, Timothy. 1990. *With Bitter Herbs They Shall Eat It.* Tucson: University of Arizona Press.

Johnston, Frank, and Setha Low. 1995. *Children of the Urban Poor: The Sociocultural Environment of Growth, Development, and Malnutrition in Guatemala City.* Boulder, CO: Westview Press.

Jordan, Brigitte. 1993. *Birth in Four Cultures*, 4th ed. Prospect Heights, IL: Waveland.

———. 1997. Authoritative Knowledge and Its Construction. In *Childbirth and Authoritative Knowledge: Cross-Cultural Perspectives*, ed. Robbie Davis-Floyd and Carolyn Sargent, 55–79. Berkeley: University of California Press.

Kay, Margarita. 1996. *Healing with Plants in the American and Mexican West.* Tucson: University of Arizona Press.

Kielmann, Arnfried. 1970. "Births, Deaths, and Causes of Death." Paper No. 12. *Ecological Assessment of the Nutritional State of a Guatemalan Finca Population.* Unpublished manuscript. Department of Nutrition and Food Science, Massachusetts Institute of Technology.

King, Nora, Anita Chary, and Peter Rohloff. 2015. "Leveraging Resources in Contemporary Maya Midwifery." In *Privatization and the New Medical Pluralism: Shifting Healthcare Landscapes in Maya Guatemala*, ed. Anita Chary and Peter Rohloff, 125–142. Lanham, MD: Lexington.

Kitzinger, Sheila. 1997. *The Complete Book of Pregnancy and Childbirth.* New York: Knopf.

Klein, Susan, Suellen Miller, and Fiona Thomson. 2009. *A Book for Midwives: Care for Pregnancy, Birth, and Women's Health.* Berkeley, CA: The Hesperian Foundation.

Kleinman, Arthur. 1978. "Concepts and a Model for the Comparison of Medical Systems as Cultural Systems." *Social Science and Medicine* 12:85–93.

Koblinsky, Marge. 1996. "Improving Obstetrical and Neonatal Management: Lessons from Guatemala. *MotherCare Matters* 5 (4): 1–3.

Kruske, Sue, and Lesley Barclay. 2004. "Effect of Shifting Policies on Traditional Birth Attendant Training." *Journal of Midwifery and Women's Health* 49:306–311.

Kunow, Marianna Appel. 2003. *Maya Medicine.* Albuquerque: University of New Mexico Press.

Laderman, Carol 1983. *Wives and Midwives: Childbirth and Nutrition in Rural Malaysia.* Berkeley: University of California Press.

Lang, Jennifer, and Elizabeth Elkin. 1997. "A Study of the Beliefs and Birthing Practices of Traditional Midwives in Rural Guatemala." *Journal of Nurse Midwifery* 42 (2): 25–31.

Lave, Jean, and Etienne Wenger. 1991. *Situated Learning: Legitimate Peripheral Participation*. New York: Cambridge University Press.

Leedam, Elizabeth. 1985. "Traditional Birth Attendants." *International Journal of Gynaecology and Obstetrics* 23:249–274.

Lock, Margaret. 1989. "Commentary: Words of Fear, Words of Power: Nerves and the Awakening of Political Consciousness." *Medical Anthropology* 11:79–90.

Lock, Margaret, and Vinh-Kim Nguyen. 2010. *An Anthropology of Biomedicine*. Malden, MA: Wiley-Blackwell.

Low, Setha. 1982. "Dr. Moreno Cañas: a Symbolic Bridge to the Demedicalization of Healing." *Social Science and Medicine* 16:527–531.

———. 1989. "Gender, Emotion, and Nervios in Urban Guatemala." *Health Care for Women International* 10:115–139.

Low, Setha, and Bruce Newman. 1985. Indigenous Fertility Regulating Methods in Costa Rica. In *Women's Medicine*, ed. Lucile Newman, 147–160. New Brunswick, NJ: Rutgers University Press.

Lowis, George, and Peter McCaffery. 2000. "Sociological Factors Affecting the Medicalization of Midwifery." In *Midwifery and the Medicalization of Childbirth: Comparative Perspectives*, ed. Edwin Van Teijlingen, George Lowis, Peter McCaffery, and Maureen Porter, 5–41. Huntington, NY: Nova Science Publishing.

Lozoya, Xavier, and Mariana Lozoya. 1982. *Flora medicinal de Mexico*. Mexico City: Instituto Mexicano de Seguro Social.

Lupton, Deborah. 1997. "Foucault and the Medicalization Critique." In *Foucault, Health, and Medicine*, ed. Alan Petersen and Robin Bunton, 94–110. New York: Routledge.

MacDonald, Margaret, Debra Pascali Bonaro, and Robbie Davis-Floyd. 2014. "Anthropological Engagement at a Global Women's Health Conference: A Report on the Women Deliver Conference, Kuala Lumpur 2013." *Anthropology in Action* 21 (2): 37–41.

Malloy, Mary Esther. 2013. "Optimal Cord Clamping." *Midwifery Today* 108:9–12.

Mangay-Maglacas, Amelia, and John Simons. 1986. *The Potential of the Traditional Birth Attendant*. Geneva. WHO Offset Publication No. 95. Geneva: World Health Organization.

Marini, Alessandra, and Michele Gragnolati. 2003. "Malnutrition and Poverty in Guatemala." Policy Research Working Paper 2967. Washington, DC: World Bank.

Mata, Leonardo. 1995. "The Santa Maria Cauque Study: Health and Survival of Mayan Indians under Deprivation, Guatemala." In *Community-Based*

Longitudinal Nutrition and Health Studies, ed. Nevin Scrimshaw, 28–78. Boston: International Foundation for Developing Countries.

Maupin, Jonathan. 2008. "Remaking the Guatemalan Midwife: Health Care Reform and Midwifery Training Programs in Highland Guatemala." *Medical Anthropology* 27 (4): 53–82.

———. 2009. "'Fruit of the Accords': Healthcare Reform and Civil Participation in Highland Guatemala." *Social Science and Medicine* 28 (8): 1456–1463.

McAdams, Ryan. 2014. "Time to Implement Delayed Cord Clamping." *Obstetrics and Gynecology* 123 (3): 549–552.

McClain, Carol. 1981. "Traditional Midwives and Family Planning: An Assessment of Programs and Suggestions for the Future." *Medical Anthropology* 5 (1): 107–136.

———. 1982. "Toward a Comparative Framework for the Study of Childbirth: A Review of the Literature." In *Anthropology of Human Birth*, ed. Maragarita Kay, 25–59. Philadelphia: F. A. Davis.

———. 1989. "Reinterpreting Women in Healing Roles." In *Women as Healers: Cross-Cultural Perspectives*, ed. Carol Shepherd McClain, 1–23. New Brunswick, NJ: Rutgers University Press.

McCourt, Christine. 2010. "Introduction." In *Childbirth, Midwifery, and Concepts of Time*, ed. Christine McCourt, 1–13. New York: Berghahn.

McCreery, David. 1990. "State Power, Indigenous Communities, and Land." In *Guatemalan Indians and the State: 1540–1988*, ed. Carol Smith, 96–115. Austin: University of Texas Press.

———. 1994. *Rural Guatemala, 1760–1940*. Palo Alto, CA: Stanford University Press.

McElroy, Ann, and Patricia Townsend. 2009. *Medical Anthropology in Ecological Perspective*, 5th edition. Boulder, CO: Westview.

McGuire, Judith. 1976. "A Dietary Survey of Guatemalan Women on the Finca San Luis." Unpublished manuscript.

Médicos Descalzos Chinique. 2013. *Con comadronas: Conocimiento tradicional de las comadronas sobre salud reproductiva*. Chinique, El Quiché, Guatemala: Cholsamaj.

———. 2015. Sexual and Reproductive Health Axis, www.medicosdescalzos .info.

Mellado, Virginia, Carlos Zolla, and Xochitl Castañeda, with collaboration of Antonio Tascon Mendoza. 1989. *La Atención al Embarazo y el Parto en el Médico Rural Mexicano*. Mexico, D.F.: Centro Interamericano de Estudios de Seguridad Social.

Melville, Margarita, and Thomas Melville. 1971. *Guatemala: The Politics of Land Ownership*. New York: Free Press.

Méndez Domínguez, Alfredo. 1983. "Illness and Medical Theory among

Guatemalan Indians." In *Heritage of Conquest: Thirty Years Later*, ed. Carl Kendall, John Hawkins, and Laurel Bossen, 267–298. Albuquerque: University of New Mexico Press.

Mintz, Sidney. 1985. *Sweetness and Power: The Place of Sugar in Modern History*. New York: Viking Penguin.

Mintz, Sidney, and Eric Wolf. 1950. "An Analysis of Ritual Coparenthood." *Southwestern Journal of Anthropology* 6:341–368.

Monteith, Richard, John Anderson, Maria Apineda, Roberto Santiso, and Mark Oberle. 1985. "Contraceptive Use and Fertility in Guatemala." *Studies in Family Planning* 16:279–288.

Moore, Harriet. 1988. *Feminism and Anthropology*. Minneapolis: University of Minnesota Press.

Morgan, Kathryn Pauly. 1998. "Contested Bodies, Contested Knowledges: Women, Health, and the Politics of Medicalization." In *The Politics of Women's Health: Exploring Agency and Autonomy*, ed. Susan Sherwin, 83–121. Philadelphia: Temple University Press.

Morgan, Lynn, and Elizabeth Roberts. 2012. "Reproductive Governance in Latin America." *Anthropology and Medicine* 19 (2): 241–254.

Morton, Julia. 1981. *Atlas of Medicinal Plants of Middle America*. Springfield, IL: Charles C. Thomas.

MSNBC. 2008. *Shocked at Deaths, Guatemala Trains Midwives*, September 19. www.msnbc.msn.com/id/26793739.

MSPAS (Ministerio de Salud Pública y Asistencia Social). 2010. *V Encuesta Nacional de Salud Materno Infantil, 2008–2009*. (ENSMI-2008/09). Guatemala City: Ministerio de Salud Pública y Asistencia Social/Instituto Nacional de Estadistica (INE)/Centros de Control y Prevención de Enfermedades (CDC).

Mumtaz, Zubia, and Sarah Salway. 2009. "Understanding Gendered Influences on Women's Reproductive Health in Pakistan: Moving beyond the Autonomy Paradigm. *Social Science and Medicine* 68 (7): 1349–1356.

Murphy-Lawless, Jo. 1998. *Reading Birth and Death: A History of Obstetric Thinking*. Bloomington: Indiana University Press.

Neergaard, Lauran. 2014. "No Rush to C-sections, New Guidelines Urge." *Philadelphia Inquirer*. February 20, A6.

Newman, Lucile. 1985a. "Context Variables in Fertility Regulation." In *Women's Medicine*, ed. Lucile Newman, 179–191. New Brunswick, NJ: Rutgers University Press.

———. 1985b. "An Introduction to Population Anthropology." In *Women's Medicine*, ed. Lucile Newman, 1–23. New Brunswick, NJ: Rutgers University Press.

Nichter, Mark. 1981. "Idioms of Distress: Alternatives in the Expression of Psychosocial Distress." *Culture, Medicine, and Psychiatry* 5:379–408.

Nybo, Thomas. 2009. "At a Glance: Guatemala. Fighting Chronic Malnu-trition among Impoverished Children in Guatemala." UNICEF website, www.unicef.org/doublepublish/guatemala_48087.html.

Observatory of Economic Complexity. 2015. Guatemala (GTM) Profile of Exports, Imports, and Trade Partners. https://atlas.media.mit.edu/en/profile/country/gtm/.

Oglesby, Elizabeth. 2004. "Corporate Citizenship? Elites, Labor, and the Geographies of Work in Guatemala." *Environment and Planning D: Society and Space* 22 (4): 553–573.

———. 2010. "Interviewing Landed Elites in Post-War Guatemala." *Geoforum* 41 (1): 23–25.

———. 2013. "'We're No Longer Dealing with Fools': Violence, Labor, and Government on the South Coast." In *War by Other Means: Aftermath in Post-Genocide Guatemala*, ed. Carlota McAllister and Diane Nelson 143–169. Durham, NC: Duke University Press.

Oliveira, Jessica. 2015. "Escuela de POWHER para las comadronas (proporcionando, cobertura en salud, la educacion y los recursos de las mujeres)." Saving Mothers. Unpublished draft.

Orellana, Sandra. 1987. *Indian Medicine in Highland Guatemala*. Albuquerque: University of New Mexico Press.

O'Rourke, Kathleen. 1994. *The Effect of a Traditional Birth Attendant Training Program on Obstetrical Practices and Perinatal Mortality in Rural Guatemala*. PhD diss., University of Massachusetts–Amherst.

———. 1995a. "The Effect of Hospital Staff Training on Management of Obstetrical Patients Referred by Traditional Birth Attendants." *International Journal of Gynecology and Obstetrics* 48 Suppl:S95–S102.

———. 1995b. "Evaluación de un programa de capacitación de parteras tradicionales en Quetzaltenango." *Boletín de la Oficina Sanitaria Panamericana* 119:503–514.

Ortiz de Montellano, Bernardo, and Carole Browner. 1985. "Chemical Bases for Medicinal Plant Use in Oaxaca, Mexico." *Journal of Ethnopharmacology* 13:57–88.

PAHO (Pan American Health Organization. 1999. *Guatemala: Profile of the Health Services System*. Washington, DC: Pan American Health Organization.

———. 2012. *Health in the Americas. 2010 Index, 2012 Edition. Country Volume: Guatemala*. Washington, DC: Pan American Health Organization.

Pansini, Jude. 1977. *El Pilar: A Plantation Microcosm of Guatemalan Ethnicity*. PhD diss., University of Rochester.

———. 1980. *Plantation Health Care in Guatemala*. Guatemala City: USAID-Guatemala and ASGROSALUD. Unpublished report.

Paul, Lois. 1975. "Recruitment to a Ritual Role: The Midwife in a Maya Community." *Ethos* 3:449–467.

Paul, Lois, and Benjamin Paul. 1975. "The Maya Midwife as a Sacred Specialist: A Guatemalan Case." *American Ethnologist* 2:707–726.

Pebley, Anne, Noreen Goldman, and German Rodriguez. 1996. "Prenatal and Delivery Care and Child Immunization in Guatemala: Do Family and Community Matter?" *Demography* 33:231–247.

Peng, J. Y., Srisomang Keovichit, and Reginald MacIntyre, eds. 1974. *Role of Traditional Birth Attendants in Family Planning*. Ottawa, Ontario, Canada: International Development Research Centre.

Pieper, Jim. 2002. *Guatemala's Folk Saints*. Albuquerque: University of New Mexico Press.

Pigg, Stacy Leigh. 1997. "Authority in Translation: Finding, Knowing, Naming, and Training 'Traditional Birth Attendants' in Nepal." In *Childbirth and Authoritative Knowledge*, ed. Robbie Davis-Floyd and Carolyn Sargent, 233–262. Berkeley: University of California Press.

Plant, Roger. 1978. *Guatemala: Unnatural Disaster*. London: The Latin American Bureau.

———. 1995. *Rebuilding Civil Society: Rural Workers' Organizations in Guatemala*. Geneva: International Labour Office. Issues in Development Discussion Paper No. 5.

Proechel, Sarah. 2005. *Voices of Maya Midwives: Oral Histories of Practicing Traditional Midwives from the Mam Region of Guatemala*. Self-published via Lulu.

Putney, Pamela, and Barry Smith. 1989. *The Training and Practice of Traditional Birth Attendants in Guatemala*. A report prepared for the Technologies for Primary Health Care (PRITECH) Project, supported by USAID (PN ABF-275). Washington, DC: USAID.

Rapp, Reyna. 2012. "Afterword." In *Risk, Reproduction, and Narratives of Experience*, ed. Lauren Fordyce and Aminata Maraesa, 231–233. Nashville, TN: Vanderbilt University Press.

Read, Merrill. 1970. "Social and Economic Characteristics of the Finca Population." Paper No. 2 in *Ecological Assessment of the Nutritional Status of a Guatemalan Finca Population*. Unpublished INCAP-MIT study. Department of Nutrition and Food Science. Massachusetts Institute of Technology.

Replogle, Jill. 2007. "Training Traditional Birth Attendants in Guatemala." *The Lancet* 369:177–178.

Rogoff, Barbara. 2011. *Developing Destinies: A Mayan Midwife and Town*. Oxford: Oxford University Press.

Roost, Mattias, Sara Johnsdotter, Jerker Liljestrant, and Birgitta Essen. 2004. "A Qualitative Study of Conceptions and Attitudes Regarding Maternal Mortality among Traditional Birth Attendants in Rural Guatemala." *BJOG: An International Journal of Obstetrics and Gynaecology* 111: 1372–1377.

Rosenthal, Caroline. 1987. "Santa Maria de Jesus: Medical Choice in a Highland Guatemalan Town." BA thesis, Harvard University.

Rosenthal, Elizabeth. 2013. "As Biofuel Demand Grows, So Do Guatemala's Hunger Pangs." *New York Times*, January 5.

Sault, Nicole. 1990. "The Evil Eye, Both Hot and Dry: Gender and Generation among the Zapotec of Mexico." *Journal of Latin American Lore* 16 (1): 69–89.

Saving Mothers. 2015. "Birth Attendant Training." http://www.savingmothers.org/birth_attendant_training.

Schieber, Barbara, Susan Colgate Goldman, and Alfred Bartlett. 1993. *Training Manual for Trainers of Traditional Birth Attendants: Quetzaltenango Maternal and Neonatal Health Project.* INCAP Publication MDI/001. Guatemala City, Guatemala: INCAP/PAHO.

Scrimshaw, Mary, and Sheila Cosminsky. 1991. "Impact of Health on Women's Food-Procurement Strategies on a Guatemalan Plantation." In *Diet and Domestic Life in Society*, ed. Ann Sharman, Janet Theophano, Karen Curtis, and Ellen Messer, 61–89. Philadelphia: Temple University Press.

Seiber Eric, David Hotchkiss, Jeffrey Rous, and Andres Beeruti. 2005. "Maternal and Child Health and Family Planning Service Utilization in Guatemala: Implications for Service Integration." *Social Science and Medicine* 6:279–291.

Selin, Helaine. 2009. "Introduction." In *Childbirth across Cultures: Ideas and Practices of Pregnancy, Childbirth, and the Postpartum*, ed. Helaine Selin and Pamela Kendall Stone, xiii–xvii. Dordrecht, Netherlands: Springer.

Sibley, Lynn, Theresa Ann Sipe, and Marge Koblinsky. 2004. "Does Traditional Birth Attendant Improve Referral of Women with Obstetric Complications: A Review of the Evidence." *Social Science and Medicine* 59 (8): 1757–1768.

Smith-Oka, Vania. 2013a. "Managing Labor and Delivery among Impoverished Populations in Mexico: Cervical Examinations as Bureaucratic Practice." *American Anthropologist* 115 (4): 595–607.

———. 2013b. *Shaping the Motherhood of Indigenous Mexico.* Nashville, TN: Vanderbilt University Press.

Sobel, Richard. 1977. "Longitudinal Ecological Assessment of the Nutritional Status on a Rural Guatemalan Lowland Plantation." Master's thesis, Massachusetts Institute of Technology.

Stuart-Macadam, Patricia, and Katherine Dettwyler. 1995. *Breastfeeding: Biocultural Perspectives.* New York: Aldine de Gruyter.

Taylor, Yvonne. 1970. "Reproductive Histories and Attitudes to Family Planning." Paper No. 14. In *Ecological Assessment of the Nutritional Status of a Guatemalan Finca Population.* Unpublished INCAP-MIT study. Department of Nutrition and Food Science. Massachusetts Intsitute of Technology.

Tedlock, Barbara. 1992. *Time and the Highland Maya*, revised edition. Albuquerque: University of New Mexico Press.

Thilagavathy, Ganapathy. 2012. "Maternal Birthing Position and Outcome of Labor." *The Journal of Family Welfare* 58 (1): 68–73.

Tran, Mark. 2013. "Guatemala's Campaign against Child Malnutrition Shows Hunger for Change." *The Guardian*, October 9. www.theguardian.com /global-development/2013/oct/09/guatemala-child-malnutrition-hunger.

U.S. Department of State. 2003. *Background Note: Guatemala*. www.state .gov/r/pa/ei/bgn/2045.htm.

USAID Deliver Project. 2013. "World Contraception Day: The Important Role of Contraceptives in Reaching MDGs." Washington, DC: USAID.

USAID-Guatemala. 1977. *Extension of Health Services to Finca Workers*. Guatemala Health Sector Assessment, Annex 5.7. Guatemala City: Academia de Ciencias Medicas and USAID. Manuscript.

UNICEF. 2015. "State of the World's Children 2015 Country Statistical Tables." www.unicef.org/infobycountry/guatemala_statistics.html.

Universidad Nacional Autonomia de Mexico (UNAM). 2014. Atlas de las Plantas de la Medicina Tradicional Mexicana. Biblioteca Digital de la Medicina Tradicional Mexicana. www.medicinatradicionalmexicana.unam .mx.

van Esterik, Penny. 1989. *Beyond the Breast-Bottle Controversy*. New Brunswick, NJ: Rutgers University Press.

Van Rheenan, P. 2011. "Delayed Clamping and Improved Infant Outcomes." *British Medical Journal* 343 (1): d7127.

Velimirovic, Boris, and Helga Velimirovic. 1978. "The Utilization of Traditional Medicine and Its Practitioners in Heath Services: A Global Overview." In *Modern Medicine and Medical Anthropology in the United States–Mexico Border Population*, ed. Boris Velimirovic, 172–185. Washington, DC: Pan American Health Organization.

Velimirovic, Helga, and Boris Velimirovic. 1981. "The Role of Traditional Birth Attendants in Health Services." *Medical Anthropology* 5 (1): 89–105.

Verderese, Maria de Lourdes, and Lily Turnbull. 1975. *The Traditional Birth Attendant in Maternal and Child Health and Family Planning*. WHO Offset Publication No. 18. Geneva: World Health Organization.

Wagner, Regina. 2001. *The History of Coffee in Guatemala*. Bogotá, Colombia: Villegas Editores.

———. 2007. *The History of Sugar in Guatemala*. Guatemala City: Editorial Galeria Guatemala: ASAZGUA.

Ward, Victoria, Jane Bertrand, and Francisco Puac. 1992. "Exploring Sociocultural Barriers to Family Plannng among Mayans in Guatemala." *International Family Planning Perspectives* 18 (2): 59–65.

Warren, Charles W., Richard S. Monteith, J. Timothy Johnson, Roberto Santiso, Federico Guerra, and Mark W. Oberle. 1987. "Use of Maternal-Child Health Services and Contraception in Guatemala and Panama." *Journal of Biosocial Sciences* 19:229–243.

Whetten, Nathan. 1961. *Guatemala: The Land and the People*. New Haven, CT: Yale University Press.

Willats, Amy. 1995. "Midwives and Community Workers in Conflict: Exploring the Cultural Appropriateness of Family Planning Programs." MA thesis, Vanderbilt University.

Wilson, Kevara Ellsworth. 2007. "Your Destiny is to Care for Pregnant Women: Midwives and Childbirth in Nahualá." In *Health Care in Maya Guatemala*, ed. Walter Adams and John Hawkins, 125–147. Norman: University of Oklahoma Press.

Wolf, Eric, and Sidney Mintz. 1957. "Haciendas and Plantations in Middle America and the Antilles." *Social and Economic Studies* 6:380–412.

World Bank 2004. *Poverty in Guatemala*. Washington, D.C.: The World Bank.

———. 2009. *Guatemala Poverty Assessment: Good Performance at Low Levels*. Report No. 43920-GT. http://siteresources.worldbank.org /INTLACREGTOPPOVANA/Resources/GuatemalaPovertyAssessment English.pdf.

———. 2014 Guatemala Overview. www.worldbank.org/en/country /guatemala/overview.

World Health Organization. 1998. "Care of the Umbilical Cord: A Review of the Evidence" (WHO/RHT/MSM/98.4). Geneva: World Health Organization.

———. 2004. *Making Pregnancy Safer: The Critial Role of the Skilled Birth Attendant, a Joint Statement of the WHO, ICM, and FIGO*. Geneva, Switzerland: World Health Organization.

Yates Doerr, Emily 2012. "The Weight of the Self: Care and Compassion in Guatemalan Dietary Choices." *Medical Anthropology* 26 (1): 136–158.

———. 2015. *The Weight of Obesity: Hunger and Global Health in Postwar Guatemala*. Oakland: University of California Press.

Young, Sera. 2012. *Craving Earth: Understanding Pica*. New York: Columbia University Press.

Zeitlin, Marian, Hossein Ghassemi, and Mohamed Mansour. 1990. *Positive Deviance in Child Nutrition*. Tokyo: The United National University.

Zola, Irving. 1972. "Medicine as an Institution of Social Control." In *The Sociology of Health and Illness: Critical Perspectives*, 6th edition, ed. Peter Conrad, 404–414. New York: Worth.

INDEX

Page numbers in italics refer to figures and illustrations.

ACAM. *See* Asociación de Comadronas de Area Mam (ACAM)

Adams, Walter, 45

agency: definition of, 9–11; of fetus, 88; of midwife, 10, 51–52, 97, 116, 122, 133, 143–144, 180, 226; of women, 9–10, 48, 116–117, 122, 133, 143, 180, 195, 203

agriculture, commercial: CAT system (corte, alce, y transporte), 30; coffee, 1, 15, 17–18, 20, *20*–21, 27, 32, *33*, 34, 37, 39–41, 43–44, 47–49, 70, 85, 100, 142, 164, 262nn1–2; man cutting sugarcane, *31*; sugar, 1, 15, 17–19, *20*, 21, 27, 30, *31*, 31–32, 38, 262nn1–2, 263n5, 263n9; woman picking coffee while carrying infant, *33*

agriculture, subsistence: beans, 27–28, *29*, 37, 39–40; corn, 13, 27–28, *29*, 37, 39–40, 70, 262n8; mother and daughter planting beans, *29*

Aguilar Girón, José Ignacio, 178

Ahearn, Laura, 10

AIDS. *See* HIV/AIDS

ajq'ij (shamans or daykeepers), 43, 48, 55, 60, 175–176, 265n4. *See also zahorín* (shaman, diviner)

alcohol and alcoholism, 2, 12, 93, 97, 194–195

American College of Nurse-Midwives, 221

American College of Obstetricians and Gynecologists, 233

anemia, 85–86, 88, 162, 179, *188*, 198, 235, 238; examination of eyes for, 64, 77, *78*, 86, 107, 245; in infants, 122–123; medicinal plants and remedies, 251, *259*

anger, 82, 90–98, 237–238, 253; and breast-feeding, 157, 163, 237; cause of birth complications, 2, 12, 78, 91–92, 97–98, 106, 131, 133, 237; *colera*, 91–92, 94, 96; *enojo*, 91, 94, 96; as idiom of distress, 2, 12, 94–95; as manifestation of life's lesions, 2, 12, 95

antojos (pregnancy cravings), *78*, 87–89

Arms, Suzanne, 117–118

Arvigo, Rosita, 269n6

Ascoli, Werner, 18, 19, 21, 263n4

asientos (diarrhea), 38, 39, 46, 47, 175, 188, 202, 238; and *bilis*, 94; and bottle feeding, 162, 170, 171; and *chipil/chipez*, 198–199; and *descompostura* (prolapsed uterus), 158, 159; and evil eye *(ojo)*, 98, 193–194; and fallen

medicalization (*continued*)
ation, 179; demedicalization, 8,
246; of distress, 95, 97; documen-
tation/paperwork, 54–55; family planning/contraception, 180–
181, 202–204; gender/status level,
6–12, 108–109, 148, 171–172,
227, 241–243; hierarchical nature
of, 2–6, 10, 11, 101, 107, 145–
146, 203, 217, 238–241; infant
feeding, 13–14, 160, 168–169,
171; injections, 104–105, 144; interactional level, 5–6, 108, 145–
146, 227, 238–240; labor and
delivery, 111, 117, 119, 123, 143–
149; models of, 4–12, 261n4; policy, 16, 67, 105–106, 111, 141–
142, 146, 167–169, 181, 216, 218,
220, 225–226, 234–235; postnatal care, 160, 169–171, 179,
180, 202–204; prenatal care, 77,
81, 83, 95, 97, 104, 106–109; risk,
145, 235–237; silencing/muting,
9; standardization, 5, 119–120,
123, 144–145; supine birth position, 4, 112, 113, 115–118, *147*,
156, 205, 224; technological level,
5, 104, 108, 143, 171, 227–231,
236, 238, 247; ultrasounds, 104,
108. *See also* biomedicine and
biomedical model
medicinal plants, scientific names of,
258–260
medicinal plants and remedies, 28,
38–39, 41, 48, 64, 67, 107, 202–
203, 219, 225, 249–256; anger,
91–92, 97, 253; *bilis*, 94, 253;
chipil, 198–199; colic, 202, 253;
cough, 254; *descompostura* (prolapsed uterus), 62; *detención* (delayed menstruation), 79, 88;
diabetes, 255; diarrhea, stomachache, worms, 200–202, 254–255;

emmenagogues, 175, 178, 180,
182, 184, 188, 250; fallen uterus,
256; family planning, 184–185,
188, 192, 250; fever, 255; herbal
baths, 149, 151, 153–158, 166–
167, 170–171, 172, 238–239; *hijillo*, 91; infant care, 253; infertility or barrenness, 125–126,
177–180, 250–251; labor and delivery, 120, 144, 146, *147*, 233,
251–252; *mal de ojo* (evil eye),
253; measles and chicken pox,
255; postpartum care, 151, 153–
158, 164, 166–168, 170–172, 252;
prenatal care, 79, 89, 91–92, 97,
99, 106–108, 251; prevention of
miscarriage, 89; *pujido*, 199–200,
253; *susto* (fright), 197–198, 253–
254; urinary tract infection, 99,
255
Médicos Descalzos Chinique (Chinique Barefoot Doctors), 222, 244
Mellado, Virginia, 198
meseros (permanent workers), 26
Messmer, Sarah, 47, 163, 169
methodology, 12–14
midwifery training programs and
policy, 6, 11, 51–52, 54, 56, 64–
68, 70–72, 86, 99–100, 107,
113, 115, 205–226, 239; Asociación Civil de Comadronas Tradicionales de Chimaltenango
(ACOTCHI, Association of Traditional Midwives of Chimaltenango), 222–223; Asociación
de Comadronas de Area Mam
(ACAM), 16, 218–220; current
situation, 220–226; Midwives for
Midwives, 217–218, 228, 240,
242, 247; MotherCare/John Snow
Quetzaltenango Maternal and
Neonatal Health project and policy, 210–215; Safe Motherhood

Ortiz de Montellano, Bernard, 178, 184
Ould, Fielding, 266n3

Pakistan, 10
Pan American Health Organization (PAHO), 11, 140, 180–181
Pan del Señor (clay tablets), 87–88, 251
panela (unrefined brown sugar), 20, 20, 26, 30, 162, 166, 254
Pansini, Jude, 15, 42
Pascali Bonaro, Debra, 123
Paul, Benjamin, 15, 59
Paul, Lois, 15, 59, 68, 135
Paz de Bocaletti, Maria E., 212
Peng, J. Y., 181
pesticides, 39, 41, 93, 264n12
pharmaceutical industry, 7–8, 39, 48, 107, 143–144, 175, 183, 193, 202
pielitis (skin infection), 264n16
Pieper, Jim, 60
Pigg, Stacey Leigh, 11
pimpinela (anise), 85, 112, 120, 146, 251, 252, 259, 268–269n4
Pitocin, 144, 229, 233
placenta, 57, 64, 65, 112–113, 115, 147, 229; beliefs about, 121–126, 136, 143, 145, 266n4; disposal, 125, 148; placental problems, 77, 81, 88, 135; retained placenta, 91, 120–122, 128–131, 189, 213, 219; timing, 231–334
Pop Wuj, 221
position of delivery: kneeling, 4, 112–113, 115, 116, 117, 147, 156, 224; squatting, 112, 115–117, 156, 224; supine or horizontal, 4, 112, 113, 115–118, 147, 156, 205, 224; vertical, 117–118, 147, 224, 247
position of fetus: breech, 77, 80, 131,

135; malposition, 77, 81, 106–107, 131–132, 141, 145, 213, 228, 235–236, 245, 265n1; transverse, 74, 80, 82–83, 86, 131, 142, 164
postpartum and postnatal care, 11, 51, 67, 70–71, 146, 221, 230, 247; abdominal binder or sash (*faja*), 148, 126, 151, 155–160, 171, 172; behavioral restrictions, 151–152; dietary restrictions, 153; fallen/prolapsed uterus, 158–160; herbal bath, 151, 153–158, 166–167, 170–171, 172; herbal/medicinal remedies, 164, 166, 167–168, 172; hot-cold balance, 2, 12, 152–154, 156–157, 159, 162–167, 170–171, 172, 237, 239; management of (comparison), *172*; massage, 126, 151, 154, 156–158, *159*, 159, 166–168, 171, 172, 239, 258. *See also* bottle-feeding; breast-feeding; placenta; umbilical cord
pre-eclampsia. *See* eclampsia and pre-eclampsia
prenatal care: emergency plans, 105–106; evil eye, 98–99; hot-cold balance, 74, 76, 78, 79, 82–87, 90–91, 93–94, 98–99, 106–107; injections, 104–105; management of (comparison), *78–79*; massage, 52, 64, 67, 71, 73–77, 78, 79, 81, 88, 89, 92, 97, 102, 106–107; nutrition, 77, 83–85, 87, 101, 107; pregnancy cravings, 87–89; prenatal clinic, 99–104; prenatal examinations, 77–81; preventative prescriptions and proscriptions, 81–86; prevention of miscarriage, 89–98; urinary tract infection, 99–99
primípara (first-time mother), 56, 114, 139, 146, 236, 242
Proechel, Sarah, 16, 146, 268–269n4

prolapsed uterus. *See descompostura* (prolapsed uterus)

Puac, Francisco, 182

pujido (condition in which infants cries and arches its back), 175, 199–200, 202, 238, 253

Putney, Pamela, 1

Quetzaltenango, 34, 47, 54, 59, 210–214, 218, 226, 244

Ramirez, Pablo, 244

Rapp, Rayna, 7, 11

Read, Merrill, 23, 25–26, 34, 36, 42, 43

Reagan, Ronald, 67, 190

Refuge International, 221

religion, 8, 15, 44–45, 93, 97, 114, 129; Catholicism, 44, 60, 98, 102, 129, 170, 190, 249, 254, 264–265n2, 268n1; evangelicalism, 44–45, 63, 93, 190; Protestantism, 45, 93, 190

religious practitioners or specialists, 8, 13, 55, 93; *ajq'ij* (shamans or daykeepers), 43, 48, 55, 60, 175–176, 265n4; midwives as, 55, 175–176; shamans, 7, 39, 43, 48, 55, 59–60, 62, 175–176, 265n4; spiritists, 7–8, 38, 39, 43, 48, 55, 59–60, 62, 104, 128–129, 175–176, 264n14

Replogle, Jill, 11

reproductive governance, 4, 106, 226

Retalhuleu, 48, 54, 81, 96, 108, 129, 134–135, 139–141, 146, 161, 185–186, 206–207, 212, 214, 222, 226, 228

risk: high risk (*alto riesgo*), 77, 86, 106–107, 137, 141, 145, 211, 217, 220, 236; local perception of, 7, 145, 235–236; medical definition or perception of, 5, 7, 8, 54, 104,

106, 145, 148, 209, 211, 228, 231, 235–236, 241

Roberts, Elizabeth, 4, 225–226

Rogoff, Barbara, 15, 83, 124, 125, 198, 264n13

Rohloff, Peter, 45, 163, 169, 216, 223, 246, 247

Rose Charities Canada, 221

Rosenthal, Caroline, 198, 200–201

Rosenthal, Elizabeth, 21

Rouse, Dwight J., 233

sacralization, 8, 45, 63–64, 74–76, 124, 129

Saenz de Tajada, Eugenia, 54, 71–72, 205, 244

Safe Motherhood Initiative, 10, 12, 15–16, 215–216, 221. *See also* World Health Organization (WHO)

Safe Motherhood Project, 221

Salway, Sarah, 10

San Cayetano clinic, 38, 47, 102, 134

San Cristobal, 34, 52

Sandstrom, Alan, 175

San Felipe, 22, 37–38, 47–48, 54, 66, 100, 102–103, 134, 137, 191, 193, 266n2

sanidades (public health centers), 185. *See also* health centers

San Sebastián, 43, 48, 87, 207

Santa Cruz, 15

Santa Lucia Utatlán, 13, 59, 98, 146, 151, 153, 166, 177, 179, 182, 236, 250, 261–262n6

Sargent, Carolyn, 1, 9

Sault, Nicole, 195

Saving Mothers, 221–222, 228, 230, 241; School of POWHER (Providing Outreach in Women's Health and Educational Resources), 221–222, 228

Savrin, Carol, 212, 221, 245